The
Power
of
Love

The
Power
of
Love

Christian Spirituality and Theology

by
Donald Goergen

THE THOMAS MORE PRESS
Chicago, Illinois

248.
Goe

The author and publisher wish to thank the following for permission to reprint:

Excerpts from THE JERUSALEM BIBLE, copyright © 1966 by Darton, Longman & Todd Ltd. and Doubleday and Company, Inc. Used by permission of the publisher.

Excerpts from the following books by Pierre Teilhard de Chardin: THE DIVINE MILIEU, English translation copyright © 1961 by William Collins Sons & Co., Ltd., London and Harper & Row, Publishers, Inc., New York. THE PHENOMENON OF MAN, English translation copyright © 1959 by William Collins Sons & Co., Ltd., London and Harper & Row, Publishers, Inc., New York. THE FUTURE OF MAN, English translation copyright © 1964 by William Collins Sons & Co., Ltd., London and Harper & Row, Publishers Inc., New York. Used by permission of the publishers.

ISBN 0-88347-108-6

Table of Contents

To Stan

PREFACE

Several years ago Aquinas Institute offered me the opportunity to teach a course in spirituality in addition to my courses in christology which had been my major area of concentration. Although I no longer teach that course in spirituality, I welcomed the opportunity since christology inevitably flows into and out of the theology of the Christian life. What I present in this book is the direction my thinking took as I was teaching. Some of my students will note development as they recall the three loves, the four loves, and now the five loves.

Spirituality is a wide field and is not easily circumscribed. It includes biblical, historical, and contemporary theologies. It is a field with interdisciplinary ramifications—theology and psychology, theology and the arts, theology and social science. It is an area of ecumenical concern, within Christianity and with non-Christian religions. It cannot be separated from the search for justice.

As some of my students may recall, the first time I taught "Spirituality and Discipleship" I tried to do too much. The course gradually became more focused. I did not want to make the same mistake with this book; thus I have focused on the core of life in Christ, the power of love. In doing this I do not mean to disregard all the other aspects of spiritual theology, nor does it imply a complete treatment of even this one topic. The pain of a systematic theologian and a writer is that not all can be said at once. The pain of one who takes developmental and organic theology seriously is that what is said cannot be said in a final way. Yet, these limits can serve a purpose. I therefore submit these limited, incomplete and unfinished reflections to you as you think about your own lives in Christ.

As you can tell, I consider this an essay not only in Christian spirituality but also in spiritual theology. Spiritual theology cannot be separated from its roots in moral theology nor from the fruit it bears in political and sacramental theology. The Christian life is based upon a theological anthropology which comes out of christology, an anthropology which is the foundation for moral, spiritual, political, and liturgical life. Anthropology and ethics are inseparable; morality and spirituality interact dialectically back and forth; so do spirituality and society—there cannot be one without the other. Likewise political/social theology and liturgy cannot risk bifurcation. They complement each other. But you can readily see that all these dimensions cannot be discussed here. I want to say something simple about how to understand love.

This is not simply an essay in *spiritual* theology; it is an essay in spiritual *theology*. Theology is both an art and a science. As science its method becomes more rational and rigorous. As art its method is also creative and intuitive. These two aspects of theological method must be constantly blended by the systematic theologian who is rooted in Scripture, history, philosophy, the behavioral and social sciences, and yet leaves the door open for creative imagination. In that sense both a theologian and a writer can be artists and it is as something of an artist that I share this work with you.

You may well ask: Another book on love? Love is better left to life where we can experience it rather than to books which can hardly do justice to its power and mystery. Yet, new ages need new books to bring the tenderness of this power home.

The greatest theologians have approached the theology of love. Most of them have made it the center of their theologies. Augustine is perhaps still the greatest theologian of love. Yet, Bonaventure, centuries later, still finds fruit in this theme. Also, as Gerard Gilleman accurately points out, love in another way is primary in the theology of Thomas Aquinas. With Anders Nygren, we would have to say the same for Martin Luther, too. Different theologians, different theologies, one mystery, one love. A more popular level of writing senses the importance of the topic, too. Immediately Erich Fromm's *Art of Loving* and C. S. Lewis' *The Four Loves* come to mind. I am writing another book about love because new ages, new people, a new consciousness sometimes need to have something said anew or in a new way.

Writing these days represents a difficulty—because one always writes as a particular person, and yet, as a Christian, a person with a universal consciousness, especially when one writes of love. Sexism is always closer at hand than we would like to believe and our consciousness of religious pluralism sometimes not close enough. Yet, in this universe, I find that I have chosen to be a Roman Catholic theologian, a fact which influences me, and rightly so. Yet, I want to acknowledge that the power of love is not a subject which is the prerogative of Christians alone—although sometimes we give that impression. Our Jewish and Moslem brothers and sisters as well as the members of our family in China, India, and Japan are ones to whom I speak and from whom I learn—although my particular affection for Jesus of Nazareth determines my own relationship with our one Father. It will also be obvious that all too often I am writing as a man. Yet, my hope is that what I say will speak to all women as well as all men, for the sexual liberation movements have been beneficial for me and for the power of love. I also speak from the background of a celibate experience, as a single man. Yet, spiritual theology must speak to both married and single people. What I have to say has all of us in mind. Again, I am a priest, but our universal priesthood can unite us rather than separate us. So I am one of you and I hope that my reflection on my experience and on the Judaeo-Christian Scriptures does not get more limited than it necessarily will be. But you can add your own experiences, meditations, and reflections to mine, and we can undertake this journey together—an adventure in the art of loving.

I would like to take this opportunity to thank my students, my teachers, my family, my Dominican brothers and sisters for their love and support.

In particular I thank Frank Berna for his assistance in preparing the bibliography, Loretta Crippes for her typing and assistance in preparing the manuscript, Diana Culbertson and Stan Drongowski for their extremely helpful editorial assistance and personal support, and also Stan for the creative diagrams.

I also thank Dan McGuire for his special and unique love which has been so important in my life and my story, Stan Drongowski for the experience of his brotherhood and friendship, and Mimi Vernon for having so well exemplified for me the power of love as service. I also want to thank Gary Adams, Jon Alexander, Bob Bolanos, Charles Bouchard, Harry Byrne, Karen and Rick Dufresne, John Gerlach, Jim Ganser, Linda Hansen, Matt Hynous, Walt Ingling, Gene Merz, Ralph Powell, Jacques Soukup, and Pat Walter, the monks of New Mellerary and the nuns of Our Lady of the Mississippi Abbey.

PART ONE

An Introduction

How beautiful you are, my love,
how beautiful you are!
Your eyes are doves.
How beautiful you are, my Beloved,
and how delightful!

Song of Songs
1:15-16
Hebrew Scriptures

Chapter One

THE GREATEST OF THESE IS LOVE

Life With Christ

The mystery of the Christian life, indeed the mystery of life itself, is the mystery of how God gradually unites us, his people, to himself, the mystery of God as sharing his life with us, of our participation in his divine nature, of God becoming one with us. The story of our lives eventually includes the story of the life of Christ, of Jesus of Nazareth, and that includes the story of God. God's story is intimately involved with our lives and our stories are intimately involved in his, whether we are aware of it, admit to it, or not. God and we are already one. Our stories and lives are intimately bound to each other's, although we are not as completely one as God longs for us to be.

The mystery of our human living begins with the mystery of God, Father, Son, and Holy Spirit; God whose very nature is to love actively. The Father is love; the Son is love; and the Spirit is love. There is one divine nature, that of love. The concluding insight into the character of God, after many years of his revealing himself, was clearly stated in the epistles of John: God is love (1 John 4:8). The nature of divinity is to love freely. In that sense, God cannot *not* love freely. It would be against his nature to do so. As this love story progresses, the Father of love sends the Son of love to share our human nature, to partake of our human existence, to manifest and to reveal the nature of love in the flesh. The Son of love becomes love incarnate. Human nature and divine nature are united in one person. We all know the story of that man, Jesus, who is part of the very history and story of God himself, as well as part of our stories: how he lived, was baptized, began to preach the love of his Father and the universal openness of his dawning Reign, how his love led to suffering as well as joy, glory as well as death.

Just as the Father sent the Son, so Jesus, before he returned to the Father upon being raised from the dead, sent us his Spirit, the Spirit of love who is still with us so that the wish of the Father and Son that we all be one with each other and one with God might continue to be accomplished. In response to the activity of the Spirit, an ecclesial people, a community of believers and lovers, was developed to keep alive the story of how God is love, how he became one of us, and how he is still with us deepening our own capacity to love so that we might respond to him and to others and live in fellowship.

The story of God, then, the story of Christ, the story of life, is the story of the Holy Spirit active in our midst. The story of the Christian life is the story of the Holy Spirit and the gifts the Spirit brings us as she makes her home with us, especially the gifts of faith, hope, and love. And the greatest of these is love (1 Cor. 13:13). The Spirit of love, sent by the Father and the Son, gives us the power to love, empowers us, and transforms us by sharing her nature, her life, her love with us. Thus we too can love and give life.

Basic to the life opened up to us by Christ is faith. Without faith, we cannot live, at least not fully. The fullness of life is what awaits us. It has been promised to us. Faith enables us to see, opens our eyes, enables us to know God and hear his story. Faith empowers us to hope. Without faith we could not live, could not hope.

It is not always easy to understand the life of faith. We are intelligent, yet the life which the Father, Son and Spirit makes available to us is more than we can grasp, more than we can ask for or imagine, frequently more than we can hope for. Yet our intelligent nature strives, as best it can, to understand even divine life. This is the centuries-old meaning of theology and the theological task—faith seeking understanding.

Without faith there is no hope, and the ability to hope is a gift more magnificent than that of faith. There are few stories of hope as dramatic as that of the Hebrew people, their small beginnings, their slow progress, that brief period of glory in the times of David and Solomon preceded by slavery and followed by exile. Theirs is a story of hope—as are all stories of hope—which defies human reason. They persevered with faith in God's promises. Their hope provides a paradigm for our hope and for the many stories of lasting hope that manifest themselves in the midst of what often appears to be a despairing world.

The fact of hope and the substance of things to be hoped for is a mystery; yet we do continue to hope, not naively but courageously. Hope makes faith visible, and eschatology becomes the horizon both for understanding biblical faith, Jewish and Christian, and for shaping the theological task of the Church. This consciousness of eschatology has led to a new definition of theology: hope seeking understanding, reason grappling with the incomprehensible mystery of hope. If the story of the Hebrew, Jewish, and Christian peoples is a story of faith, it is even moreso a story of hope—faith made visible. But it can also be said that just as those stories are stories of hope, so too are they stories of love, love that springs from faith and hope, love stories which are as much a mystery as faith and hope are, love stories that are the fruit of hope. Just as hope is faith visible, so love is faith and hope alive, active. And these are the gifts the Spirit brings: faith, hope, and love, and the greatest of these is love, for love requires and presupposes the other two. Love is faith and hope at work. It is the fruit of faith and the glory of hope. Faith and hope empower us to love with a kind of love that only the Father, Son and Spirit can create. The story of our ability to love is the story of our hope, the story of our faith, the story of God himself in love with us. God is love and it is into union with his love that we have all been called.

Gifts of the Spirit

faith

hope ———— love

Just as theology is faith seeking understanding and, even moreso, hope seeking understanding, so theology is love seeking understanding. What is love? From where does the power to love come? How do we love? Can we love? Can we believe in love; can love be trusted? Can we hope in the triumph of love or are hatred and indifference more powerful? Will we love?

Are we loveable? What are the effects of loving? These are existential and theological questions. Theology, as a reflection on God, is a reflection on love; it is love, our love seeking to understand itself. Within ourselves we are all lovers. The Spirit of love lies deep within our hearts. It may be buried or not yet fully alive, but it is there longing to recreate us in the image of the Spirit. We are lovers, although as sinners we are not always faithful to who we are as lovers. We fail to give flesh and bones to the spirit of love within us. She remains a Spirit unincarnate. Yet, she longs to break through, and frequently enough does, and we find ourselves being transformed and living a new life marked by joy, peace, patience, kindness, goodness, trust, gentleness and self-control (Gal. 5:22).

This incomprehensible drive, the fruit of this remarkable power, the roots of this mysterious energy: this our intelligences seek to understand. This search is theology: love seeking self-understanding. It is the story of how we are all one, all unique, and not yet fully formed. This story is *our story,* the *story of God,* and the story of the life we share in common. Although God and we are different, we are created in his image and destined to become his likeness. We have different natures but share one life, his life, which for us is a supernatural life and for him a natural life, but yet one life. His love runs through our veins. If only we have the courage to live with the strength it gives us.

There is nothing, no story so moving, so powerful, as that of love and its history. It is that which the Christian life, all life, is about. Part Two of this book explores the notion of our love, human love, and Part Three the nature of God's love, divine love.

Human love manifests itself in a variety of ways, five of which are central.

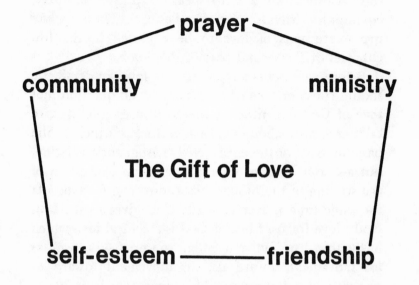

The Five Loves

The fundamental goal of moral and spiritual living is to love and to deepen our capacity for love. This goal is stated quite clearly in Scripture and in theology. Thomas Aquinas, for example, sees the centrality of love as the goal of the whole of Christian life.[1] Although love is the goal of life in Christ, it manifests itself in many ways. In the Scriptures we find five basic loves. Though this does not mean that there are not others as well, yet there are five in terms of which most relationships can be understood. We are not speaking here of the loves C. S. Lewis explores nor the loves such as *eros* and *agape* that Christian tradition makes much of.[2] The five loves in Scripture to which I refer are love of God, neighborly love, communal love, particular love, and self-love. These are the core of Christian spirituality. Another way of expressing these Gospel values is to speak of prayer, ministry, community, friendship, and self-esteem. These are the five expressions of love to be explored in the five chapters of the second part of this book.

Before we discuss any of the five loves in detail, we should consider each briefly. There is no question that love of God is central in the Scriptures. We are not talking simply about God's love for us which is the basic message of the entire New Testament revelation, but also our love for God. Prayer is an expression of the stirring of the human heart, our love for God. At the same time prayer is a gift God gives to us. It is God's love for us. Love of God is a central love which has within itself our movement toward God as well as his movement toward us, his movement toward us always being initiatory. God's love for us is grace. Grace, however, is not ineffective. It enables us to reach out toward God, the kind of reaching out that is described as prayer. There can be little doubt that this love of God is essential to the Scriptures if we simply look at Jesus' summary of the Law and the prophets in the great commandment.

Love of neighbor is also central and, in the biblical tradition, of equal importance to love of God. Love of neighbor does not refer to all forms of human response to the other but to the other who is in need. Love of neighbor is a universal love. The Scriptures ask, "Who is our neighbor?" and the response is: any person who is in need (Luke 10:29-37). This love might be better described as love of the poor, the needy and the oppressed—the human heart reaching out to those who are outcasts and in need. It is ministry. This does not imply that ministry is one-directional. Just as God first loves us so that we can reach out to him, so in reaching out to others, we too are enriched. Nevertheless, love of neighbor is based primarily upon the need of the other rather than upon the "equality" of the other with us, that is, our need for each other. Love of neighbor is also included by Jesus in his summary of the Law.

Within the general area of love of others there are three kinds of love—friendship (*philia*), community (*koinonia*) and ministry (*diakonia*). Friendship is

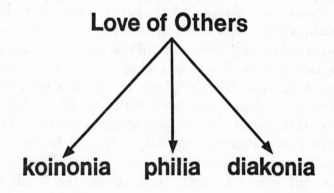

Love of Others

koinonia philia diakonia

that kind of relationship between two based upon intimacy and reciprocity. In ministry the relationship with another is based upon need. The basis is not mutuality, not self-disclosure and not commitment, but responsiveness to a need which is perceived or felt. Between these two kinds of love, friendship and ministry, there is the love that exists between brothers and sisters, whether we think of this in terms of our family life, or as we become aware of how brotherly or sisterly a particular relationship might be. This is a love which is not easy to describe although it does relate to our experience. This third love is fellowship or community.

Another consideration in understanding this love is that of understanding family life. Family connotes those with whom we interact at a certain level of significance without the same necessary degree of commitment to self-disclosure as might exist in friendship. Although intimacy must always be seen in terms of degrees and though there is a sense in which every human relationship involves an element of intimacy, intimacy is a word more appropriately associated with the psychology of friendship than with the psychology of brothers and sisters. In fact, there is a sense in which brothers and sisters are those with whom we are not intimate but with whom we still share and upon whom we can depend. There is a kind of love here, then, less erotic than friendship can be, perhaps even less affectionate than some relationships might be, but a love that values the companionship potential. The word *family* connotes not only biological family but also the entire human family and thus we will see later that our true community is a family, the family of humankind.

The fourth love, with which we might be less familiar as far as biblical material is concerned, is the love of friendship or particular love. This can be contrasted with the universal love that lies within the notion of ministry. In addition to love which reaches out to those who are in need, there is the love that builds a bond between those who are perceived as equal, those whom we love with a special love. It is a love that cannot be shared with all. We might feel that this love is not evidenced as strongly in the Scriptures and yet it is expressed in the Song of Songs and is also exemplified in concrete relationships, such as that which existed between David and Jonathan, Ruth and Naomi, Jacob and Rachel. In the New Testament we find exemplified in the life of Jesus himself the particular love he felt for his friends at Bethany as well as for the disciple John. Love of friendship is one of the supreme Christian loves.

A fifth love which we are even more likely inclined to omit when discussing the Scriptures is love of self. We need to remember that each of these loves can exist in an ambiguous and distorted way as well as in a healthy and truly Christian way. Particular love can become a masked selfishness; ministry can fulfill one's own needs rather than those of the other; community can become superficial commonality; prayer can lead to self-righteousness rather than to acceptance of justification through grace. Self-love can exist in a distorted form, such as false pride, yet, in its positive sense, it is essential to the biblical message. It is included in the great commandment when we are instructed to love others as we love ourselves. The biblical intuition is that no one can authentically reach out to the other unless this reaching out is based upon a healthy acceptance and love of one's own self. The word "self-esteem" is perhaps too technically psychological a word for expressing this biblical notion; yet it suggests a starting point for all the other loves. Love of God and love of others cannot be separated from love of self or they will all be distorted by those unconscious needs which lead us to manipulate others, including God. The problem of self-esteem is basic in spiritual theology; ignoring this problem will distort the other four loves.

We do not imply that there are no other variations

of these five loves. For instance, we know of the love of parents for children, children for parents, teachers and students for each other, love of nature or animals, and study or the love of learning. Yet these loves often partake of one of the other loves or are analogous to one of the other loves. Love of enemies is also a supreme form of love to which the Scriptures refer; yet love of enemies is simply an exemplification of love of neighbor. The Scriptures are calling us to respond to those who are in need whether or not they are our friends. What good does it do simply to love those who love you? Ministry cannot be based upon those who love us but must be based upon those who are genuinely in need. Thus these five loves provide the core of Christian moral and spiritual living.

We can reflect upon Jesus' summary of the Law and the prophets. Mark writes:

> One of the scribes who had listened to them debating and had observed how well Jesus had answered them, now came up and put a question to him, 'Which is the first of all the commandments?' Jesus replied, 'This is the first: Listen, Israel, the Lord our God is the one Lord, and you must love the Lord your God with all your heart, with all your soul, with all your mind and with all your strength. The second is this: You must love your neighbor as yourself. There is no commandment greater than these.' The scribe said to him, 'Well spoken, Master; what you have said is true: that he is one and there is no other. To love him with all your heart, with all your understanding and strength, and to love your neighbor as yourself, this is far more important than any holocaust or sacrifice.' Jesus, seeing how wisely he had spoken, said, 'You are not far from the kingdom of God.' And after that no one dared to question him any more (Mk 12:28-34).

Here Jesus responds to the questioner by pointing out his own understanding of the biblical ethical tradition.

He says that we must love God with all our being, we must love our neighbor, and we must love our neighbor as we love ourselves. These are the basic components of the Law. This should not surprise us since Paul himself later says that three things are important: faith, hope and love, and of these three the most important is love. This is what Jesus is saying as well. There is no reality more important. Looking at Matthew's version of the great commandment we read:

> But when the Pharisees heard that he had silenced the Sadducees they got together and, to disconcert him, one of them put a question, 'Master, which is the greatest commandment of the Law?' Jesus said 'You must love the Lord your God with all your heart, with all your soul, and with all your mind. This is the greatest and the first commandment. The second resembles it: You must love your neighbor as yourself. On these two commandments hang the whole Law, and the Prophets also' (Mt. 22:34-40).

Again Jesus quotes the two commandments upon which the entire Hebrew and Christian traditions rest, love of God and love of neighbor, love of neighbor including a love of self.

Luke's version is the same:

> There was a lawyer who, to disconcert him, stood up and said to him, 'Master, what must I do to inherit eternal life?' He said to him, 'What is written in the Law? What do you read there?' He replied, 'You must love the Lord your God with all your heart, with all your strength, and with all your mind, and your neighbor as yourself.' 'You have answered right' said Jesus, 'do this and life is yours' (Lk. 10:25-28).

We therefore see the similarity within the Synoptic tradition as well as the implication of this similarity.

A theological problem that often emerges in discussions of these loves is the priority that should be given to one or the other. It is true that in a way each has a certain priority. There is, however, a definite sense in which Jesus is opposed to putting these five loves in any kind of hierarchy. Every person is called to love in all five ways. There is no escape from this basic commandment.

There is certainly priority associated with the love of God. Jesus himself refers to this love as the first and the greatest of the commandments. This priority stems simply from the definition of God himself. For the Christian, God is the one who deserves to be loved, the one who is supremely loveable, the one who is truly adorable. Even a rudimentary understanding of who God is should motivate us to give God priority.

On the other hand, the second commandment also has priority. The second commandment is like and equal to the first and in Luke's version is actually included within the first. Love of neighbor is as important for the Christian as love of God. Jesus here shows a profound unity between the two commandments and not a hierarchy. This unity is exemplified when Jesus teaches the parable of the Good Samaritan and when John instructs us, "A man who does not love the brother that he can see cannot love God, whom he has never seen" (I John 4:20). Even Paul, who in his epistle to the Galatians is so fundamentally concerned with the life of faith and the human response to God in faith, astounds us when he summarizes the Law in a single command—love your neighbor as yourself (Gal. 5:14). Paul, for whom love of God is supremely important, summarizes the Law simply as love of neighbor. This priority exists not because of the deservedness of our neighbor, but rather because of the inauthenticity that can exist if we attempt to separate

our response to God from our response to his creatures and friends. Our God is the one who loves us,
who loves men and women, who loves our neighbors.
No Christian response to God can be separated from
loving those whom he loves. The prophetic tradition
is quite explicit in this. It points out that love of God
can be too readily separated from a response to those
in need. Thus, we already find in the first chapter of
Isaiah a criticism of that hypocritical religion which
attempts to separate the two, giving a higher priority
to our love of God, which then simply becomes external:

> What are your endless sacrifices to me?
> says Yahweh.
> I am sick of holocausts of rams
> and the fat of calves.
> The blood of bulls and of goats revolts me.
> When you come to present yourselves before me,
> who asked you to trample over my courts?
>
> Bring me your worthless offerings no more,
> the smoke of them fills me with disgust.
> New Moons, sabbaths, assemblies—
> I cannot endure festival and solemnity.
> Your New Moons, and your pilgrimages
> I hate with all my soul.
> They lie heavy on me,
> I am tired of bearing them.
> When you stretch out your hands
> I turn my eyes away.
> You may multiply your prayers,
> I shall not listen.
> Your hands are covered with blood,
> wash, make yourselves clean.
>
> Take your wrong-doing out of my sight.
> Cease to do evil.

> Learn to do good,
> search for justice,
> help the oppressed,
> be just to the orphan,
> plead for the widow
> (Is. 1:11-17).

Love of God includes a search for justice. A love of God separated from love of neighbor becomes religious formalism and hypocrisy. This principle is again reiterated in the New Testament when Matthew instructs us to leave our gifts at the altar and to reconcile ourselves with our neighbor before offering sacrifice (Matt. 5:23-24). He is emphasizing the intrinsic relatedness between two loves. One cannot exist without the other.

Can the same principle be extended to friendship? Just as Jesus says, "Do not tell me you love the one whom you do not see if you do not love the one whom you do see," so we can hear him saying, "Do not tell me you love everyone in general if you love no one in particular." Particular love is also a supreme form of love and one could say in John's gospel the supreme exemplification of what love is. For John *philia* (particular love) is *agape* (universal love) and *agape* is *philia*.[3] They are inseparable and the two words are quite interchangeable. To see the point, we can look at two Bethany stories. In Luke's gospel, we read:

> In the course of their journey he came to a village, and a woman named Martha welcomed him into her house. She had a sister called Mary, who sat down at the Lord's feet and listened to him speaking. Now Martha who was distracted with all the serving said, 'Lord, do you not care that my sister is leaving me to do the serving all by myself? Please tell her to help me.' But the Lord answered: 'Martha, Martha,' he said 'you worry and fret about so

many things, and yet few are needed, indeed only one. It is Mary who has chosen the better part; it is not to be taken from her' (Lk. 10:38-42).

Often we interpret this story as the superiority of the contemplative life over the active life. This is a common interpretation in preaching as well as in the mystical tradition. We find this interpretation in the writings of the great mystics of the fourteenth century, such as the author of *The Cloud of Unknowing*.[4] Yet we know that the intention of the Gospel's author is not to resolve the problem of action versus contemplation. This is a problem of monastic theology and of monasticism moving in an apostolic direction. The problem of action and contemplation would not have been envisioned by Luke. What then can the text mean? We can gain understanding if we can look at John's gospel:

Six days before the Passover, Jesus went to Bethany, where Lazarus was, whom he had raised from the dead. They gave a dinner for him there; Martha waited on them and Lazarus was among those at table. Mary brought in a pound of very costly ointment, pure nard, and with it anointed the feet of Jesus, wiping them with her hair; the house was full of the scent of the ointment. Then Judas Iscariot —one of his disciples, the man who was to betray him— said, 'Why wasn't this ointment sold for three hundred denarii, and the money given to the poor? He said this, not because he cared about the poor, but because he was a thief; he was in charge of the common fund and used to help himself to the contributions. So Jesus said, 'Leave her alone; she had to keep this scent for the day of my burial. You have the poor with you always, you will not always have me' (Jn. 12:1-8).

Is the meaning of this text that Jesus invites us to be unconcerned about the poor? Of course not. Jesus is vitally concerned about the poor; there are numerous texts to that effect. Jesus is concerned about the poor, but he is aware here that Judas' concern fails to respond to the poor on the basis of real love for them. If Judas really loved the poor, if Judas really loved, then Judas would recognize love when he saw it. Judas would recognize the love that exists in the relationship between Jesus and Mary. What Jesus is saying in both of these instances is that his relationship with Mary was a valid form of love and was not to be separated from love of neighbor and love of God. In an objective sense, both Martha and Judas are correct. Mary could readily have helped with the work that Martha was legitimately engaged in. Judas also was correct. The ointment could have been sold and the money could have been used for the poor. But, if we were to talk about theology and economics in the New Testament, spending money on a friend is, according to Jesus, one of the few justifications for an expense. In these Bethany stories Jesus validates friendship. He is saying to Martha, not that her work is unimportant, but that what Mary is doing is also important, a fact which Martha has not perceived. Martha has distorted the religious understanding, not by being aware of the value of hospitality, but by being unaware of the value of friendship.

So with Judas. Love of the poor is always important. Yet there are those who distort the text, saying that the poor will always be with us and thus we need not be overly concerned about this reality. We know that this is not the message of the text. Jesus constantly calls us to justice. Yet, when there are those who distort this call by giving it a priority over love of friendship, then the compassionate, kind, loving, and tender Jesus becomes assertive and even takes the offensive. Jesus is

simply validating the kind of relationship of particular love that contributes to ministry and to friendship
with God. The school of particular love is the school
in which we frequently learn how to love God, who
loves us with a particular love, the love of friendship.
In John's gospel, love of friendship is the supreme
form of love. For Paul, love of friendship, particularly
conjugal friendship, is supreme because of its sacramental dimension. It is a sign of the kind of love that
Christ himself has. Love of friendship then has priority.

Community, or brotherly and sisterly love, can also
take priority since it summarizes so well all our relationships, with head and with members. It is a universal love based on equality and creates a family, a
universe, or, as Paul envisions, a body in which all are
united. Community is Paul's image of the end, the
final shape of things, that for which all exists, almost
the final cause of all creation, the body of Christ and,
in that sense, it is prior in importance to all other
loves.

Self-esteem or self-love can also be seen as prior
since, for Jesus, love of neighbor cannot be separated
from it. This priority of self-esteem is found in both
Hebrew and Christian Scripture. Somehow Jesus'
acute psychological insight is that we cannot reach out
to the other with a damaged self-esteem. Love of self
is equal to love of neighbor and in one sense precedes
it. Each of these loves has priority depending upon the
perspective from which it is viewed.

It should be emphasized that there is always danger
in attempting to hierarchize one love as more important than the other. There is no question that God is
more important than human beings. On the other

hand, all five loves, although distinguishable, are inseparable and of equal importance in the Gospel accounts of the life of Christ. To separate these loves and to hierarchize them is to run the risk of distorting them. For Jesus of Nazareth there is only one love, one outpouring of the Spirit within us, which reaches out in many directions. There is only one love that reaches out to God, to those in need, to those who enter our lives in a particular and special way, to our brothers and sisters, and to our own selves. That one love can be manifested in many ways depending upon the objects of that love. That one love is an outpouring of the Spirit within us that pours forth love towards God, neighbors, friends, brothers, and sisters and self.

If we attempt to say that prayer is more important than ministry, then Jesus, angered at our distortion of his understanding of love, will reply that we cannot love God without loving those whom we see. If we say that love of the poor is more important than love of a friend, then Jesus will reply that the poor we will always have with us and point to the responsibility for friendship. If we reply that the other is more important than ourselves, then Jesus will simply quote Hebrew Scripture and tell us that we are called to love others *as* we love ourselves (Lk. 19:18). These five loves are so interrelated that we are called to love in all five ways. Jesus' anger surfaces when we distort this intuition of the nature of love by separating its manifestations. To attempt even to envision talking about one in its fullness apart from the others is already to have misunderstood the message.

The God of whom the Scriptures and Jesus speak is a God who is inseparable from his presence in others and in ourselves. To not grasp this revelation is to not yet have penetrated the life of Christ's God.

We have heard before of the four cardinal moral virtues as the hinges of the moral life. In Christian spirituality it has often been the three evangelical counsels that have provided the basis in terms of which striving after perfection could be understood. My approach is to base Christian spirituality on these five loves. The first reason for doing so is that this basis is biblical. A second major reason, however, is that this approach can overcome the double standard that has crept into the history of Christian spirituality once celibate Christian life emerged as the radical form of Christian response to which not everyone is called.

In the early Christian tradition a radical response to Christ was expected, and manifested in martyrdom. The society or culture in which Christian life took shape was one in which Christians were persecuted and total response to Christ was found in the gift of martyrdom. Martyrdom became less of a possibility when Christianity became accepted in the Roman empire, and virginity and monasticism, which had already begun, surfaced as the supreme form of Christian witness. It became the equivalent of martyrdom. When celibacy emerged as that kind of radical response, however, it inevitably led to a double standard: some were called to a radical response and some were called to a minimal response, since it was obvious that not all were called to celibacy. But today, any Christian spirituality must be equally applicable to conjugal as well as celibate lives, to single as well as married men and women.

Not only have we had the struggle of action versus

contemplation in the history of Christian spirituality, we have also had the struggle of celibacy versus marriage. Christian spirituality must finally move out of that destructive tension which sets actives over against contemplatives and celibate against married rather than seeing all of us in partnership within the body of Christ. We need each other. We are friends, not enemies in the body of Christ. The most important statement any of us can make about our lives is that we are in Christ and moved by the Spirit. This we all have in common. These five loves enable us to biblically challenge all Christians to accept their call to perfection. To be in Christ, no matter what our life style, is to desire total union with him. Thus, self-esteem, friendship, community, ministry and prayer give us the context in terms of which each of us can understand our particular life style in its unique relationship to our response to God's grace. This response is Christian spirituality, our response to the grace of God, a spirituality which will always manifest itself in a diversity of ways within the one body.

The theology of spirituality which is developed here is a theology of spirituality truly applicable to all Christians, a theology of spirituality in terms of which contemplative monks and nuns can understand their lives. It is a spirituality in terms of which mendicant and apostolic celibates can understand their lives. It is a spirituality at the heart of Christian marriage, and a spirituality for single men and women. Christian spirituality at its core is one reality lived out by many people in diverse ways. Christian spirituality cannot be monastic spirituality watered down for apostolic celibates, watered down more for married men and women and even more for singles. Christian spirituality has to make available the fullness of the Gospel life to all, whatever shape or form our life or call takes.

The Five Complements

Many times, in approaching an inquiry, it is not so much the content or answers which we seek that is important but the very way in which we pose the question or set up the problem. The way of posing the question or conceptualizing the problem can determine the direction in which we go. This is true of the nature of love as well. How can we conceptualize the reality of love and how should we think about it?

There are different ways of thinking. We will speak only about two of these. Both are insightful and valid. One does not necessarily rule out the other. In fact, some issues, questions or problems may be better handled by one mode of thinking than the other. What is important is not that we choose between the two but that we recognize the validity of both. One is thinking in terms of exclusive opposition and the other is thinking in terms of complementarity. There is no need to choose one or the other since both are central to the human quest for understanding. Yet the fact remains that in the West one mode of thinking has predominated, frequently to the exclusion of any other. I shall emphasize the one which has been the less influential position in Western intellectual history.

The common Western way of thinking for centuries is what I would call thinking in terms of "either/or." This is a categorical, discursive, logical and rational mode of thought. It is satisfying to the intellect which searches for clarity because its tendency to categorize and, therefore, to dichotomize helps us to establish clear and distinct ideas. One can already see the triumph of this way of thinking within the philosophy of Descartes. In this form of discursive, oppositional and rational thought we define one reality over and against another, in opposition to another, in distinction from another. We see a reality in terms of specific differences rather than in terms of that which it might have in common with or how it might complement other realities. The propensity toward rationalism in the West, the emergence of rationalism with the Enlightenment in Western philosophy, and the impact of Cartesianism on all of us cannot be dismissed. Whether we admit to it or not, most of us tend to think in terms of "either/or."

Placing realities in opposition to each other when this opposition is unnecessary, frequently means that to affirm something, we must deny something else. Is there no way in which both realities might be affirmed, a way in which we can think in terms of "both/and" rather than "either/or?" I develop this notion of two ways of thinking further in the first appendix rather than here where it may be unnecessary. The "either/or" thinking dichotomizes and opposes realities. The "both/and" thinking allows realities to complement each other. (See Appendix 1 for further discussion.)

Perhaps some examples will help us to understand this tendency in Western thought to dichotomize. For example, we make easy distinctions between masculine and feminine, defining masculinity over and against femininity. The more masculine one is the less feminine one is and vice versa. Although that mode of thinking can be appropriate, it is not necessarily appropriate at every level of reality. Thus at the biological level it is certainly true to say that we are either male or female, although even then that is not always clearly the case. Yet, generally speaking, material and biological realities can be fairly well grasped by "either/or" ways of thinking. The higher up the evolutionary scale we move, however, such as into the psychological realms beyond biology alone, the more we see that this mode of grasping reality is less adequate. Realities which are either male or female need not be either exclusively masculine or exclusively feminine. It is possible to be both and the two need not be defined over against each other.

We dichotomize also the intellectual life and the emotional life. The more intellectual I am, the less emotional I will be, and the more emphasis I give to emotion, the less I am likely to give to intellect. This dichotomy flows from our way of thinking, an unnecessary and inadequate way of thinking also evident in the traditional Western relationship between mysticism and rationalism. In the East, the history of philosophy includes much of what we in the West include within the history of religion, namely mystical development. It is, however, our Western tendency again to define the two over and against each other rather than seeing the way in which, although distinct, mysticism and rationalism, religion and philosophy mutually relate to and support each other.

Another reason for emphasizing the importance of our complementarity is that frequently "either/or" thinking does not avoid value-free judgments although it might pretend to do so. When we define masculinity over and against femininity, we usually evaluate one side of the opposition more highly than the other. In this case masculinity becomes a value rather than femininity. The same is true of intellectuality which becomes more valued than emotion. In

Aristotle's sense, therefore, it becomes more tyranical rather than democratic.[5] Rationalism is likewise more esteemed than religion or mysticism. The same problem manifests itself as we look at the relationship between physicality and spirituality, or the body and soul problem, as it was manifested in the dualistic metaphysics. This tendency often accompanies Western philosophical thought, e.g., Plato as well as Descartes later. We can hardly overemphasize the importance these traditions have had upon all of us whether we admit to them or not. In that sense we are probably all Platonists and Cartesians. Yet this way of posing the body and soul problem leads to subtle evaluations in such a way that we think first in terms of the higher nature and the lower nature. In the West, theologians debated the relative value of contemplation and action. When the two are seen over and against each other evaluation inevitably enters in and one is seen as higher rather than seeing both as interdependent, distinguishable but not separable in the concrete.

Complementarity takes concreteness, development, solidarity, and wholeness seriously. We are not saying, however, that complementarity is a better way of thinking. This would be a manifestation of the "either/or" mentality. Both ways of thinking are necessary if we are to grasp any reality. It is simply that the one has been left in an inferior or unused position in much of Western thought. It is now rebelling.

Now we can consider the nature of love. In the previous section we made some distinctions which will become more apparent as we proceed. There are not five loves, but only one love, one gift of the Holy Spirit, which manifests itself in five, and even more, ways. Although we emphasize that each of the loves, which we have distinguished in a somewhat rational way, interpenetrates and relates to each of the other loves so that no one love can be totally separated from any of the other loves, which is indeed the wisdom and insight of Jesus of Nazareth, yet there is a danger that in speaking about each of them we will fail to search for its complement, in terms of which its completion or wholeness can best be seen. In other words, we run the risk of misunderstanding each of the loves unless we raise the question of how that love might be completed and what its complement is. We need to answer this question to understand the love itself of which we speak.

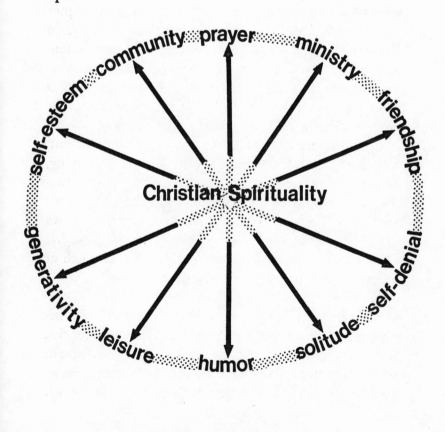

As we take a look at the loves of which we have already spoken, the following are the complements to which we will refer. Self-esteem needs to be balanced by self-denial; intimacy needs to be balanced by generativity; community by solitude; ministry by leisure or play; prayer by humor and joy. Just as we can speak of the five loves, so too can we refer to the five loves joined with their complements as the ten pillars of the Christian spirituality which we will consider in the second part of this book. We are aware that nothing can be understood in terms of itself alone and understanding means standing under the distinctiveness as well as the relatedness into which the life of the Spirit leads us.

PART TWO

The Five Loves

Father of all, Master supreme. Power supreme
in all the worlds. Who is like thee?
Who is beyond thee?

I bow before thee, I prostrate in adoration;
and I beg thy grace, O glorious Lord!
As a father to his son, as a friend to his
friend, as a lover to his beloved, be
gracious unto me, O God.

The Bhagavad Gita
11:43-44

Chapter Two

SELF-ESTEEM

The Psychology of Self-Esteem

I have previously pointed out the diversity that exists within psychology,[1] not only in the continuing dialectic between psychoanalysis, behaviorism, and humanistic psychology, but in the differences within these traditions as well. Thus there is no one psychology of self-esteem, although all psychologists affirm its importance. We need to consider some psychological reflections in order to understand our lives at this level as well as prepare ourselves for life in Christ.

Abraham Maslow, one of the most significant humanistic psychologists, gives us a clarification of the human person's basic needs. I have explored Maslow's basic hierarchy of needs elsewhere and there is ample material written on the subject.[2] He is responsible for making us aware that needs exist in a hierarchy. Some needs do not become such until other needs are satisfied.

> At once other (and higher) needs emerge and these, rather than physiological hungers, dominate the organism. And when these in turn are satisfied, again new (and still higher) needs emerge, and so on. This is what we mean by saying that the basic human needs are organized into a hierarchy of relative prepotency.[3]

For Maslow, the basic human needs are the physiological needs of hunger and thirst. Until these are met, other needs are less necessary for the organism. When they are met and we are no longer physiologically deprived, then other needs arise which become significant. It is as if the higher needs do not exist until the lower needs have to some degree been met. After physiological needs come safety needs. We will risk safety, if we are hungry. If, however, hunger and thirst have been met, safety, security, stability, protection, freedom from fear and anxiety become significant. These now are the important needs. In this same way, gratification of needs is important in Christian development, since gratification releases or frees us from the domination of lower needs and discloses more human, social, and spiritual goals.

After the safety needs comes the entire range of affective needs, the needs to belong, to love and to be loved. It is at this time, as Maslow points out,[4] that we feel more keenly absence from friends or significant others. We now need more strongly affectionate relationships in general and will strive after these with greater intensity. We now attach more importance to the emotional quality of relationships when previously love and acceptance might have been less important. Loneliness becomes more real and rejection more threatening. We now need to belong, to love, and to be loved.

When these needs seem to be more or less adequately met, the need for self-esteem emerges. Self-love is not only a root for love of others; being loved by others is also essential to love of self. In other words, the five loves interact. It is not as if one is chronologically prior in such a way that it can simply be resolved once and for all. Love of self enables us to love others more effectively and we can then love God more deeply. But it is also true that loving God enables us to love others, and loving others and being loved by them promotes self-love. There is constant dialectical interaction. The esteem needs emerge as basic within Maslow's hierarchy. These are not the most important needs, not needs in the same way as food and drink, but still basic as far as self-actualization and spiritualization are concerned. Self-esteem is a need that must be met prior to self-actualization. The desire for self-actualization, or even spiritualization, will not surface until we feel self-respect.

For Maslow the esteem needs are classified into two groups. First come the desires for strength, achievement, adequacy, competence and confidence. The second area of esteem needs is for respect from others in the form of recognition, attention, reputation, and appreciation. He writes, "Satisfaction of the self-esteem need leads to feelings of self-confidence, worth, strength, capability, and adequacy, of being useful and necessary in the world."[5]

Behind Maslow's frame of reference, however, is Alfred Adler's psychology which attempts to deal with the feelings of inferiority innate within all of us.[6] Adler's starting point is the feeling of inadequacy and man's striving to compensate for this feeling in order to feel a sense of self-worth, an upward striving which is the fundamental motivational force in the life of a person. Adler, in some ways the father of humanistic psychology, already sets the stage for the importance we attach here to self-esteem.

From a Christian point of view, we must be aware that the need for self-esteem is important psychologically if we are to be freed for higher and further development. After the esteem needs comes the need for self-actualization for which every Christian should be freed, the freedom to develop our potential as well as to develop our life in Christ. As Christians, we may well go beyond Maslow's framework and say that the need for self-actualization must be met in order to achieve freedom for life in Christ. If we are starving, we will risk safety; if we feel totally unprotected, we will be less aware of being loved; if we feel unacceptable and unloved, self-confidence and achievement will be less significant; if we feel badly about ourselves, there will be less desire for actualizing our potential. If the human potential is frustrated, the potential for life in Christ is damaged. The need for contact with God emerges as the basic human needs are met and as grace continues to build upon the human nature that prepares its way. Maslow, discussing the need for self-actualization, comments:

> Even if all these needs are satisfied, we may still often (if not always) expect that a new discontent and restlessness will soon develop, unless the individual is doing what *he*, individually, is fitted for. A musician must make music, an artist must paint, a poet must write, if he is to be ultimately at peace with himself. What a man *can* be, he *must* be. He must be true to his own nature. This need we may call self-actualization.[7]

Self-esteem is not the most basic need in the human person's functioning, but is basic in terms of the higher needs, this is, the human and spiritual needs, and hence cannot be neglected by Christian theologians and spiritual writers. Impaired self-esteem impairs union with God.

Societal attitudes are not totally responsible for the way we accept ourselves. In fact, the two subsidiary aspects of self-esteem which Maslow points out are interrelated, but the second is in some sense less significant. The second aspect of esteem needs is the desire for respect from others. Maslow clarifies this point.

We have been learning more and more of the dangers of basing self-esteem on the opinions of others rather than on real capacity, competence, and adequacy to the task. The most stable and therefore the most healthy self-esteem is based on deserved respect from others rather than on external fame or celebrity and adulation.[8]

The healthiest form of self-esteem flows from our positive self-affirmation. Blaming society for our impaired self-esteem is usually a way of avoiding the task involved in affirming ourselves.

Nathaniel Branden makes emphatic the same principle: "There is no value judgment more important to man—no factor more decisive in his psychological development and motivation—than the estimate that he passes on himself."[9] Self-esteem, a sense of personal efficacy and personal worth, an integration of self-confidence and self-respect, a feeling of competence, is essential for the human spirit.[10] Too many become prisoners of their own self-negation. They see themselves as weak or mediocre or unmasculine or unfeminine or ineffectual. Overcoming this self-negation involves self-affirmation. At the core of the problem of self-alienation is the disowned self.[11]

For Branden, self-esteem involves self-acceptance and self-acceptance is an acceptance of the whole of and not simply a portion of oneself. One needs to be thoroughly in touch with oneself in order to accept the fullness of self. The problem in self-esteem is usually that we have alienated ourselves from a portion of ourselves, that we have disowned a portion of ourselves and thus made it unavailable to us. We remain divided within and are never capable of giving undivided attention to the Lord. This process of self-alienation involves a denial of our feelings and repudiation of our experience.

The problem of the disowned self can exist not only in blocking off aspects of our experience, but also aspects of our feelings. This is the starting point for self-negation. The tragedy is that this self-negation leads not only to the negation of one aspect of self but eventually to the negation of many aspects. Branden points out, "To diminish one's capacity to experience pain is to diminish also one's capacity to experience pleasure."[12] Different areas of our emotionality resonate with others. Not opening myself to myself impairs not only that portion of myself which I disown, but other portions of the personality as well. Stifling my capability for experiencing pain can impair my capacity for pleasure, joy, union. A denial of who I am is the creation of an unreal self.[13]

No matter how difficult it might be to accept the facts of the case, we are called upon to accept ourselves as we are before God. Self-protective denial in this psychological sense cannot be the basis for life in Christ. When we repress certain thoughts, fantasies, experiences, when we disown a portion of ourselves, it is often in the name of protecting the self without realizing that we are in fact damaging the self. We tend to repress that portion of ourselves which threatens our concept of acceptability, maturity, or perfection. Yet this repression never leads to self-esteem. Theologically, this is to base self-love on self-justification rather than on justification through grace. Salvation only comes when we accept who we are. In this sense we need to take a thorough look at the whole question of what striving for perfection means in the Christian tradition. Branden's fundamental assumption is theological in nature, "Self-esteem cannot be built on a foundation of self-alienation."[14]

Rollo May also recognizes this false avenue to self-acceptance. The gradual progress toward perfection, if perfection implies a denial of that which is socially or personally unacceptable in terms of our values, is destructive. May points out that the saints were not talking nonsense when they called themselves sinners. When we look at them, we see their sanctity; when they look at themselves, they see their reality and their sinfulness and their imperfection. It is in our ability to accept ourselves as we are that sanctity becomes a possibility. Sanctity is not based upon the need to deny to ourselves who we are in order to give the image of sanctity. True sanctity is always humility. It is never a false self-understanding. The goal of perfectibility, then, can frequently be a bastardized concept even for Christians. Striving for perfection does not mean a denial of the negative side of ourselves, the seamy side of our lives, the less public side of who we are. Perfectibility is rather acceptability and integration of every aspect of the personality. Perfection in St. Matthew's sense means to be completed, to be finished, to have arrived at one's goal. The Greek word for perfection is *teleios* which does not mean to be perfect in the sense that we so often think. It means rather to arrive at one's goal, that is, to accept the self in order to realize salvation through God's grace.

Like Nathaniel Branden, Rollo May points out quite clearly that "the most important criterion which saves the demonic from anarchy is *dialogue*."[15] For self-acceptance we need to enter into dialogue with ourselves, into dialogue with the disowned portions of ourselves, lest those disowned portions, through our inattentiveness, begin to take over and become demonic. The demonic for May is that portion of the self which has the power to take over the whole self. It can cause anarchy unless it is tamed, accepted, integrated, loved. This is why Rollo May points out that an acceptance of oneself requires a fundamental humility.[16] The Greek injunction to know oneself is important for everyone. May also points out,

> Traditionally, the way man has overcome the demonic is by naming it. In this way the human being forms *personal meaning* out of what was previously a merely threatening *impersonal chaos*. We need only recall the crucial importance historically of knowing the particular *name* of the demon in order to expel him. In the New Testament Jesus calls out Beelzebub![17]

The question arises: from where does self-esteem come? What are its sources? Psychologists list these differently. For Maslow the esteem needs are related to achievement, mastery, reputation, recognition, appreciation. Branden is more explicit and states that there are five areas which allow a person to experience life in a self-affirming way. These are productive work, human relationships, recreation, art, and sex.[18] For Victor Frankl, self-esteem is related to meaning. Sources for meaning are the sources for self-affirmation and self-transcendence. For Frankl these are three. "We can discover the meaning in life in three different ways: 1) by doing a deed; 2) by experiencing a value; and 3) suffering."[19] A significant portion of meaning in one's life is derived from activity. Experiencing a value could include contemplation of a work of art or experiencing a friend or lover. This combines several of Branden's sources. Love enhances self-esteem, hence the importance of friendship and relationships in the life of every man or woman. To seek sex apart from love can too readily be a vehicle for harming one's self-esteem. Sex in itself does not lead to self-esteem for Frankl, only sex in the context of a loving relationship.

The third source, suffering, is worth further consideration. Frankl is not referring to suffering that can readily be changed, but rather unavoidable suffering.[20] We are not talking about an unhealthy masochism, but rather about a realization that suffering can sensitize us to deeper realities in life and that instead of blocking that sensitization process we need to support it. Meaning and self-esteem go beyond simple rationality. As Frankl writes, "What is demanded of man is not, as some existential philosophers teach, to endure the meaninglessness of life; but rather to bear his incapacity to grasp its unconditional meaningfulness in rational terms."[21] Meaning cannot be reduced to logic. Suffering carries us to the limits of rationality in such a way that we can be opened as persons to the suprarational areas of life. This is why some people cannot always accept the fact of being loved even in a relationship. They might question, "But why do you love me? Why am I loved?" The impossibility of answering the question rationally can prevent them from allowing themselves to feel love. This is why it is better sometimes to ask not *why* are we loved but *how* are we loved. This question enables us to feel and grasp the love and to allow ourselves to be grasped by the fact of being loved.

The Theology of Self-Love

Self-esteem may seem an inappropriate word for a Christian who is aware of the reality of sin and the call of humility and holiness. Self-esteem is not to be confused with the sin of pride. Rather than being an obstacle to Christian growth, self-love is at the heart of the Gospel message. We can recall the summary of the Law given by Jesus in which he asks us to love ourselves, quoting the law contained in the book of Leviticus: Love your neighbor as yourself (Lv. 19:18) . There are at least two other New Testament texts with which we should be familiar. The first of these is Matthew 25:14-30.

It is like a man on his way abroad who summoned his servants and entrusted his property to them. To one he gave five talents, to another two, to a third one; each in proportion to his ability. Then he set out. The man who had received the five talents promptly went and traded with them and made five more. The man who had received two made two more in the same way. But the man who had received one went off and dug a hole in the ground and hid his master's money. Now a long time after, the master of those servants came back and went through his accounts with them. The man who had received the five talents came forward bringing five more. "Sir," he said "you entrusted me with five talents; here are five more that I have made." His master said to him, "Well done, good and faithful servant; you have shown you can be faithful in small things, I will trust you with greater; come and join in your master's happiness." Next the man with the two talents came forward. "Sir," he said "you have entrusted me with two talents; here are two more that I have made." His master said to him, "Well done, good and faithful servant; you have shown you can be faithful in small things, I will trust you with greater; come and join in your master's happiness." Last came forward the man who had the one talent. "Sir," said he "I had heard you were a hard man, reaping where you have not sown and gathering where you have not scattered; so I was afraid, and I went off and hid your talent in the ground. Here it is; it is yours, you have it back." But his master answered him, "You wicked and lazy servant! So you knew that I reap where I have not sown and gather where I have not scattered? Well then, you should have deposited my money with the bankers, and on my return I would have recovered my capital with interest. So now, take the talent from him and give it to the man who has five talents. For to everyone who has will be given more, and he will have more than enough; but from the man who has not, even what he has will be taken away. As for this good-for-nothing servant, throw him out into the dark, where there will be weeping and grinding of teeth."

In this parable in Matthew, which has its parallel in Luke 19:12-27, we find the call to self-actualization and self-development. Each of us in our personal lives is given gifts in proportion to our ability. The Lord expects us to develop these gifts in order to show our appreciation for them. The development of our talents is not an act of pride, but a way of giving honor and glory to God. The Lord does not want us to be undeveloped, but developed. The man who hid his master's money and thus bore no fruit was considered to be the good-for-nothing servant. The Lord expects us to reap the benefits of the gifts he has given us so that when he returns, we can give to him the actualization of those gifts. This parable is a biblical call to actualize our human potential, seeing it as a gift from God.

We can also consider the text from Matthew 5: 14-16.

You are the light of the world. A city built on a hilltop cannot be hidden. No one lights a lamp to put it under a tub; they put it on the lamp stand where it shines for everyone in the house. In the same way your light must shine in the sight of men, so that, seeing your good works, they may give the praise to your Father in heaven.

Here again Jesus invites us to let our gifts shine before the other members of the body of Christ. We too readily think of Christian spirituality only as a call to self-abnegation and not as a call to self-development. Both, however, are central to spiritual theology as pointed out by Teilhard de Chardin:

> Books about the spiritual life do not as a general rule throw this first phrase of Christian perfection into relief. Perhaps it seems too obvious to deserve mention or seems to belong too completely to the natural sphere. Quite possibly it is too dangerous to be insisted upon—whatever the reason, these books usually remain silent on the subject or take it for granted. This is a fault and an omission . . . it is a truly Christian duty to grow even in the eyes of men and to make one's talents bear fruit even though they be natural.[22]

The first principle of Teilhard de Chardin's ascetical theology is that of growth and development. Both self-development and self-denial are at the heart of the Christian life. Teilhard writes:

> Why separate and contrast natural phases of a single effort? Your essential duty and desire is to be united with God, but in order to be united you must first of all *be*—be yourself as completely as possible and so you must develop yourself and take possession of the world *in order to be*. Once this has been accomplished, then is the time to think about renunciation, then is the time to accept diminishment for the sake of *being in another*. Such is the sole and twofold precept of complete Christian asceticism.[23]

Development and denial belong together with a rhythm, "They harmonize, like breathing in and out in the movement of our lungs. They are two phases of the soul's breath, or two components of the impulse by which the Christian life uses things as a springboard from which to transcend them."[24]

Self-development, self-acceptance, self-actualization, and self-love are central to life in Christ. God wants us to build up our nature, to actualize it to the fullest, and he sends the Spirit into our lives not to destroy but to perfect. This is not a semi-Pelagian doctrine but a realization of the power of God's grace and the desire to let it take root in the hearts and souls of human beings. Central to the Christian life is the polarity that exists between sin and grace. Yet the doctrine of sin need not be a barrier to self-esteem. Sin does affect the totality of who we are. There is no question that, with respect to God, it leaves us undeserving. God, by definition, is the One who deserves to be loved. We are ones who do not deserve to be loved. This does not mean, however, that we are worthless, that we are lacking in value. We are also images of God. Justification by grace is a psychologically healthy doctrine, which implies total self-acceptance based neither upon self-rejection nor self-righteousness but upon self-affirmation. Doctrines of self-acceptance, whether psychological or theological, that imply striving after perfection through denial of either our goodness or our sinfulness lead only to falsification and self-righteousness. Jesus condemned such doctrines. Sinfulness does not necessitate self-hatred. Once and for all we need to uproot this pseudo-Christian masochistic attitude that associates holiness only with self-negation.

The doctrine of sin means that we do not deserve the love of God because we are so frequently unfaithful, that God's love always comes as a gift and not as something to which we have a right. Sin means undeservedness. Our mistake is to identify undeservedness too readily with unworthiness. We have intrinsic worth as human persons and as creatures of God but this worth does not justify us before God nor does it allow us to conclude that we deserve the gifts that God has given. Undeservedness does not mean worthlessness. The doctrine of man's sinfulness does not deny the value of self-esteem. In fact the Christian is called upon to esteem himself, to appreciate his worth, and to actualize his potential to the fullest that he might return greater honor and glory to God. The Christian injunction is to love ourselves.

Obstacles to Self-Esteem

Obstacles that disrupt self-acceptance and hinder self-love fall within eight areas. Each of the following have entered into my own personal experience and my experience in providing counseling and spiritual direction. The eight areas are 1) one's attitude toward one's body, 2) parental messages, 3) passiveness, 4) a sense of incompetence, 5) neurotic guilt, 6) fear, 7) self-alienation, and 8) sin.

One's attitude toward one's body. Our attitude toward our physical self is of extreme importance. Little progress can be made toward self-affirmation if we do not face our bodily and physical attributes. An inability to feel good about, to enjoy, to respond favorably toward the bodily and physical dimension of life and life's experience gets in the way of feeling good about and enjoying ourselves. How do we feel about our physical selves? Do we like ourselves from this perspective? Not only is our physical self important, so is our sexual self. How do we feel about our sexuality? Do we see ourselves as sexual persons? Is it ok for us to be sexual?

One hesitates to raise the question of sexual adequacy because we already overemphasize it. Much depends upon what we mean. Somehow, however, we must feel sexually "adequate." The character and frequency of orgasm is not the only nor the most important question in sexual functioning. Some theories of sexual inadequacy probably do more than anything else to make us feel sexually inadequate. The overall area of my sexual self, however, is important. Do I feel good as a sexual being? As a sexual lover? As one who can bring pleasure to another person?

We must face also the question of our personal attractiveness. Do I feel that I am physically and sexually attractive? Again, as with the question of sexual adequacy, one almost hesitates to discuss this since so much in our society over-emphasizes physical appeal. By sexual attractiveness we do not mean that we must conform to a particular image of physical beauty. Yet, we need to know that no matter what our physical features are, we can be appealing, attractive, to another person.

Body language is also significant. What I communicate bodily can lead to affirmation from others which can enhance self-esteem. A lack of self-esteem can be communicated through my body language. If I feel good about my bodiliness, my body will communicate that I think that I am a significant person, that I like myself, that I am worthwhile.

The value of sexual love and physical love should not be diminished. It is an important avenue through which many people come to self-esteem. There are few substitutes if any for the feeling of worth which develops within the context of sexual love, the realization that my body can be a source of pleasure to someone, that someone can value my body and enjoy it. Then I too can feel good about myself; I can enjoy my body no matter what the physical characteristics because it is an enjoyable dimension of who I am. In the spiritual life this means that we must once and for all overcome manichaeism.

Parental messages. We can place too great an emphasis or too great a blame upon parents. Yet, whether we are Freudian or not, the importance of the parental role in the life of children can hardly be denied. Messages that are communicated early are highly influential in the development and formation of personality. Eric Berne has contributed much toward understanding the role of parental messages.[25]

Many parental messages are constructive, helpful, and necessary. Yet, as adults, we begin to realize that parents are human. To children, parents appear omnipotent and omniscient. When, as adults, we play our own role as parents, however, we see how vulnerable and limited we are. We too are human beings. Parents do play significant roles in the development of personality. Yet, the more adult we become, the more we realize that, precisely because parents are human beings, we need to sift through and sort out the messages that we received from them. Not all of these messages have been for our good and not all of them were intentional. Parents may have communicated something based upon false information. Even with accurate information, however, and the best of intentions, parents are sometimes going to miscommunicate—perhaps non-verbally—what they want. Parents communicate much through their attitudes toward their children, and attitudes are seldom constant. When parents are disturbed by struggles in their own lives, when they are dealing with issues in their marital relationship, when they are working through their troubles with their own parents, when they are attempting to grow more themselves, when they are burdened and irritated, they are going to communicate some things which in the best of circumstances they may want to avoid.

It is very probable, moreover, that parents are not going to have the same attitudes toward all their children. Sometimes we have the romantic notion that parents should feel exactly the same about each child. Yet we know that we love people differently, and it is very probable that a father or mother will love each child differently. These various and almost inevitable attitudes are picked up by the children and can be comforting or disturbing. This is a part of sibling rivalry. At the delicate and formative stage of childhood, parental messages are internalized, however unintentional they may have been. Sometimes parents are later judged to be guilty or responsible for that over which they themselves may have had little control. As we become adults, we need to realize how little responsibility our parents must bear for some of their attitudes. We must sort out those feelings of acceptance and rejection, those feelings of confirmation and abandonment, which may have been communicated. We should begin to separate ourselves from those messages which now presently prove destructive in our lives. If we do not feel that our parents were proud of us, if we do not feel that they liked us, if we do not feel that we were their favorites, there is no reason for those messages to continue to tell us that therefore we are unlikeable, unacceptable or failures. We need to face the messages which have come through to us from our early life experiences, messages which we may have distorted or overemphasized because of our own dependency. We cannot allow perceived parental attitudes to determine how we perceive ourselves as adults.

Passiveness. A certain type of passivity is another obstacle to self-growth. Passiveness, like body language, can be both cause and effect, sometimes the cause of diminished self-esteem, sometimes the effect. We should note that passivity can be a value when balanced with activity. The goal of personal growth is neither to be a totally active or a totally passive person, but to achieve a balance. Edrita Fried analyzes some of the destructive aspects of passivity in *Active Passive,* although she tends not to appreciate the constructive side of passivity.[26] Passivity, as used here, implies that one is relatively incapable of being assertive even when a situation calls for self-assertion. Passivity has its value, but by itself it puts us in a precarious position as far as seeing that our needs are met. Passiveness can be an important obstacle to self-esteem in religious people who, for some reason or other, feel that to become too assertive is to be less Christian.

We all have needs; we are all important people; we are thus all responsible for seeing that some of our needs are met. Too often we can diminish or disregard our own needs rather than attend to them. The passive person is one who too readily sets aside the importance of his or her own self, who communicates a sense of not being worthwhile, who opens himself or herself to being taken for granted. Being taken for granted is the responsibility of the one who is taken for granted.

Assertiveness is the mean between the two extremes of aggressiveness and passivity.[27] In the past we identified passivity with femininity and aggressiveness with masculinity. In fact, the goal of personality development for both men and women is to be neither aggressive nor passive but assertive. Thus if we have difficulty with self-esteem, we should look at our capacity for assertive behavior and communication.

Passivity is not simply the opposite of aggressiveness, for many passive people can be quite aggressive. It is simply that their passive forms of being an aggressor are less direct and less capable of being confronted; both passivity and passive aggression are enemies of self-esteem. The capacity for initiative, affirmation, and attention should be developed.

Sense of incompetence. In addition to our attitudes toward our bodily and physical and sexual self, to sorting through parental messages which we have internalized, and to developing our capacity for assertiveness, we need to explore our feelings about our personal competence. There is a growing emphasis in psychology today upon this value which some would list as being *the* value in terms of which the personality can be understood.[28] Competence is very closely related to one of the three areas which Frankl discusses as sources of meaning, the sense of accomplishment.

Whether one is male or female, the sense of satisfaction which comes from feeling competent in an area of activity, ministry or work is necessary for self-esteem. Here is the value of ministry or work for every human person. One of the important gratifications or satisfactions, and hence sources for a healthy self-concept, comes precisely from what we do. We are not simply what we do, but what we do contributes significantly to who we are and how we perceive ourselves. This is why, from any psychological or theological perspective, unemployment is an extremely serious social problem. Unemployment over a long period of time is destructive to one's self-concept. Another social problem is how alienating work has become in our technological society.[29] Too often the word "work" connotes burden rather than enjoyment. The liberating value of enjoying one's work and feeling a participant in one's work and acquiring a sense of competence and satisfaction from one's work has become difficult in our society.

It is important to feel a sense of competence. Our work is an extension of ourselves. How we feel about our work has much to do with how we feel about ourselves. This is why, in spiritual theology and in the spirituality being developed here, the word *ministry* is used. We should see our contribution to the world as being ministry, a value, significant and important, not simply something that has to be done to earn a living. Work is intended to be enjoyable. Work is enjoyable. This is why the unemployed, those who are students for a long period of time, or those separated from ministry have crises in self-esteem; they fail to perceive how competent they are.

Neurotic psychological guilt. Guilt can be either constructive or destructive. Psychologists, seeing the destructive effects of neurotic (or irrational) guilt, often use the word *guilt* pejoratively, whereas moralists use the same word in a different way. The ensuing confusion has led some psychologists to blame religion for leading to neurosis, and it has led some liberal theologians and moralists in the twentieth century to develop a theology of sin that does not lead to guilt. Both of these avenues are destructive because they look at guilt too univocally, as if psychologists and theologians are talking about the same reality. In fact they are talking about two different realities.

Psychological guilt, generally speaking, is feeling bad about ourselves, imposing upon ourselves irrational disapproval. Psychological guilt is a feeling, an emotion which leads me to feel bad about myself. Moral guilt, however, is not primarily a question of emotions but rather a question of responsibility, owned responsibility. Moral guilt, or the assumption of responsibility, implies freedom, a will.

Guilt, as theologians use the word, implies freedom and responsibility. Psychological guilt then, in the sense of bad feelings about ourselves, is destructive and the psychological appraisal of its destructive character and neurotic potential is valid. Yet the moralist, in his or her appraising of the constructive value of owned responsibility flowing from freedom, is also clarifying a value. We need more and more to realize that a sense of responsibility does not have to lead to self-rejection.

It is true that often the preacher and the moralist have confused these two terms and allowed rhetoric to confuse moral responsibility with psychological guilt. The goal of ethical teaching, however, is not to lead people into psychological guilt but into moral guilt, that is responsibility, the ability to own and expand their freedom.

Moral guilt is constructive because it leads to changed behavior and hence is an avenue to self-esteem. A sense of moral responsibility means that if we do something which we perceive to be destructive, there is no need to *feel* bad about ourselves as persons but that there is value in saying to ourselves that this could have been otherwise; we could have acted differently. I can change my behavior! Moral guilt is owned freedom and responsibility and can lead to change.

Psychological guilt, on the other hand, accomplishes little. It seldom leads to changed behavior. Speaking theologically, it too quickly allows us to atone for our sins by feeling bad without doing anything differently in the future. We have made up for what we have done by feeling bad rather than doing anything that might make the future different. The movement toward deepened self-esteem means that we come to own our freedom, become responsible for our behavior, assume a sense of responsibility and thus perceive that we are capable of guilt in a moral sense; but becoming guilty in the psychological sense, in the sense of having bad feelings about ourselves, is an irresponsible way of avoiding facing the responsibility which is ours. Both the psychologist and the moralist, therefore, have valid perspectives.

When we or someone whom we counsel or direct is struggling with psychological guilt, it is paramount that such guilt be alleviated. At the same time this does not mean that the person move in the direction of irresponsibility. The client must begin to assume responsibility for his or her life and face the fact that they need not feel bad about themselves because of individual acts of irresponsibility. The most responsible way of dealing with individual acts of irresponsibility is not to feel bad but to change. We can own and accept responsibility for certain aspects of our life but we do not equate those actions with the totality of who we are. Feeling that we are bad persons is destructive. I am a good person: this is valid psychologically and theologically. Yet we are good persons who are capable of inappropriate and irresponsible behavior, sometimes extremely irresponsible or pathological. Yet much guilt is only psychological and neurotically self-destructive, destroying rather than enhancing self-esteem.

Fear. Another area within the personality which needs to be explored as we come to face ourselves is what we fear. We all are afraid at times; fear is natural in the course of growing. As children we are dependent and defenseless within an adult world. Tragedies, moreover, do happen which lead us legitimately to be afraid of the world in which we find ourselves where parents may come and go, where disease is painful, where death is inevitable. Yet we need to become conscious of our fears so that they do not destroy how we feel about ourselves. One's fears too readily lead to self-defeating and defensive behavior.

Fears can lead us to develop self-destructive patterns of activity which might enable us to avoid facing what we fear, patterns which allow us to put people at a distance so that we are not hurt. If we ask the question why people don't like us, there is no value in answering that question by saying we are unlikeable. We may well have some unlikeable characteristics which we developed defensively and protectively, but which we can change.

We can ask: What are the defensive and self-defeating forms of behavior that we have developed? Why have we developed these defenses? Upon what fears are they based? Are those fears realistic? Can we face those fears? Are there other ways of coping with those fears? In other words, we need to raise the question: What are we afraid of? To avoid facing these fears, what patterns of communication and behavior have we developed?

Such destructive self-protection includes arrogant behavior, for example. Some people cover up inner fear, inner fragility, insecurity, through what psychoanalytic theory calls reaction formation, developing the opposite characteristic, a communication of exaggerated self-importance, a sense of arrogance. Few people like arrogance or respond to it favorably. Thus arrogance is self-defeating, although the arrogant person is seeking self-affirmation and affection.

In addition to arrogance, and closely related to it, is hostility. Some people seem to be hostile, negative, whether overtly or passively. Hostile people are not likeable people, whether that hostility is manifested by passive aggression or pervasive conscious hostility. We all have a right to be angry and how we cope with anger is important.[30] In fact, one might list as an obstacle to self-esteem an inability to handle and communicate anger. If, however, we see ourselves as hostile or if others perceive us in that way, a style of behavior has developed which has taken over too great a portion of the personality.

Another self-defeating defense which is probably not as obvious as the others is cerebralization. Many who have an intellectual capacity and are sufficiently intelligent frequently use that particular strength in order to cover up their own unaccepted weaknesses. Those who tend to cerebralize every aspect of life are as distorted as those who sexualize every aspect of life. Cerebralization puts people at a distance because it does not allow for a free exchange of emotion. If we are going to love ourselves, we must *feel* good about ourselves and sense that others feel good about us. This communication of feeling will be impaired if we avoid emotional expression. Cerebralization, hostility, arrogance, are simply ways of avoiding our fears and avoiding the risk of emotional exposure. Too often self-defeating behavior can take the form of self-fulfilling prophecies. We might be afraid that people won't like us. Then we develop patterns of behavior which are unlikeable and which prove a point. Self-defeating behavior is not easy to work through because there is a certain psychic gain and investment in the behavior because of what it helps us to avoid, whether that be a fear, an anxiety, imperfection, weakness, or insecurity.

Self-alienation. Nathaniel Branden's notion of the disowned self is extremely important, not only for psychology but for spirituality as well. Within each of us there are portions of ourselves that are harder to face because they are less socially desirable or acceptable. We are talking here about the unacceptable portions of ourselves, the disowned portions of ourselves, that self from which we can be alienated and from which we want to be distanced, that portion of self which we do not accept. It is precisely this disowned self, however, that must be owned in the process of personal integration and self-affirmation.

Psychologists describe alienation in different ways, the shadow side of ourselves, the psychological self, the private or less public self. In each of us, however, there is that portion of ourselves of which we are less proud, which we are less ready to communicate, which we want more easily to conceal. What is important is not that we make this or that aspect of self public but that we ourselves face it, accept it and begin to own it as being indeed a portion of ourselves. To do other than this is to pursue a false road to self-acceptance. Our path toward self-esteem can never lead us to deny portions of ourselves which might appear to be less capable of esteem.

We need as adults to realize that both of these aspects, the positive and negative, are *me*. We are multi-faceted selves or persons. It is only in getting to know ourselves and face ourselves that we come to genuine self-esteem. "I'm ok" can only be said at the end of a process of self-owning.

Freedom and responsibility, so important to psychological well being, remind us that we are not determined by our past. It is certainly true and obviously so that our previous life experience, family life and history, have deeply entered into who we are. At the same time these experiences do not completely limit or determine who we will be in the future. We can own portions of ourselves but we need not say that they will continue to limit or destroy us. We can face them and thus rob them of their power because the main power they have is precisely our own personal attitude towards them. We are not determined by our past in terms of how we feel about ourselves. Healing can take place when we begin to love ourselves, all of ourselves, the unacceptable within ourselves, when we can say that's who I am and that's ok.

Sin. For the spiritual director, the moralist, and the theologian, this last reality points to an ultimate internal disorder which is destructive to self-esteem. For psychology or theology to fail to deal with the reality of sin is to fail to take a holistic approach to the subject of self-esteem.

The difficulty here, as in discussing guilt, is that we have many popular misunderstandings and even unhealthy theological expressions about sin. Although a complete theology of sin is not offered here,[31] in approaching the subject of our relationship with God, relationship with others and relationship with self, and in terms of disorder within those areas, we must first divest ourselves of any preconceived notions of sin which we may have.

Sin leads to self-alienation. It is a further and deepened alienation than psychological self-rejection. Sin is that which separates us or divorces us from a portion of ourselves, cuts us off from ourselves, frequently at an unconscious level. We sometimes readily dismiss the psychological aspect of sin because its effect might not be conscious and yet sin works its harm in the personality.

Sin has at least two dimensions. The sinner is victim as well as participant. Traditionally, we have always accepted the passive aspect of sin, more often discussed under original sin, that which affects us for which we are not responsible but which victimizes us. We also considered, traditionally, actual or personal sin, that for which we are responsible. We must constantly keep both of these aspects of sin in mind. As sinners we are victims of the disorder and participants in the disorder which manifests itself in our world, in our environment.

Being victimized by this disorder and participating in it, however, leads to depersonalization and desensitization. No matter what form it takes, sin is destructive because it does not lead to the further personalization of the individual. Ultimately it in fact cuts us off from our true self. In personality theory as well as in spiritual theology we talk about our many selves. There is the empirical self, the conscious self, the self which is perceived by others, and the shadow or disowned self. But beyond all these there is what may be called our divinity, our share in the divine life, the gift of divine life which has been given to us and which is also now in us at our deepest levels of interiority.

Each of us is both human and divine and what sin does is separate us from our divinity. Granted we are divine by grace and not by nature, but sin still sep-

arates us from the life of grace or that created participation in the divine nature, our deepest self. Insofar
as sin separates us from our deepest self, puts us out of
touch with our deepest self, and leaves us sometimes
unaware of that depth within ourself, sin is self-alienat-
ing. It alienates us from our total self, from divinity,
from God's love. Sin is destructive of self-esteem and
a reality which a counselor, director, or individual
cannot neglect. We must come to grips with our sin
and the reality of sin as we grow in realistic self-
appraisal.

Self-esteem is a basis for spiritual growth and for
the life of love to which we are called. Love others as
you love yourself. Begin then to love yourself. This is
what Jesus asks of us. Love yourselves as I have loved
you. To move in the direction of self-love we need to
overcome what obstacles lie in our paths. We can think
of these as the eight capital sins against self-esteem.
What can we do then to become more self-accepting,
self-affirming and self-loving? We can develop healthy
attitudes toward our body and our sexuality. We can
form adult self-concepts free of destructive parental
messages. We can become more assertive in our behavior and communication. We can develop areas of
competence and enjoyment. We can affirm our freedom
and become responsible. We can change self-defeating
defensive behavior. We can face the disowned and
unacceptable within ourselves. We can reach out to
God with continuing prayer so that we stay in touch
with our divine life.

Self-Denial and Self-Sacrifice

Because of the human condition, the sin of the world
in the midst of which we find ourselves, the path to-

ward authentic self-development and authentic esteem can be frequently filled with the illusions of the sinful person. Thus, although the Scriptures affirm self-love as a value and a necessity, we must sort through the meaning of loving ourselves. It may seem that psychology affirms the importance of self-esteem, self-affirmation, self-fulfillment, whereas traditional spiritual theology speaks of denial, sacrifice and renunciation. We need to consider an apparent conceptual opposition. Thus many have abandoned the traditional spiritual wisdom for the wisdom of contemporary psychology. This is unfortunate because it represents a Western way of thinking in which we tend to dichotomize. Authentic self-esteem cannot endure without self-restraint. To the degree that any psychology or theology of self-esteem abandons the importance of its complement, self-denial, to that degree we are led in a false direction. Likewise, the degree to which any spiritual theology affirms the value of self-denial to the detriment of self-affirmation, to that degree that spiritual theology misleads us.

We have considered, both psychologically and theologically, the importance of self-esteem. What, however, are we to say within the context of our Christian tradition about those values which have variously been labeled as asceticism, detachment, mortification, self-abnegation or self-renunciation? These expressions and others point to the emphasis that this dimension of experience plays in the spirituality of the Christian tradition. Can such a value be easily discarded?

By no means. The insight of Teilhard de Chardin again helps us restore the needed balance.[32] Teilhard speaks about attachment and detachment, about self-development and renunciation, as being two phases of a single effort. They are like rhythm within our lives or two sides of a coin. He uses the analogy of breathing in and breathing out, which we can again employ here. For life, which is more important, exhaling or inhaling? Why contrast two natural phases of a single reality? Which is more important, self-affirmation or self-negation? Self-actualization or self-emptying, self-development or self-abandonment? What Christians realize is that we can't have one without the other.

We can indeed live an illusory life, a blind life. Yet the primary function of the desert experience, the emphasis on mortification, is precisely that conversion of heart or change of consciousness which leads us to a new way of seeing, an altered state of consciousness, a different way of perceiving the world in which we find ourselves, a way which opens us to discovering our true self.[33] There are two ways of being self-centered: egoism and self-love. We encounter many selves in the course of our spiritual journeys. There is the false self, the sinful self, the selfish self; and it is not this self which we need to affirm, which we seek to esteem, precisely because this self is false. Growth requires the uprooting of our selfishness, the uprooting of our egoism, purification of self to discover who we are and who we can be.

Face to face with a sinful human condition within which we find ourselves, each of us needs to undergo a process of transformation in which we move from self to Self, in which we become our Selves. We are unfinished, not yet done, not yet fully created. This means that in the rhythm of life, in each stage of growth, in each turning point, the old self must be set aside for the new self to emerge. The coming to be of who we are is a rhythm of self-creation and self-destruction in which the old self is let go and the new self put on. Authentic self-esteem only comes by searching for our authentic Self. It is this search for authentic self-esteem which is at the heart of the Christian mystery of love. Self-love is not selfish love. One can only find that healthy, mature, and spiritual form of self-esteem by seeing the value of both self-affirmation and self-purification. Self-denial need not lead to a lack of self-esteem. Self-denial, in fact, can only be based upon healthy self-esteem. To divorce or separate these two natural phases of a single love is to distort the work of the Spirit within us, who gifts us with the capacity to embrace the totality of ourselves so wholeheartedly that in the process we ourselves are transformed and become the Selves that we can be.

Chapter Three

FRIENDSHIP

A Theology of Friendship

For Teilhard de Chardin, centration or individualization and excentration or socialization are aspects of personality growth, parts of a rhythm, like breathing in and breathing out.[1] This same rhythm is described biblically when the Scriptures refer to love of self and love of others. We cannot have self-love apart from other-oriented love; nor can we have other-oriented love apart from self-love. As the self moves out, both particular love and universal love are discovered. We have looked at that love referred to as self-esteem. Let us now examine particular love, the love of friendship, one form of excentration. In the next chapters we will look at community and ministry, universal loves.

In discussing friendship as one of the core Gospel values, we should remember that friendship is a Christian reality. We think too readily of friendship as a human value, but not as a religious value in itself. Friendship is not only a human value, however; it is a Gospel value as well.

One of the earliest theologies of friendship is that of the Yahwist whose understanding of the creation of woman places friendship in the context of a relationship which overcomes loneliness and thus gives glory to God. The Yahwist states that it is not good for man to be alone; friendship and intimacy provide the environment within which loneliness can be overcome. Hence, friendship completes a human person.[2]

Theologically, we must begin with the Scriptures.

73

John is the starting point for a biblical theology of friendship and it is not surprising that his Gospel should so emphasize it since John himself was one of Jesus' intimate friends. We frequently miss the value of friendship when reading the Scriptures because we are not looking for this value, which does not surface as a major theme in the teaching of Jesus. It does emerge, however, as a major part of his life. Especially helpful in understanding the role of friendship in Jesus' life are the Bethany stories to which I referred in Chapter One.

Not only Scripture but Christian tradition affirms the value of friendship. The work of Aelred of Rievaulx gives us one of the most complete theologies of friendship in the Christian tradition.[3] Aelred, almost exaggerating, writes, "Among the stages leading to perfection, friendship is the highest."[4] He also writes, "Scarcely any happiness whatever can exist among mankind without friendship."[5] Whether Aelred is correct in his assessment of friendship or not, we can at least see the significance he assigns to it.

We find similar observations in many other texts. Gregory Nazianzen writes "If someone were to ask me what is the most beautiful thing in life, I would reply that it is friends."[6] John Chrysostom writes, "Nothing is so injurious to mankind as to undervalue friendship."[7] Pourrat notes Lacordaire's preaching on friendship: "Friendship is the most perfect of human experiences."[8] Thus there is sufficient reason to theologize on this subject; theologians and saints have seen friendship as a particularly significant Christian value.

We notice the Christian quality of friendship also when we read the language associated with it, a theological language very similar to that used in the discussion of Christian marriage, which is one form of Christian friendship. Aelred speaks of friendship in the context of what God has joined together, of two becoming one.[9] Augustine speaks of one soul in two bodies, talks about a friend as half his soul, and as one's other self.[10]

We shall not dwell here on the biblical and historical aspects of friendship, but we shall examine a systematic theology of Christian friendship centering around the nature of friendship as gift as well as its nature as duty, the sacramental theology of friendship, eschatology and friendship, and the apostolic and ascetic character of friendship.

Theologically, friendship is always a gift. It is not something that a human person can achieve by effort alone. In that sense friendship assumes the characteristics of grace. It is always something that comes to us from another, something for which we can dispose and prepare ourselves, but not something that we can achieve by ourselves. It is always something given by another, and ultimately given to the human person by God. This does not mean that every person is necessarily given the gift of friendship, but it does mean that God, because of his love for us, wants to give that gift to each of us. If the gift is not found in one's life, it is generally because of human obstacles that have been placed in its way. God wants to endow us with friends because he sees them as the completion of ourselves. There is a sense in which one can also speak of friendship as a charism that some people within the Christian community are given for the sake of the whole.

Friendship as a gift, however, does not imply that there is no responsibility on our part to seek this gift, to pray for it, and to develop our lives in such a way that we might be capable of receiving it. Friendship is also a duty in the sense that human persons as creatures of God have the responsibility for developing themselves in such a way that they can give greater glory to God. As Christians we have the obligation to perfect ourselves in order to give greater glory to God, and that effort includes the responsibility to overcome loneliness so that the Lord's creation might be more complete. Christians have the responsibility to seek friendship, to develop friendship, and to make every effort to sustain friendship, always, however, with the realization that friendship exceeds our powers. In the end it remains gift; our duty is to prepare ourselves for this gift and to sustain it when it comes. Friendship is a balance between grace and responsibility.

Friendship is also sacramental. First, it is a sacrament of God's love *ad extra*. Aelred of Rievaulx paraphrased John's Gospel by saying that God is friendship.[11] Friendship, then, is a mirror of God Himself. It is one of the best visibilizations of who God is, a sacrament of God and his way of loving. God's way of loving is a sustained, ongoing, committed fidelity to his creatures. Friendship as a sustained unselfish love is a sacrament of this way of loving. Friendship, like God's love, lasts. Human friendship is an analogue of God's love for us and Christ's love for his people.

Friendship is not only a sacrament of God's love *ad extra* but also a sacrament of the inner life of God himself, God's trinitarian life. This point can be abstract, but we should recall the Christian affirmation of God as Triune. Affirming the trinitarian life of God within himself is necessary if we assume the mystical insight of John that God is love. Love by its nature is personal. No human being experiencing personal love can affirm that God's love is impersonal. God's love exceeds human love, is an even more personal love than we generally experience. This is why Christians affirm the personal character of God who cannot be less than we ourselves are. If he is love, he is Person.

Yet today we realize psychologically that being personal implies being interpersonal or relational. God is not simply individual; God is personal. Personal reality implies social reality. The affirmation of personal existence is at the heart of Christian faith. If God is personal, he is social being. This interpersonal and relational character of God is what the Christian tradition refers to as Trinity. Too often in modern conceptual categories we translate personality as individuality and when we think of the three Persons in God we think of three individuals. This is not at all what Christian tradition means. God is not three individuals, three persons in that sense, three Gods. God is one person in the way we generally speak of Person, one Being, but he is three relationships. This is the basic meaning of person in Thomas Aquinas' theology of the Trinity. Person is relationship. The relationship between the Father and the Son which is productive of the Spirit is that quality of love which is exemplified in the relationship of friendship where the lover and the beloved are generative of something beyond themselves alone.

Thus friendship is a sacrament of God's inner life as well as of His love for us. When we speak of the human person as the image of God or of God's creating us in his image (Gen. 1:27), and when we read in Paul that we are the image and glory of God (1 Cor. 11:17), we have to affirm that friendship is the perfection of this image. Man is not an image of God individualistically but only in relationship. It is in friendship that our ability to mirror God is most accomplished. Friendship is a sacrament. Friendship, moreover, is a sacrament of election. It is in friendship that we discover what it means to be given something which we feel we do not deserve, when we discover what it means to be chosen. The genuine experience of being loved is often an experience of feeling unworthy. We are not someone's friend because of what we deserve but because of the gift that someone has chosen to give us. Friendship is a grace.

Friendship is also eschatological. Biblical theology today points to the eschatological character of existence, almost as if eschatology has become a category within which we must understand Christian life. Eschatology is primarily concerned with the coming of the Kingdom, the single reality for which we all wait, that final reality which the Jewish people expected. Biblical eschatology, however, is of two sorts. The first points to the future. The Kingdom is not now here in its fullness. This future character, however, was affected by Jesus of Nazareth in whom the Kingdom of God is already here, has already come. This tension between the present realization of God's Kingdom and the fact that it is not yet here in its fullness is characteristic of Christian eschatology. The Kingdom has been inaugurated and is already here at work in our midst although not in its final form. Both realized and future eschatological elements permeate the New Testament.

Friendship, then, if it is to be understood theologically must be understood eschatologically. Considered eschatologically, it has a two-fold dimension. The first is realized eschatology; friendship in that sense is the realization of the Kingdom already present in our midst. Friendship is one reality in which Christ is already present to us. In friendship we discover Christ. Christ is friendship and wherever Christian friendship is there Christ is. Friendship is the realization of the Kingdom and God's presence in our lives.

Yet friendship as we know it is still in this life never totally perfect, if only because we can never be totally present to the ones we love. In other words, friendship in its perfected form is that for which we still long and wait. Just as friendship is a sign of the presence of Christ and is Christ himself present at work, so friendship is also a sign of the unfinished character of our lives since we never achieve the perfection that friendship can offer. It is only in the future of God's reign that we will enter fully into the life of friendship. Catherine of Siena writes that in heaven "the blessed will have a special sharing with those whom they closely loved with particular affection in the world."[12] What is remarkable about the life for which we wait is that then we will be once again together with those whom we love with particular love. We long for the heavenly eschatological banquet so that we can once and for all be totally present with those we love in an embodied way. Friendship is both already here and not yet fully here; it is an eschatological reality.

Not only must we look at the sacramental and eschatological character of friendship, but we must also keep in mind its apostolic quality. Paul Hinnebusch has provided a good contemporary study of friendship and especially the apostolate of friendship.[13] Friendship is a gift that is always given to us for the sake of building up the body of Christ. It is not private. It is a gift granted for the good of the Christian community as St. Paul notes in his first letter to the Corinthians (1 Cor. 12:4ff). We can see then the important apostolate that friendship itself can be. The entire Christian community is possible only through the building blocks which provide us with the body of Christ. The Christian community is built up through interlocking relationships. Only when we move out in love to one other do we enter into the kind of relationship which opens us to the friends of our friend. Friendship is not a closed community but provides the concrete stones from which community flows. Friendship is not simply to be seen as the perfection of one's self, but something which we are obliged to perfect as a gift given to us for the sake of others. It is not simply a gift given to an individual; it is given to someone for the sake of the community.

Another apostolic aspect of friendship is that God may well want to save someone through me. We are called in a special way into the lives of those whom we call friends. Perhaps we can do nothing greater in our lives than to be a friend. John points out this apostolic aspect of friendship. Jesus calls his disciples friends and then immediately asks them to go out and bear fruit that will last (John 15:16). Jesus does not say I call you my friends and I want you to love me alone. Friendship is always nonpossessive; it is for the good of others, not merely for the good of self.

A further theological aspect of friendship is the spiritual and ascetic. Traditional forms of asceticism are now being redirected. If asceticism includes the values of self-denial, self-discipline, self-sacrifice, surrender to the other, we find no better environment for the practice of the ascetical life than in friendship. In fact, we can go so far as to say that someone who is not ascetic is incapable of being a friend. Anyone who has attempted to develop a significant relationship is aware of that.[14] If we consider the psychological tasks involved in the development of relationships, clarifying expectations, being open to development within a relationship, the feelings of jealousy and hostility, the need for working through our own feelings of dependency, the need for independence, the realities of separation, we see the painful aspects of friendship.

The Song of Songs, one of the supreme biblical exemplifications of the kind of love of which we are speaking here, points not only to the joy but to the pain of particular love (Song of Songs 3:1-4). Often when we speak about friendship it is something that we welcome; we want friendship. In the concrete, however, no reality is so painful in the process of living it out as is particular love. It is only the person who is capable of surrender and disciplining self for the sake of another who is able to be friend. Friendship is not only eschatological and apostolic; it is ascetic as well. The reason many friendships do not succeed and many marriages are not sustained is that the value of asceticism has not been developed. Friendship is not only a fullness of life but is a way of the cross.

Friendship is not simply a human reality; it is an extremely important value in the Christian community. It is a divine reality. The basis of friendship is God himself. There is no sacrament as revelatory of the social structure of the universe and the social nature of God as is true Christian friendship. Friendship allows us to partake of the divine nature. It can be an entrance into union with God.

The Kinds of Friendship

Just as there are different kinds of love, so there are different kinds of friendship. Friendship, or to use the more psychological word, intimacy, manifests itself in a variety of ways. It is that relationship between equals which involves reciprocity, two giving themselves to each other for life, for better or for worse. Intimacy and friendship admit of degrees. In our society we use the word friendship in a wide sense—more than simply the one, two, three or several to whom we might give ourselves with a consciously sustained commitment. In a sense, then, we can speak of friendship that exists between parents and children—and this is a unique kind of friendship—or the friendship between clients and those to whom they come, whether counselors, therapists, or spiritual directors. One can even speak of divine friendship, that which exists between the human person and God, as the human person enters deeply into sharing the divine life. The sublime exemplification of friendship, however, is the inner life of God himself and not simply the divine friendship that God has with us, but divine friendship in the sense of an inner life within himself.

Committed and reciprocal human intimacy between equals—partnership—is the kind of relationship now under consideration. We can distinguish conjugal friendship and celibate friendship. When we describe friendship in terms of the highest levels of human intimacy, Christian marriage is one supreme exemplification of this. Marriage is a significant Christian exemplification of this Gospel value. On the other hand, celibate life can also share in the deepest levels of human intimacy and in the supreme forms of friendship. Celibate friendship is not a lesser kind of friendship than conjugal friendship. Marriage is one form of friendship, but not the only form. Every true marriage is a friendship and every friendship is in some sense a marriage.

Another important distinction is that between friendship with someone of the other sex and friendship with someone of one's own sex. Friendships we have with people of the other sex are heterosexual relationships. This is not to say that the expression of sexuality is specifically genital, nor that this is the most important element in a particular relationship. The most significant aspects of friendship may be mutual sharing, support in times of stress, and the opportunity for deepened spiritual living. Nevertheless, there can also be a sexual character to friendship just as there are spiritual and emotional characteristics. We can describe that sexual quality in some relationships as being heterosexual and that quality in other relationships as being homosexual.

Heterosexual friendships, however, can also be of two sorts. There can be the relationship between two heterosexual people of different sexes. This is what we usually think of when we think of a heterosexual relationship, the relationship between a heterosexual man and a heterosexual woman, which may be either conjugal or celibate. There are also, however, heterosexual relationships into which homosexuals enter. In other words, a homosexual man can have a heterosexual relationship with a heterosexual woman or with a homosexual woman and vice-versa. Too often the stereotype leads us to think that homosexual men and women can only enter into deep affective relationships with their own sex. A healthy homosexual person has the capacity to enter into affective relationships with people of the other sex although his or her own genital preference is for people of the same sex.

In this same sense we can talk about homosexual friendships. Homosexual relationships can exist between two heterosexual people, a heterosexual man and another heterosexual man, who enter into affective bonds, although their genital orientation is toward someone of the other sex. We can speak also about a friendship between two people of the same sex who are homosexual in that their genital preference is for the same sex. It is this final example which we most often think of when we speak of homosexual relationships.[15]

We should recognize the importance of a bisexual aspect to the personality.[16] A homosexual person who prefers genital relationships with the same sex is still capable of affective bonds and sometimes even genital bonds with the other sex. Likewise a heterosexual person who prefers genital involvement with the other sex is capable of deeply affective and sometimes also genital bonds with someone of the same sex. To be limited in one's capacity to love is destructive. Homosexually oriented persons are called upon to develop their capacity to relate to the other sex, just as heterosexually oriented persons are called to deepen their capacity to relate to the same sex.

The Qualities of True Friendship

Having looked at the subject of friendship theologically and with the realization that there are many manifestations or varieties of friendship, we can consider nine qualities that describe or at least are striven after in a genuine Christian relationship.

Reciprocal and Equal: The first quality of genuine friendship is that it is a relationship between equals. Even if there is inequality in some ways between the two persons, this inequality does not exist within the dimensions of their friendship. A genuine friendship can exist between an employer and employee despite inequality within one aspect of the relationship. Equality is basic to reciprocity in genuine friendship. Friendship involves mutuality between the lover and the beloved, mutual response. This mutuality is so central to the Christian tradition that Paul places it at the center of his understanding of Christian marriage. The spouse does not have sole rights over his or her own body, but the other has rights too. In other words, in a relationship of friendship, mutuality is so central that decisions pertinent to the relationship cannot be made unilaterally. This does not mean that there will be no variation of feelings within the relationship or that the level of affection and emotional response between those who love will not vary. But the desire to sustain the relationship is something mutually agreed upon and clarified.

Lasting: Spiritual writers frequently point to this quality of friendship, although permanence or commitment is a seriously questioned value today. Yet, Christians insist upon the permanent, sustained, faithful, lasting character of a relationship because only in that way can a relationship actualize itself to the fullest. Only when there is mutual understanding that there is a commitment to sustain the relationship, a willingness to enter into risks, can the relationship achieve its sacramental potential of embodying and giving witness to the kind of love that God himself is. Human relationships achieve their highest potential when they are sacraments of God's love and thus exist in a sustained rather than a temporary way. This is the sustained love of which the Song of Songs speaks, and the kind of love that Paul and Aelred refer to.

Developmental: Not only is friendship reciprocal and ongoing; it is developmental; it passes through stages. It is extremely important for two partners to realize this developmental aspect lest they enter into a relationship and are deluded by the fantasy that some level will be achieved at which the relationship will remain for life. Thus there needs to be more to a relationship than simply an emotional response. Love is not simply affection and sexual responsiveness. The high level of emotional intensity that is involved in the early stage of a relationship cannot be sustained for life and yet ideally friendship should be sustained for life. Understanding the concept of "stages" makes us aware that no relationship is automatic; it is something to which we give ourselves, something we are willing to work with and work through. Relationships are always in the process of becoming other than what they presently are. Hinnebusch points to the different stages of a relationship as it moves from attachment and fear and possessiveness to genuine friendship itself.[17] Aelred of Rievaulx speaks of four stages of development within friendship.[18] Here we shall consider four other stages.

The first stage in a relationship is frequently the honeymoon phase, the phase of falling in love, of being in seventh heaven, a stage of being high, as if nothing can go wrong. We are in love. Both are emotionally intense with a full experience of positive emotional qualities. During this time we can be convinced that we are going to love this person for life and that nothing can change the depth of our commitment. It is a good phase in the relationship but also a phase during which it is not wise to make a final decision. This is the phase of high sexual excitement. At this time those who love will experience desire for genital interaction, although genital interaction at this stage is inappropriate since it has a way of sustaining emotional intensity without giving the relationship the chance to discover whether or not there is a mutual desire for commitment.

Eventually one person comes down from the stage of heightened emotionality and positive affection to more normalized feelings. The other will then feel threatened, insecure, and jealous. Thus, the honeymoon phase gradually moves into the phase of jealousy and possessiveness. Since the only way in which we have experienced the other person was at that heightened emotional state, we now no longer know whether or not the other loves us since he or she is no longer experiencing emotions in the same way. We can be frightened, not knowing whether there is more to the relationship than the initial affection. We begin to feel unsure of the future of the relationship, jealous that the other no longer gives us the same kind of focused attentiveness. We become more conscious of the attention that our friend gives to others. It is only gradually that we begin again to be assured that although the emotional responses of the other have changed, that he or she is still committed to the relationship. Gradually, then, after a period of time, the second phase can move into greater security. This second phase, which involves jealousy and during which relationships can frequently move apart, often includes substages as well. Just as one person can go through the period of jealousy and eventually comes to grips with it, so the other can become jealous as he sees the changes in the beloved's emotional responses.

It is in the second phase that one begins to experience the anger and hostility which flow from the hurt that is involved with jealousy. The first two phases in a relationship are altered states of emotional living, apart from the range of emotional life that we ordinarily experience. The third phase is the beginning of a reconciliation of our experience of this wide range of positive and negative emotional qualities. Now we are aware that this other person is someone whom we can and do love intensely but also a person at whom we get angry. In fact, we may get more angry at this person than at any other we know. Opening one's self to the depths of positive emotions opens us also to a deeper experience of negative emotions. This third phase is the phase of ambivalence, the love-hate aspects described by Karl Menninger. We need now to accept, reconcile, and resign ourselves to both aspects of the relationship—the love and the possible anger. We can see that this is someone whom we love and with whom we want to live. We can also see that there are some days when we wish we had never met this person. It is only in allowing ourselves to experience the full level of this emotional range that we can really move to that phase in a relationship where authentic decisions are possible. It is only after an acceptance of ambivalence that genuine decisions can be made as to whether we want to commit ourselves to this person for life. In that sense, the third phase of the relationship prepares for the decision-making process of whether to move this relationship in the direction of friendship or not. It is really only the fourth phase that is properly called friendship, after the decision has been made to commit ourselves to each other for life.

It is not best to make the long range decision about a relationship during the first two phases simply because the heightened emotionality disturbs our ability to know whether this is a person with whom we want to work through a friendship for the rest of our life. It is only in the third phase that we begin to integrate our experience of the positive and negative, so that we can eventually come to a decision as to whether this is someone with whom we do or do not want to spend our life. It is only after the phase of ambivalence that a genuine decision can be made. A decision does not change the experience of ambivalence within a relationship but simply clarifies for the other that he or she is someone to whom we are committed for life. This fourth phase, then, is really the stage of mutuality, reciprocity and permanence. Once we enter into the fourth stage of the relationship the developmental quality does not cease, however. The two people are still going to have to work through their communication systems, the rhythm within the relationship, and the emotional changes that are still in store.[19] The relationship will continue to develop and those changes will always be a difficulty within the relationship. Although we can speak very positively these days about change, there is a way in which all of us resist changes within our relational network. Yet, relationships will continue to change because the persons within them continue to grow. Being open to and responding to the growth of the other will be an ongoing part of friendship. Yet friendship will at least have stabilized itself to the point that one feels the assurance and the love and the commitment of the other within this developmental process.

Communicative: The fourth quality we should examine is communication. There is no genuine love without communication. Love wants to communicate itself and the deeper the ability of two people to communicate the deeper the capacity to love. In fact, communication is probably the most concrete central problem in a human relationship. Whether or not a relationship can be sustained for life will depend upon whether two people can arrive at a mutually understood communication pattern. Each of us enters into any new relationship with our own communication system, learned as we were growing up and in our previous experiences of relating. Our own communication system reflects the unique person that we are. When we enter into a relationship, however, we must learn the other person's communication pattern, both verbal and nonverbal. It is only when we can enter into and understand and respond to the other's communications and feel that we can be free and open and honest in communicating ourselves that the relationship is cleared for deepening. Breakdowns in communications—inevitable in any relationship—prevent growth. They can be healed, however, and can become breakthroughs into deeper levels of love. One of the fundamental tasks that two friends always have is to learn how they best communicate and this is an ongoing life process, not something that is accomplished once and for all.

Limited: We cannot be friends with the intensity and intimacy described here with dozens of people. Friendship must be limited numerically. This observation is not necessarily good news, but we should realize that the person who attempts to befriend everybody will be a friend to nobody. We gradually learn that a task in life is to love a few people deeply, and that we cannot love everybody with the love of particular friendship. We can indeed and must indeed love everyone but not with the particular love that friendship is and the intensity it demands. We can care for and love everyone with a universal love but not with the particular love of friendship. Friendship implies a conscious choice about those to whom we are going to commit ourselves for life and with whom we have the desire to sustain an ongoing kind of relatedness. As human beings we are limited in the number of people with whom we can sustain that kind of intimacy. To love one person deeply may mean not loving someone else in the same kind of way. Thomas Aquinas recognized this limitation, "Amicitia intensa non habetur ad multos" (Intense friendship cannot be distributed among many) .[20] He was following Aristotle:

> One cannot be a friend to many people in the sense of having friendship of the perfect type with them, just as one cannot be in love with many people at once (for love is a sort of excess of feeling, and it is the nature of such only to be felt towards one person); and it is not easy for many people at the same time to please the same person very greatly, or perhaps to even be good in his eyes. One must, too, acquire some experience of the other person and become familiar with him, and that is very hard.[21]

Moral: Another genuine quality of friendship is that it strives to live life in a morally good way. Morality is not an easy subject to discuss today because some people have an unhealthy and mistaken notion of what moral life is. It often suggests a repressive and oppressive kind of life. Being moral, however, means striving after human goodness. The moral person is the good person. We certainly want, within friendship, to enhance the goodness of the other. If friendship is love, and if immoral activity is destructive of love, then no friend desires to allow immorality to enter into a relationship. The problem is not so much whether a relationship be moral or not; the problem is that many of us have not sufficiently thought through what moral goodness means. Yet striving after ethically good expressions of love is important. Immorality impedes growth in love; love implies concerted and responsible efforts to grow in the moral life.

Generative: Another characteristic of friendship already pointed to in John's Gospel is that friendship bears fruit.[22] In fact, this is the best criterion as to whether friendship is genuine friendship and Christian. It is basically an application of Paul's principle of discernment, "by their effects you shall know them."[23] When Jesus addresses his disciples as friends he then goes on to say, "Go out and bear fruit; fruit that will last" (John 15:16). In other words, friendship is not a closed circle for two. Although friendship is the intense particularity that exists between two, friendship is always called to be creative and productive. Friendship is given as a gift not simply for the sake of the two but for the sake of the community; it is intended to be public and not simply private. Although there is no question that friendship needs privacy in order to grow, just as the individual needs solitude, friendship is not simply a private relationship. It is a value that should be acknowledged, recognized and pointed to in the community at large.

Interpenetrating: Eventually friends no longer see themselves apart from the other. We cannot define ourselves by ourselves alone. If you ask me who Don Goergen is, I cannot tell you who he is apart from those others who have become part of me. Others—and this is very much affirmed in process philosophy—are not simply those who are there but those who are here. This quality of friendship also points to a form of bilocation. We are not simply in one locus of space-time. We are not simply in one place alone. We are where we are loved, although with a different modality of presence. In fact it may be as significant to say that we are where we are loved as to say that we are here, although our physical presence might be more discernible here. A friend is someone who has become a part of us. This is a stern realization during the process of grief when we either separate or lose someone we love.[24] We realize how much a part of us they have become. In other words, friends are those who are so totally present to each other that they can no longer be conceptualized apart from the other. I am the others in my life as much as I am myself.

Spiritual: The final quality we need to examine is that friendship is always spiritual. In a post-Cartesian age we so readily misunderstand spirituality. Spiritual does not imply non-physical. Spiritual means rooted in the Spirit, being guided by the Spirit. A better expression than spiritual for us could be Christian since it appears more holistic. The word spiritual, for someone like Aelred, did not imply a non-emotional, non-erotic, non-physical kind of relationship. "Spiritual" implies an effort to root out relationship in Christ, and a vision of this friendship as not simply ours but as coming from Christ, created by Christ, and existing for Christ. Christ must always be a part of any friendship. The spiritual quality of friendship means that we are not only concerned about the physical, emotional, reflective, and moral support of the other, but that we also want to give ourselves to the spiritual journey each of us has undertaken. To be a support to each other's spiritual living is an important aspect of friendship.

Intimacy and Generativity

Intimacy in its falsified expression can readily lead to possessive love, both because intimacy is closely related to *eros* and affection, and because emotion can easily lead to dependency and possessiveness. For friendship, however, to become what it can be, the capacity to let be, to let go, to not own, completes friendship.

In one sense this aspect of the love of friendship could be designated as its creative aspect. Generativity, therefore, is an appropriate term to apply to the complement of intimacy. In addition to the way in which friendship is fulfilling to the two who are involved and mutually related, friendship finds value in the creativity it promotes, the outpouring it unleashes, which transcends the two alone, which goes beyond them. This outpouring is obvious in conjugal friendship where the procreative activity symbolizes the generative dimensions of the relationship. Intimacy without generativity is masked selfishness, *egoïsme à deux* as Teilhard would put it.

The notion of generativity has been developed by Eric Erikson in his psychology as well as by Don Browning in *Generative Man,* which is based upon the Eriksonian concept of generativity.[25] Generativity for Erikson is the task to be accomplished within adulthood. Don Browning coins the expression *generative man* as the model of the mature man in modern society. For Browning the essence of the generative person is to generate and maintain a world which both includes and transcends one's own issue, family, tribe, nation and race.[26] Generativity is that which enables us to include those with whom we are immediately identified and yet enables us to go beyond that particularized self-identification. Both identity and intimacy are stages which must be crossed by the adolescent and young adult before the adult can become generative. Generativity then refers not simply to the results of genital love but to the result of all love. It flows from the intellectual and spiritual life as well as from the genital life. Generativity does not mean letting go of our friends. It enables us to be with and in our friends and still to transcend that friendship. Browning writes: Generativity is not only the instinctive source behind biological pro-creation and care; it is also the ground for man's higher attempts to create a total environment ecologically supportive of the general health—not only of family and tribe, but of the entire human species."[27]

It may be helpful here to outline the different conflicts which Erikson developed so that we can see them in the progression within which he discusses generativity.[28]

Age	Nuclear Conflict	Virtue
1. Infancy	Trust vs. Mistrust	Hope
2. Early Childhood	Autonomy vs. Shame	Will
3. Play Age	Initiative vs. Guilt	Purpose
4. School Age	Industry vs. Inferiority	Competence
5. Adolescence	Identity vs. Identity Confusion	Fidelity
6. Young Adult	Intimacy vs. Isolation	Love
7. Adulthood	Generativity vs. Self-absorption	Care
8. Old Age	Integrity vs. Despair	Wisdom

A sense of competence emphasized in the consideration of self-esteem above is seen here as a virtue which must be acquired to some degree before one can move toward fidelity. Fidelity and love are the words most closely associated with friendship discussed in this chapter. Identity and intimacy must be engaged before one actualizes one's generative potential. The danger of neglecting generativity is that our intimacy will remain at a level of self-absorption. Just as self-esteem without self-sacrifice can be selfishness, so friendship without a generative consciousness can be a preoccupation with the relationship, which eventually will lead to stagnation.

The virtue which Erickson uses to resolve the tension between becoming generative and being self-absorbed is care. The word *care* connotes the inner essence of love. We are to care about ourselves, about our friends, about our brothers and sisters, about those who are in need, about God himself. Care is a helpful term here because the word love has become so associated with romantic love or emotion alone. Care points to that transcendent quality which shows that one has moved beyond self-preoccupation and self-absorption. Thus the virtue that emerges when generativity triumphs over self-absorption is care.[29] Browning even speaks of the ethic of care.

We need self-esteem and self-sacrifice if we are to grow. And we need intimacy and generativity. Just as we suffer diminution when our need for intimacy is left unfulfilled, so we suffer a kind of death when our need for generativity is not met. Generativity is the complement of intimate love, friendship. It creates realities which transcend the relationship itself, and which enable the lovers to discover a world beyond their love for one another.

Chapter Four

COMMUNITY

The Meaning of Community

We now come to the third love, brotherhood and sisterhood, *koinonia,* community or fellowship. In contrast to the particular love which friendship is, community is more universal in scope. Community is a word which can have varied meanings. There are at least four implications to the term: the body of Christ, fellowship, significant others, and those with whom I consciously choose to live.

Each of these relationships is valid for interpreting the meaning of community. The first two are explicitly biblical, *soma* or *koinonia,* both in the Pauline sense. If we ask ourselves about the character of our community, the most fundamental reality is that we are in Christ, that we are members of Christ, that we are Christ, that we are his Body and that our community is truly the fellowship of the Body of Christ. My fundamental ontological community is Christ in his fullness, the total Christ, head and members. Community in this sense has a potential universality to it in that all have been grafted into the body of Christ whether they are conscious of this relationship or not. In this sense, all are my brothers and sisters if I am living in Christ. As Christian I am explicitly called to live in union with all members of the human family because all have been invited into the Kingdom of God, into the embodied reality of Christ on earth.

Closely associated with this more universal notion of community, the human family, and specifically the human family as rooted in Christ, is the biblical notion of fellowship. Christians are those with whom we interact at a level of significance because we have something in common, one faith and one baptism. Fellowship as a word, however, does not necessarily have the connotation that "body of Christ" might have. We share fellowship with all within the body of Christ but fellowship connotes those with whom we are immediately and presently interacting, those who have come together at a particular time for a particular purpose. Fellowship is a particularization, concretization, of the more universal concept of Christ's body. In one sense it is almost a contrast between the Church universal and the Church local. Community in fact connotes both. Yet fellowship need not imply an explicitly religious reality. There are those whom we may love as brothers and sisters with whom we do not have one faith and one baptism. This may mean a degree to which the brotherhood and sisterhood, the sharing, the communality, is diminished but it does not mean that in this relationship there is no authentic fellowship.

To continue the notion of community as a more particularized or experiential reality such as fellowship denotes, we could speak more sociologically of our community as being significant others, those others who are important to our self-definition, apart from whom we do not tend to define or understand ourselves, those who enter into our lives at a level of significance and with whom our interaction establishes a strongly valued interdependence. In this sense my community is that network of relationships which constitutes who I am. Another may be a member of my community but his or her community and mine need not be the same. We can see how this network can expand. If we take all the significant others of all the significant others of my significant others, my relational network expands and expands. Yet community here would connote those who enter more immediately into my relational network. Although all our relational networks overlap and interact and we all have something in common, we might not immediately think or feel that all others are my brothers or sisters. Yet there is still the universal potential of brotherly and sisterly love which is not there within the notion of friendship as particular love.

Community can also mean those with whom I consciously choose to live and to establish workable living relationships—life together. We tend often to think of community in this sense. Yet neither fellowship nor significance need imply physical or geographical proximity or immediacy. "Those with whom I live" can point to variations of community as well. We immediately think of celibate communities, the history of religious communities established by single men and women in order to live the common life based on certain goals they share in common. Life together, however, is not only shaped through celibate communities but also through conjugal communities. In fact, this is what conjugality seeks today. It seeks an expansiveness, a capacity for universality without which it suffocates. Celibate community seeks intimacy without which it cannot survive and conjugal community seeks to own the communal character of life to which it has a right. The most immediate conjugal community is the whole family, not simply the communion between husband and wife which is more appropriately described as love of friendship. When that love of friendship is generative in such a way as to lead to children, we have a particular form of communal love, not only children for each other but parents for children and children for parents. Conjugal community is often described in our society as a nuclear family but other descriptions are applicable as well, such as the extended family, a more extensive conjugal community.

A third form of community in this last sense would be the commune—not always celibate groupings where the motivation is explicitly religious and not always the family whether considered as a nucleus or in its full extensiveness, but groups of men and women, single and married, who choose to come together in order to share life. Communes have had different degrees of success or failure. Nevertheless, they do manifest another aspect of the meaning of community as life together.

There is no need to reduce these four ways of speaking about community into one. For Christians, community can take place with those with whom I live as well as with those with whom I share a deepened level of commonality, with whom I may or may not live, whether these be significant others whom I can clearly identify on the basis of past experience or those who might come together in a new way with whom I share fellowship. Community in all of these senses still implies a relationship of familiarity, communality, a way of loving which is not based on need nor on full self-disclosure but is still mutual and interdependent. This kind of love is always open to further universalization in such a way that all are seen as my brothers and sisters whether or not I have yet come to feel this kind of love for all my brothers and sisters.

The reality of fellowship or communal love is closely

related to but still distinguishable from identity and intimacy, two tasks of psychological growth. Identity very much pertains to the struggle for self-love; intimacy is based on knowledge of others, reciprocal love and mutual self-disclosure. The task of identity needs to be faced and wrestled with so that one can begin to see what intimacy is going to mean in one's life. Similarly, intimacy needs to be faced before one can love with a communal love in an adult fashion. In other words, the task of identity (self-esteem) needs to precede the task of intimacy (friendship) which needs to precede the task of community (fellowship), although all three continue to interact dialectically as well.

The more we move into intimacy, the more it can both threaten and enhance our self-esteem. The more we move out toward fellowship, the more it can both threaten and enhance friendship. Community can contribute to self-esteem and self-esteem to community. Intimacy can contribute to community and community to intimacy. Self-esteem and intimacy contribute to each other. These three realities interact. Yet facing ourselves and identifying ourselves need to take place before we begin to give ourselves to others. We need to open ourselves and give ourselves in that disclosing kind of mutual depth before we can give of our depth more universally.

Community and personal identity are interrelated because our identities are influenced by those with whom we interact at a certain level of significance. Community or fellowship does imply necessarily a group of people with whom we identify. Rosabeth Kanter emphasizes this dimension.[1] Community provides our most immediate personal environment and thus contributes to the process of our self-identification. The more blurred the boundaries of our community, the more difficult it is to sustain or maintain our identity. The more stabilized our identity, the greater the risk we are able to take in terms of moving out of previously defined forms of communal existence. In other words, there is a dialectic between self-identification and self-transcendence. Our identities both contribute to and benefit from the definition of our community. Yet community and identity are not the same reality. I am not my community and my community is not me. As persons, however, we are always individuals in community. The two, individuality and community, provide the poles for personal existence. They can be distinguished but they cannot be separated.

Just as the boundaries of self or ego need to be firm while at the same time remaining open, so the boundaries of relationships need to be both firm and fluid. We need to be able to identify not only ourselves; we need to be able to identify who our friends are as well. In the same way community also interacts with friendship or intimacy. There is a degree of intimacy within every relationship that is personal, that is truly human. Communal love is personal love and hence intimate love. Yet it is not precisely the intimacy of the mutual bond which is the basis for communal love or fellowship. The basis of such love is much more something outside of ourselves which members of community have in common.

In self-love the focus is, in the beginning, interior. Teilhard de Chardin describes this focus as centration or individualization. Friendship, for Teilhard, is an excentration opening the depths of our interiority to encounter the depths of another's interiority, reaching out to an other outside but reaching out to the within of the other. Although there is a union of interiorities in communal love, such union is not the basis on which communal love is maintained. Rather the basis is the common goals outside the members of community. Community is not explicitly a kind of intimate love as much as it is interdependence for the sake of common goals or values. Community is a network of mutual dependency, a relational network, which provides the most immediate context for living, a context which establishes interpersonal ties, but ties established for the sake of something other than self, for the sake of something other than you or me alone. What binds us together is the cause, goal, or meaning which has called us to one another. Ultimately this goal is Christ himself.

Communal love involves intimacy. Yet intimacy is not precisely that for which we search in community. In fellowship or companionship, with brothers and sisters, we search for those who share our values. It is because of Christ that our community can be truly universal. He is not only the historical Jesus but the universal Christ as well. Community, then, is not intimacy as such but it is a profound way of loving.

Before examining the concept of community or fellowship in Teilhard de Chardin and in the Scriptures, we need to remind ourselves of an important distinction. Too frequently we tend to idealize community, communal love, indeed idealize love itself. We should look at each of the five loves idealistically but also from the perspective of experiential realism. In other words, the theory, the theology, the meaning, the attractiveness of each of these ways of loving draws us forth. Yet the concrete, existential, daily living of that love is what enables us to see that love demands that kind of selflessness which is the mark of an ascetical person, the self-sacrifice which is the complement to self-esteem. Community is an ascetical experience just as friendship and self-esteem are. Indeed, we do not come to self-love apart from the ascetical wrestling with the totality of our inner selves. We do not come to the love of friendship apart from openness to the reality of pain. As there is an ascetical theology of friendship, so there is of community. Communal love is an experience of asceticism (or purgation) and union (or integration). It is as much an experience of purification as it is of unification.

As we look at the value of community in Teilhard de Chardin's theory of personality and in the Scriptures, we should not lose sight of the process through which we come to love others as brothers and sisters. That process involves the asceticism of communication and dialogue as does friendship and self-esteem. Underlying each of the loves is communication. Any principle which enhances communication enhances the capacity to love as well. There is an old scholastic axiom that says goodness tends to communicate itself, love tends to communicate itself. Anything that makes that communication more difficult or less possible or more inhibited will inhibit, destroy or interfere with our capacity to be lovers.

Koinonia In The New Testament

Koinonos in Greek is a fellow or participant, one who participates in, who shares with. *Koinonia* is fellowship or participation—brotherhood, sisterhood, community. *Koinonia* in the New Testament can be distinguished both from *philia,* friendship, and from *diakonia,* service or ministry. *Koinonia* implies participation in the life of the community, a sharing of life in common, fellowship. It is not the same as friendship or ministry.

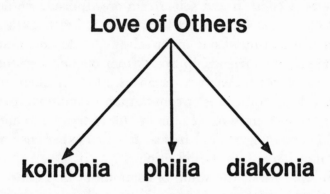

Love of Others

koinonia   philia   diakonia

There is a sense in which friendship can be seen as an expression of *koinonia.* We experience fellowship with our friends. Yet fellowship implies the possibility of universal communion. The strength of friendship, *philia,* is its depth, its intimacy, its particularity, while the strength of *koinonia* is its potential for universalization. We do not envision *philia* with all members of the body of Christ, yet we realize that we experience or can experience *koinonia* with all members of Christ's body. Both kinds of union are extremely important and valid ways of loving.

The same can be said in contrasting *koinonia* and *diakonia.* We can see ministry or service as a supreme form of love to which we are called as we respond to those who are in need. In fact, the imperative to love our enemies indicates the extent to which love of neighbor or *diakonia* calls us. Whereas both *philia* and *koinonia* imply a relationship based upon mutuality, diakonia does not necessarily have such an implication. *Diakonia* calls us to selflessness. In each of these forms of love, therefore, we see a particular strength, the capacity for particularization (*philia*), the capacity for universalization (*koinonia*), or the capacity for self-transcendence and self-giving (*diakonia*).

We should not attempt to make one way of loving a more noble form of Christian love than another, as the Scriptures themselves testify. For John, *philia* is a supreme form of love. It is *agape*. There is no love greater than *philia*, that between friends, and John uses *philia* to describe our own relationship with God himself. The supreme compliment is that God calls us into friendship with him. If we were to articulate a theology based on experience, this emphasis of John should not be surprising. The particular friendship between John and Jesus himself would have given John an experience of a kind of love which he could then use to articulate the depths and heights to which this kind of love can go. John uses *philia* to express his understanding of union with Christ, union with God, as well as union between two people.

Paul on the other hand, uses the word *koinonia*. Fellowship and community are the focal points for much of Paul's theology of the Christian life. Again, if we begin with the root experiences of these authors, their emphases should not surprise us. Paul, never having been a personal disciple of the historical Jesus, does not speak so much of his *philia* or friendship with Christ but of his fellowship or *koinonia* with Christ. That into which Christians are called is the community of believers, fellowship with one another. Just as John can talk about love as friendship, Paul can talk about love as fellowship. When we discuss ministry and service in greater detail, we will see that the synoptic gospels tend to speak about love of neighbor and love of enemy, about love as *diakonia*.

Thus, in the Scriptures, we find all three loves valued. We may experience fellowship with our friends or those to whom we minister. Yet ministry does not necessarily imply reciprocity or fellowship. We may find ourselves ministering to or at the service of our friends and yet friendship itself connotes mutual reciprocity more than it does a response based on need. Thus we have three kinds of love: intimacy, fellowship, and service. Fellowship is that kind of relationship which implies a bond based upon the sharing or participation in a common enterprise, a bond established on the basis of sharing something in common. If we look at the New Testament we see two directions which *koinonia* takes. One is union with God, the other is union with fellow Christians. In 2 Peter, 1:4, fellowship is a participation in the divine nature itself. In Acts 2:42, fellowship is the brotherly and sisterly accord expressed in the life of the Christian community. Paul gives us a developed theology of *koinonia* and both of these directions are found within his theology, the first being christocentric, participation in the life of Christ, and the second, fellowship shared among Christian believers.[2]

It is the second of these two directions which is our primary concern here since the first relates more to the fifth kind of love of which we shall speak later, love, union, friendship, fellowship with God. Yet, as we proceed, we must see that all forms of Christian love, whether love of self or of others, are based on love of God. The beginning of *koinonia* for Paul is being grafted into Christ himself. It is because of our participation and fellowship with Christ that we experience fellowship or communion with one another.

Paul, the New Testament author for whom the language of *koinonia* is highly important, uses this term for religious fellowship or the participation of the man or woman of faith in Christ. He talks about being *in Christ* and sees the believer as a member of the body of Christ. These are Paul's efforts to express how we are united to Christ, and his imagery flows from his own experience as well as the type of relationship with Christ to which we are called.

Paul uses *koinonia* also for the fellowship which arises in the Eucharist, the Lord's Supper. For Paul, fellowship with Christ primarily comes through faith, but it is experienced and enhanced and made visible in the Lord's Supper. Thus *koinonia* implies table fellowship. In table fellowship we see both implications of *koinonia*. The Eucharist implies both fellowship with Christ and fellowship with our brothers and sisters. The Eucharist, in the sense of our fellowship with Christ, grounds and makes real the basis of our fellowship with one another. Those who partake of the life of Christ in the Lord's Supper become the companions of Christ and hence the companions of one another. Fellowship can be closely related to companionship. Christ is our companion just as other fellow Christians are.

Fellowship with Christ, however, is achieved not only through faith and through the breaking of the bread. It is achieved through suffering. For Paul, participation with Christ means participation in the phases or events of the life of Christ. Mystical participation is still real participation. It means literally sharing the life of Christ, both his suffering and his glory, entering into the very death and resurrection of Christ himself.

This union of the Christian with Christ which is the basis for Christian union and communion helps us to discuss love of God. One of the effects of this fellowship with Christ is fellowship among Christians, the mutual fellowship of members in the Christian community. Fellowship among Christians is a bond that is not simply friendship; it is a bond based upon spiritual union because of one baptism and one faith. *Koinonia,* fellowship, community is that love by which we love our brothers and sisters in the faith. It is those brothers and sisters in the faith with whom we share one baptism who are our community, although we might only experience fellowship with them on an *ad hoc* basis, when we concretely enter into one another's lives, such as at a Eucharistic celebration. The Eucharist is a concrete expression of fellowship and it is in the local church that fellowship is experienced and made manifest. Yet this fellowship is that which we share with all our brothers and sisters who are members of Christ. The expression then, body of Christ, in addition to its reference to the historical body of the earthly Jesus, has two other primary significations for Paul: the body of Christ which we all are through our fellowship with him in faith; and the body of Christ that we each partake of in the Eucharistic worship.[3]

Personality and Community in Teilhard de Chardin

Neither the importance of an individual in a society's history nor the importance of the society in an individual's history can be denied. An individual is always an individual in a community, and a community is always a community of individuals. The individual exists *in relationship* to a group, a community, a society, without losing any distinctive and distinguishable individuality. We are *different from* the others but *related* to the others. We are *distinguishable* from the others but *not separable* from them. The prominence and mutual relatedness of both individuality and community can be seen in the thought of Teilhard de Chardin.

Teilhard describes individuality as inexpressible characteristics, as a personal molecule, as the incommunicable singularity of being which each of us possesses. Each of us is a natural unity with his or her own responsibilities and incommunicable possibilities.[4]

Teilhard takes seriously the importance of individuality. In 1927 he wrote, "Each person, though enveloped within the same universe as all other persons, presents an independent centre of perspective and activity for the universe."[5] In 1939 he writes, "Thus socialization, whose hour seems to have sounded for humankind, does not by any means signify the end of the Era of the Individual upon earth, but far more its beginning."[6] In *The Phenomenon of Man* in the late forties, he stresses that our goal is to find "the utmost limit of ourselves."[7]

His essay on the personalistic universe attempts to present the human personality as the significant element within his system. He asks the question: "Isn't it an essential duty to perfect, within oneself, the individuality entrusted to one?"[8] The essay on the rights of man speaks of "the absolute duty of the individual to develop his own personality."[9]

Teilhard emphasizes the importance of recognizing the individual in any concept of fraternity. We see a classic example of this conviction in *The Phenomenon of Man* where he opposes collective massification within society.

> We have 'mass movements'—no longer the horde streaming down from the forests of the north or the steppes of Asia, but 'the Million' scientifically assembled. The Million in rank and file on the parade ground; the Million standardized in the factory; the Million motorized and all this only ending up with Communism and National Socialism and the most ghastly fetters. So we get the crystal instead of the cell; the anthill instead of brotherhood.[10]

If due regard is not given the individual, if he or she is not seen as a significant element within any group, one cannot have unity. The individual is important. Society and sociality center around the individual.

Spirituality also centers around the individual. "Our God, on the contrary, pushes to its furthest possible limit the differentiation among the creatures he concentrates within himself. At the peak of their adherence to him, the elect also discover in him the consummation of their individual fulfillment."[11]

Teilhard realizes that the individual is significant, that the individual is an integral center in any wholesome totality, that individuality has to be developed rather than denied. Individuality, the singularity within our personality, is that which makes each person unique. The social, relational, or communal dimension complements the individual dimension of our personalities; the two can never be seen as separable from one another but only in correlation with each other. Individuality is one pole for our personality; sociality or relationality, another.

The personality process begins for Teilhard with individuality. The giveness or uniqueness of the individual is the alpha of personality development. Personality, however, is more than individuality. Teilhard stresses not only individuality but also personality. "The goal of ourselves, the acme of our originality, is not our individuality but our person."[12] 'Individual' and 'person' are not identical concepts.

Personality development is a process of discovering, growing towards and arriving at one's person. Person here is the omega of development. This process involves focusing on the self—a process of centration as Teilhard calls it—in which we, our individualities, our "selves" continually evolve. This dimension of personality growth centers on self-development.

Lest personality growth become selfishness, however, we move from centering on our own selves to centering ourselves upon others—moving the center of ourselves outside ourselves or beyond ourselves—a process of excentration: "The individual, if he is to fulfill or preserve himself, must strive to break down every kind of barrier that prevents separate beings from uniting. His is the exaltation, not of egotistical autonomy, but of communion with all others!"[13] The self (individual) finds Self (person) outside his or her own self. The more "other" we become, the more we find our Self. "The true ego grows in inverse proportion to egoism."[14] Selfhood finds its fulfillment in co-existence, collaboration, interdependence. The Self or person includes more than the self or individual.

For Teilhard, both the individual and the other are focal centers. We can be completely ourselves only by ceasing to be isolated. Excentration begins as the center of our existence begins to move outside ourselves. "But one thing is certain: despite our fears, it is in the direction of 'groupings' that we must advance."[15] Excentration is the socialization of the individual. Teilhard's synthesis enables him to emphasize both individuality and community. Individualization (the process of developing our strengths, our uniqueness, our individuality) and socialization (the process by which our individuality is socialized) are not mutually exclusive. They harmonize like breathing in and breathing out. They are two components of a single process. The community is a part of the individual and the individual is a part of the community. By ourselves we are incomplete and unfinished.

Human socialization is not an impersonal or depersonalizing process. "The egocentric ideal of a future reserved for those who have managed to attain egoistically the extremity of 'everyone for himself' is false and against nature. No element could move and grow except with and by all the others with itself."[16] "According to the evolutionary structure of the world, we can only find our person by uniting together."[17] "No evolutionary future awaits man except in association with all other men."[18] The process of personalization includes both individualization and socialization, individuality and relationality.

Teilhard writes, "Man becomes a person in and through personalization."[19] As we have examined it thus far, there are two components to this process going on simultaneously.

$$\text{Personalization} = \frac{\text{centration (individualization)}}{+} \text{excentration (socialization)}.$$

For Teilhard, all evolution is a process of unification. Atoms unite to form molecules and molecules unite to form mega-molecular substances. Evolution moves in the direction of increased complexity and increased consciousness. Growth implies increased integration and unification. The problem is whether this can be achieved without destroying the individuality of the elements united. For Teilhard, true union does not destroy, but perfects, creates, and personalizes. It is in this process of unification that individuals discover who they are. "In any domain, whether it be the cells of a body, the members of a society, or the elements of a spiritual synthesis—*union differentiates*. In every organized whole the parts perfect themselves and fulfill themselves."[20] True union, the union of heart and spirit, does not enslave, nor does it neutralize the individuals which it brings together. It super-personalizes them.[21]

> If you consider the mutual fulfillment of two beings who love one another; if you analyze philosophically the effect of a center on the elements it gathers together and note that it does not dissolve but inevitably completes them— in every case you will come to the conclusion that directly contradicts what first seemed to be indicated. True union does not run together the beings it joins, but rather differentiates them more fully.[22]

Teilhard distinguishes union from fusion. Fusion merely absorbs the elements it contains; it de-personalizes. "Creative union does not fuse together the terms which it associates. . . . It preserves the terms. It even completes them."[23]

The question of how this is possible brings us to the phenomenon of love. Love, for Teilhard, is the energy underlying the process of evolution. "Love alone is capable of uniting living beings in such a way as to complete and fulfill them, for it alone takes them and joins them by what is deepest in themselves."[24] "The forces of love have the property of personalizing by uniting."[25] "To love is to discover and complete oneself in someone other than oneself."[26]

> It is through love and within love that we must look for the deepening of our deepest self, in the life giving coming together of human kind. Love is the free and imaginative outpouring of the spirit over all unexplored paths. It links those who love in bonds that unite but do not confound, causing them to discover in their mutual contact an exaltation capable, incomparably more than any arrogance of solitude, of arousing in the heart of their being all that they possess of uniqueness and creative power.[27]

Love, at the basis of personality, is the energy of personalization, bringing about the transformation from impersonality to personality.

We are individuals, but also more. We are other-oriented individuals. Centration, individualization, self-development, moves in the direction of excentration, increasing unification, self-transcendence. Personalization or personality growth accompanies and is accompanied by socialization or social growth. There is nothing personal that is not also social. Personality, as a process, is based upon the individuality of a person. With this starting point, it moves in the direction of unity and community for all. Centration does not find its fulfillment within itself, but culminates in an excentration from the self. This excentration, however, is still centered and integrated within the self. One takes leave of the self, the actual or present self, to arrive at the Self, the potential or to-be-achieved Self.

Our "selves" as processes must be seen as developing between an alpha and an omega, between a term from which and a term to which, both termini of which we ourselves are. We are what we are and we are what we are becoming. Both focuses are important if we consider the alpha not only as a point in time but also as

our individualities. Our individualities are our starting points as persons. Our "persons" then are our
omegas, that in the direction of which we move. Today's personality is tomorrow's individuality; today's
accomplishment is tomorrow's starting point; our persons are always evolving realities. Our individualities
are what we are. Our persons are what we become.
Personalization as a process must respect both who we
are and who we are not yet. Personality grows forth
from our individualities integrating more and more
into us as individuals. There is always that which we
are (individuality) and that which is still left to become part of us (the rest of the world). As we grow
we become progressively concerned with the world outside our present selves. The development of the self
is achieved through the transcendence of the self until
it culminates in the fulfillment of the self as Self. Self-
development is self-transcendence, self-actualization.

Individuality is a starting point but is also the incommunicable, the unique, the precious within us.
True unity never destroys this incommunicable element; it never destroys us. Yet the incommunicable,
the individual, can still be personalized. For a healthy
universe, each individual must be a healthy center,
healthily self-centered. To affirm individuality, however, is not to affirm individualists or egoists, those
"who seek to grow by excluding or diminishing their
fellows whether individually or nationally or racially."[28]
Personality is always in community. To be an individual and nothing more, we need not be so concerned
with community. To be a person we must always be
in-process-within-community. Love, which perfects and
personalizes the individual, brings us into relationship
with others to be perfected and completed. This is a

never ending process. As Teilhard writes, "A universal love is not only psychologically possible, it is the only complete and final way in which we are able to love."[29]

Love by its nature universalizes the person. It is the fulfillment of the person. Personalism is an emphasis upon the importance of love in personality fulfillment. To be a person means to love and to be loved. It means to love as a fully human person in a totally human way. Love by its nature, however, is a universalizing force. To be a person is to become universal. "The ego only persists by becoming ever more itself in the measure in which it makes everything else itself."[30]

Personalism must lead an individual to the communal, the social, the universal dimension if it is to be authentic. On the other hand, those who emphasize the social have to realize that there is no such thing as true humanity, community, a universe worth building separated from human affection and human individuals. We can have no true society that is not a personal society nor a true person who is not a social person. "No evolutionary future awaits mankind except in association with all other men."[31]

Solitude

We saw in Chapter Two that we could not have a proper appreciation of the self, of self-esteem, apart from self-denial. In a similar fashion, in Chapter Three we saw that the notion of intimacy is inseparable from the notion of generativity, if we are speaking about Christian intimacy, about authentic intimacy. We need now to emphasize a similar complementarity between being together and being alone, between community and solitude.

For those versed in Christian spirituality, there is probably little need to emphasize solitude as a value. For those, however, highly enculturated into the twentieth century, solitude is more often than not something from which we escape rather than something which we welcome and it is necessary for us to rediscover the value of solitude, to appreciate its necessity in order to live deeply communal and social lives.

Solitude bears fruit within all five of the loves of which we are speaking. Perhaps one of its greatest benefits is that it leads to self-discovery. One of the early roles of solitude within the desert tradition of spirituality is that it provided the opportunity for facing oneself, for wrestling with one's devils, for learning to be with one's own self and learning to be compatible with oneself. Our inner fears often prevent us from doing so, and yet it is precisely these fears which we need to tame, with which we need to become friends, for these are the fears which reveal us to ourselves. Self-discovery achieved apart from solitude is inauthentic. This does not mean that solitude is the only route to self-discovery, but that it is one route and a necessary route along with others. We do not discover who we are completely by ourselves; we discover ourselves in the presence of and in union with others. At the same time, however, we do not discover ourselves completely if we are always and only with others; we also need to be alone.

This solitary side of ourselves needs room to grow. Thus it is that, even within a human and Christian intimacy, two people need at times to be apart. Solitude is not only important if we are to grow in self-love; it is also important if we are to grow in intimate love. Although friends are literally a part of us and we are

119

not who we are apart from them, it is also true to say that our friends are not all of us, that sometimes we need to be apart from them. Marriage—as an important example of Christian friendship—too often ignores this need to be alone, and to be apart. A frequent problem in marriage is finding time to be alone together. An equally important problem can be finding time to be alone with ourselves. Both problems reflect the need to find time to get away from the distractions of life and the business of raising a family. Rearing a family, work, and our own interior fears about ourselves and relationships can prevent two people from getting to know each other more deeply and getting to know themselves. Intimacy requires solitude.

When we discuss love of neighbor, we shall see that ministry is also in a rhythm with solitude. Jesus is the supreme example of this as he manifests his need to get away from the crowds. He who attempts to minister all the time ends up ministering none of the time. This is the important role that leisure and play provide as a complement to a life of ministry, for leisure and play manifest themselves in both solitary and social ways. Leisure often suggests a more solitary and appreciative stance; play, a more active and social stance. A life of service cannot be lived apart from a respect for the need for solitude and leisure.

Love of God is a clear example of the need for such solitude. Just as we do not develop a human relationship in depth if two are not alone together at times, so we do not develop a relationship with God if we do not take time to be alone with God. Solitude is extremely important in the life of prayer and when we discuss prayer we shall see that the prayer of solitude is a fundamental form in which loving God and being loved by him is experienced. Thus solitude contributes to self-esteem, friendship, ministry, and prayer. It is, however, the fundamental way in which community or fellowship is balanced to be complete. Dietrich Bonhoeffer makes this clear when he writes, "Let the one who cannot be alone beware of community. Let the one who is not in community beware of being alone."[32]

Being alone and *being with* are two sides of life—like breathing in and breathing out. It is important to realize that solitude is a social concept. In its essence, it is not antisocial. A solitude which springs from a fear of others, or a hatred of others, or an inability to be with others, is a destructive running from others rather than a constructive being with oneself. The very purpose of solitude is social so that we might return to our friends, to our brothers and sisters, and to those to whom we minister, that we might be more completely present and more deeply there than we would be if we had not taken time for ourselves. The emphasis which traditional Christian spirituality has placed on this value of solitude can be seen in the early solitary tradition and the eremetical life. Although not all are called to such lives of solitude, some are called to this kind of solitude in order to make more clear, to witness, to make sacramentally visible this particular aspect of Christian existence. Not all of us can witness to all the facets of Christian life with equal clarity. This is why some are called to make more visible one aspect than another.

The hermit makes visible the socially responsible type of solitude which is central to all Christian living just as Christian marriage makes visible the generatively responsible type of intimacy or friendship which is also a part of Christian life, as friars and sisters make visible the apostolic character of Christian existence, and as monks and nuns make visible the communal character of Christian life. Although communal, ceno-bitic monasticism became the dominate form in the West, in Christianity, monks and nuns find that they can live their vocation as solitaries or in communities. In other great religious traditions of the East, the life of solitude was seen as a supreme path to spiritual liv-ing, the value that balances community. There is no Christian solitude which sees itself apart from others and no Christian community which can define itself in such a way as to exclude the right of each to be alone with themselves and with their God.

The important question that we must ask when we are with others, whether as friends, as brothers and sisters, or for the sake of ministry, is the question of whether we are there to be *with* others and *for* others, or there out of desperation, to be away *from* ourselves. Often we are with others to avoid the self—and that avoidance is inauthentic social existence—just as being with ourselves in order to be away from others is in-authentic solitude. Loneliness is a current which runs through life, a fact of life about which we too seldom speak, perhaps the most fundamental negative fact about life. It is probably a superfluous quest to attempt to define the ultimate source of negativity in human experience. Kierkegaard talks about boredom in this fashion.[33] Others might list depression or anger. We might easily build a case for fear, or in philosophical terms suggest finitude.

Biblically, however, negativity is pictured as lone-liness (Gen. 2:18). Are not boredom and loneliness closely related? Is there not a greater chance for bore-dom when there are no significant others for the sake of whom we live our lives? Is not an exaggerated dependency upon our need for others greater when there are no other constructive sources of stimulation in our life? Are we bored because we are lonely? Or lonely because we are bored? And something similar could be said of depression. Although much depression is anger, is it not an anger at or a fear of this fundamental fact of aloneness which confronts us and from which we cannot escape. How much depression is wrapped up with estrangement from others? Or dislike of self? A fear that I might ultimately be unlikeable, or unliked, or unloveable, or unloved? Is the issue of how we face ourselves, our aloneness and loneliness, not at the root of our emotional responses in many situations? Certainly a fundamental fear for all of us is that incapacitating fear of loneliness. Ultimately, is loneliness the fundamental fact about human existence? It is hard for us even to raise these questions, and yet these are the questions which will surface when we find ourselves alone. The time must come, however, when these need to be faced, wrestled with, and overcome, not to overcome our *need for aloneness* but in order to overcome our *fear of loneliness*.

There are so many kinds of loneliness in life, and there is no need to delineate these here other than to emphasize how pervasive loneliness is in human existence, and thus how important it is for us to face, and we cannot face it when we are running from ourselves. Loneliness is faced in solitude, and when confronted we are better prepared for social existence, which is the core of Christian life. Loneliness manifests itself as a life without intimacy, as an inability to love or be loved, as the loss of identity or the "notyetness" of having established an identity or the anxiety which comes from split identity. Loneliness can also be the loneliness of failure, of career failure or career change, of a breakdown in a human relationship. There are few sufferings as painful as significant changes within intimate human relationships growing at different rates or with different rhythms. There is the loneliness of separation, the loneliness of loss, the loneliness of not liking oneself. There is the loneliness of creativity, of unorthodoxy, of the manifold ways in which each of us is different, the loneliness of being different, the loneliness of being unable to communicate our innermost selves, unable to find ways of making ourselves known, or expressing ourselves. There is the loneliness of the artist and the loneliness of the one who is not an artist. There is intellectual loneliness, emotional loneliness, the loneliness of the absence of God. These are ways in which our individualized and unique existence can be perceived as threatened rather than as gift, as alienating rather than as creative, as isolation and separateness. The fear of loneliness is a devil which must be met head on. How we incorporate this fact of life, or how we fear it, or how we transform it, this fact of aloneness and individualization will be central to how we are with others and whether we are with others as present to them or as running from our inability to be apart from them.

Solitude, like leisure and humor, like generativity and self-restraint, is a truly Christian value, the counterpart of community or fellowship. There is no love which can develop without respecting the other's need to be alone.

Chapter Five

MINISTRY

The Qualities of Ministry or Love of Neighbor in the Scriptures

As I discuss the fourth of the loves, I use love of neighbor and ministry synonymously. In ministry we reach out toward those who are in need. Three qualities are especially associated with love of neighbor in the New Testament: compassion, hospitality, and service. To minister is to love one's neighbor, to be a compassionate, hospitable, servant. This fourth love is a gift of the Holy Spirit who dwells within us enabling us to move out of ourselves and reach out to those who are in need, opening ourselves to them with compassion, inviting them to us with hospitality, and placing ourselves at their service.

Just as fidelity is central to a discussion of friendship, so compassion is central to a discussion of ministry. Just as God's love is revealed to us as faithful and constant, so his love is revealed as caring and compassionate. And as John's Gospel is a focus for a biblical understanding of friendship, so is Luke's Gospel a focus for a biblical understanding of compassion. A commentary could be written on Luke's Gospel entitled "The Compassionate One," for the central quality of God that comes through in Luke's message is the compassion of our Father.

In the discourse on the Beatitudes, Jesus' heart fixes itself on those who are in need: the poor, the hungry, the sad, the rejected. This discourse, however, which lists the blessings and the woes, continues into a dis-

cussion of love of enemies, a love which I have not
listed as a separate love although we do find it, not only
in Luke's Gospel but also in Matthew's. Matthew 5:43
says, "You have learned how it is said: you must love
your neighbor and hate your enemy. But I say this to
you: love your enemies and pray for those who persecute you." We find a similar emphasis on love of
enemy in Paul's Epistle to the Romans, 12:14, "Love
those who persecute you: never curse them, bless
them." And in the first Epistle to the Corinthians,
4:12, Paul states, "When we are cursed, we answer
with a blessing; when we are hounded, we put up with
it. We are insulted and we answer politely."

The first Epistle of John, 3:16-18, includes a similar
emphasis: "If you refuse to love you must remain dead;
to hate your brother is to be a murderer. And mur-
derers as you know do not have eternal life in them.
This has taught us love that he gave up his life for us
and we too ought to give up our lives for our brothers.
If a man who is rich enough in this world's goods saw
that one of his brothers was in need but closed his
heart to him how could the love of God be living in
him?" This is the heart and core of ministry or love
of neighbor. If one of our brothers or sisters is in need,
how can we harden our hearts? Such rejection would
mean that the gift of the Spirit was not within us.

Luke, in chapter 6:27-35, like Matthew, makes love
of enemies explicit. This love is not, however, another
kind of love; it is simply the degree to which love of
neighbor will go. Love of neighbor responds to need
wherever it **is** perceived and thus responds even to
needs within those who do not love us. There is no
limit to the extent of love of neighbor. The discourse
in Luke beginning with the beatitudes and continuing

with a dialogue about love of neighbor comes to an important summary statement in 6:36, "Be compassionate as your Father is compassionate." The parallel to this statement in Matthew reads, "Be perfect as your Father is perfect." Although we cannot determine which text reflects most accurately the words of Jesus himself, it is clear that Luke describes the perfection of the Father as his compassion.

The Father is the compassionate One. This compassion means not judging, not condemning, but granting pardon, being merciful. This quality of mercy so readily attributed to God in the Old Testament is now to be imitated by us. In the Old Testament traditions, mercy is attributed to God and rarely to humans. Jesus now points out, through Luke, that mercy is not to be God's alone. We too are to be merciful. Luke's teaching on mercy or compassion in chapter 17:4 is one of forgiveness. "If your brother wrongs you seven times a day and seven times comes back to you and says 'I am sorry' you must forgive him." Likewise Matthew 18:22, a different version but with just as great an emphasis, writes, "Then Peter went up to him and said 'Lord how often must I forgive my brother if he wrongs me? As often as seven times?' Jesus answered 'Not seven, I tell you, but seventy-seven times.' " The quality of mercy, forgiveness, compassion, is a central attribute of God. And to share in the perfection of God is to be compassionate as he is compassionate.

This quality is by no means the only attribute of God in Scripture. God is revealed as Creator; his activity is creative. He is revealed as faithful; his promises are kept. He is freedom. His love frees us to be ourselves and frees us from the burden of sin, and it is freely given to us. God's love is creative, faithful, and free; it is also compassionate. Love is a mystery and escapes being defined. Yet, if we speak of a descriptive definition based on Scripture, we can say that love is God who is creative, faithful, free and compassionate.

This quality of God's love, compassion, is already manifested in the psalms just as his fidelity is. In Psalm 50 we read, "Have mercy on me God in your goodness, in your great tenderness wipe away my faults." In Psalm 25:6, "Remember your kindness, Lord, your love, that you showed long ago." And in Psalm 40:11, "For your part, Lord, do not withhold your kindness from me! May your love and faithfulness constantly preserve me." The constant fidelity of the Lord and his kindness are two of his central qualities expressed in the Psalms. In reading the Scriptures, the quality described here as compassion is sometimes called tenderness, mercy, forgiveness. In 2 Corinthians, Paul addresses the God and Father of Our Lord Jesus Christ as "A gentle Father and a God of all consolation." In his lists of virtues Paul writes, "You are God's chosen race, his saints; He loves you, and you should be clothed in sincere compassion, in kindness and humility, gentleness and patience" (Colossians 3:12). These qualities reflect God himself.

Compassion in a man or woman is one sign of integrated sexuality.[1] Abraham Maslow points out that many times intrapsychic conflicts are manifested in the conflicts which we experience in our external world.[2] If a man does not feel comfortable with women, it may be that he does not feel comfortable with the woman inside of himself, with the feminine dimensions of his personality, or with his own mother. Someone who does not feel comfortable with homosexual men and women may not have faced the homosexual dimension of his or her own personality. In order to reach out in tenderness and openness to others we need to have fully accepted ourselves. Once again we see the importance of that first love, self-esteem and self-acceptance. The one who has not yet accepted all aspects of his or her self, who has not achieved that quality of humility that true self-knowledge provides, is one who is not yet able to reach out to others with compassion. As the expression goes, "There is so much bad in the best of us, and so much good in the worst of us, that it ill behooves any of us to talk about the rest of us."

True self-knowledge which moves in the direction of self-acceptance, total self-acceptance, accepts the totality of the self in such a way that one is not easily threatened. Whatever I encounter in the world I have already encountered, already fought, and already come to grips with, within myself. If I have fought the interior battle of self-knowledge, self-discovery and self-acceptance, I am prepared to reach out to others, to respond to my neighbor, to minister to those in need, and to do so with compassion. Compassion then is a sign of a person who has accepted self, who loves self, and who has an integrated self.

Love of neighbor is a compassionate love. It is not only compassion, however; it is hospitality. Hospitality was one of the supreme virtues in ancient Israel. The stories of Mamre and Sodom in the Old Testament are stories of hospitality and inhospitality.[3] There were people in Israel who were frequently the subject of the concern of the prophets: the widow, the orphan and the stranger. Not to be concerned for these was to violate one of the most fundamental moral codes in the Scriptures. Hospitality assumed an extremely important role in Judaeo-Christian writing; the way one responds to a stranger reflects the way one responds to the Lord. The strangers at Mamre are revealed to be the Lord himself.

In the New Testament this same motif emerges in the 25th chapter of Matthew, the story of the final judgment. The basis for the Father's judgment about those who are to be on his right hand and those on his left depends upon whether they have fulfilled the corporal works of mercy. I was hungry and you gave me to eat. I was hungry and you did not give me to eat; I was thirsty and you did not give me drink. Whatever you did to the least of these you did to me. Jesus' identity in these texts is with the one who is in need, with the stranger, the naked, the hungry, the thirsty. The story of the final judgment is not so much a story of God's wrath as it is a story of his values. The way we respond to those who are in need is a reflection of the way we respond to God himself.

We can look further in the Old Testament for similar references. Job, in attempting to defend himself before God, pleads in chapter 31:31-32, "The people of my tent, did they not say 'Is there a man he has not filled with meat?' No stranger ever had to sleep outside; my door was always open to the traveler." Job defends himself before God on the grounds that he has obeyed the law of hospitality. The footnote in the Jerusalem Bible to this text states: "Hospitality was the prince of virtues in the Ancient East." The Jerome Biblical commentary states, "These verses affirm Job's constant practice of the virtue of hospitality—sacred and all important in that society."[4] Love of neighbor is hospitality.

Just as compassion knows no limit, indeed extends even to enemies, so hospitality knows no limit, either.

Love of neighbor or ministry is a universal love. This universality is reflected in Luke, 10:29-37, the story of the Good Samaritan. The question raised is who is one's neighbor, and Jesus teaches that anyone who is in need is one's neighbor. Love of neighbor or ministry knows no bounds. Such love does not select its object on the basis of race, color, creed, sex, sexual orientation or any other distinction. All are my neighbors because all are my brothers and sisters. Love of neighbor is a universal hospitality, allowing all others to make themselves at home with me because we have one Father. Love of neighbor is a compassionate, hospitable and universal love.

Henry Nouwen in *Reaching Out* describes the movement from hostility to hospitality as one of the three fundamental movements of the spiritual life. He writes, "Hospitality therefore means primarily the creation of a free space where the stranger can enter and become our friend instead of an enemy."[5] Hospitality involves creating space for others, even psychic space in the sense that excessive preoccupation is an enemy of hospitality. It gets between me and the other. Just as hostility can be an enemy of compassion, so preoccupation can be an enemy of hospitality. Nouwen points out that movement in Christian life is from hostility and self-preoccupation to compassion and hospitality. He also emphasizes the extensiveness of hospitality, of love of neighbor. Hospitality can include the hospitality of parents to children, teachers to students, professionals to clients. And yet it goes beyond these. It is reaching out to anyone in need, universal love; it is ministry, inviting and compassionate. Hospitality welcomes others into our lives.

Ministry also sees itself and defines itself as service.

The Christian minister is a servant. The one who loves is one who *suffers with* as a servant, as servant of others, servant of the world, servant of the Gospel, servant of the Father. The Greek word in the New Testament for ministry is translated as service, *diakonia*. The word primarily means to wait on someone. This meaning is reflected for example in Luke 12:37 where the verb is used. "Happy those servants whom the master finds awake when he comes. I tell you solemnly he will put on an apron, sit them down at table and *wait on* them." In Luke 12:8 we read, "Get my supper laid; make yourself tidy and wait on me while I eat and drink." The verb translated here as "wait on" is *diakoneo*. Matthew 8:15 reads, "He touched her hand and the fever left her. She got up and began to wait on him." There are many references to this kind of service in the Scriptures.

In Acts 6:2 service is taking care of someone or caring for someone. In Luke 8:3 we see service as helping to support someone. In I Timothy 3:10 it has become more defined as a specific ecclesial service, related to the office of deacon within the Church. The notion of service necessary to preparing a meal is found in Luke 10:40, "Martha was distracted with all the serving." In that passage Martha is the example of service, the examplar of hospitality, the one who has lived up to what the Old Testament asks. The supreme model of service, however, comes in John's Gospel, 13:1-20, where Jesus himself washes the feet of the disciples. John writes about Jesus after having concluded the washing of the feet, "When he had washed their feet and put on his clothes again he went back to the table. 'Do you understand,' he said, 'what I have done for you? You call me Master and Lord and rightly so. I am. If then, the Lord and Master, he washed your feet, you should wash each others. I am giving you an example so that you may copy what I have done to you.' " Jesus points to service as a work of his disciples. Discipleship is compassion, hospitality and service—ministry is love of neighbor.

One final aspect to this notion of love of neighbor is that *it is the one to whom we minister with whom Christ identifies himself*. The Scriptures point to the presence of God in the stranger; to the presence of Christ in the hungry and the thirsty. The Father and the Son identify in our world with those who are in need, not exclusively with the one who ministers.

Ignatius of Antioch spoke in the early centuries of Christianity about the presence of Christ in the Eucharist and also in the martyr. As the virgin became the new martyr in the history of Christian spirituality, Christ was seen as present in the virgin, the virgin who was the spouse of Christ himself. Later, as the monastic movement became active in the world—apostolic—Christ was seen as present in another way, in ministry.[6] The imitation of Christ is the imitation of that kind of service, hospitality, compassion and ministry to which he calls us.

Hence Christ became identified with the minister. In the Scriptures, however, Christ's identity is with the one to whom we minister. The minister, although responding to the need of the other, is never in a position of superiority. We always see ourselves as the servant of the other. The basic motivation for the Christian's reaching out to others in need is that Christ is there. As we respond to our neighbor, we meet and encounter Christ. This is why religion which emphasizes encounter with God only in prayer and in worship is deficient and hypocritical. The basic encounter with God himself is found in ministry, compassionate and hospitable service to those who are in need. The real presence of Christ is in the poor, the needy, the oppressed, the widow, the orphan, the stranger, the lonely, the homosexual, the divorced, the prisoner, etc. These are the presences of Christ in our world today and the basis upon which the final judgment will be made as to whether we indeed have loved.

Love of Neighbor and Ministry in The Mission of Jesus

To understand the implications of the fourth love—love of neighbor—within a Gospel spirituality, we need to examine this value in the life of Jesus of Nazareth himself, in his three-fold ministry: preaching, presence, and prophecy.

In Mark 1:29-31, we see Jesus' compassion. "On leaving the synagogue he went with James and John straight to the house of Simon and Andrew. Now Simon's mother-in-law had gone to bed with fever and they told him about her straight away. He went to her, took her by the hand and helped her up and the fever left her as she began to wait on them." In Mark 1:33 we read, "The whole town came crowding round the door, and he cured many." A similar reference in Mark 3:9 shows Jesus asking his disciples to have a boat ready for him to keep him from being crushed by the crowd. Jesus obviously was one to whom people could go and Jesus undoubtedly saw himself as being there for the sake of others.

Mark 1:35 continues "In the morning, long before dawn he got up and left the house, and went off to a lonely place and prayed there." We see here another important ingredient in the life of Jesus, the fifth love, love of God, prayer. Ministry and prayer are always intermingled in the life of Jesus and provide a rhythm similar to that of breathing in and breathing out. He spends time with his Father in prayer and he spends time with others in ministry.

Then the text says that Simon and his companions set out in search of Jesus and when they found him they said "Everybody is looking for you." This again exemplifies the extent to which Jesus has already been known as one who was a man for others. The crucial verse, however, is verse 38: "He answered, 'Let us go elsewhere to the neighboring country towns so that I can preach there too, because that is why I came.' " Here we have Jesus explicating his understanding of his own mission. Jesus takes time to be alone in prayer. Yet, when there is need, he says "Let us go on." He sees himself as one called to minister. Yet the fundamental ministry to which he sees himself called is that of preaching. "Let us go elsewhere so that I can preach. This is why I came." Mark 1 then continues in verse 39 with Jesus going through all of Galilee preaching in the synagogues. The Gospel of Mark and the Scriptures as a whole give witness to Jesus seeing the ministry of preaching as being his primary mission, the public ministry for which he was sent.

Preaching was the primary and central thrust in the consciousness and mission of Jesus in history. He saw himself as one called by the Father to preach, especially to preach the good news of the coming Reign of God. We see this consciousness in the very first chapter of Mark's Gospel.

We can place this consciousness of ministry and preaching within Jesus' life in the context of his developing and unfolding consciousness as a whole. As we know today, the consciousness of the man Jesus is an important biblical discussion.[7] Although we cannot explore the matter extensively here, we can examine something of Jesus' self-understanding by a consideration of his life of prayer. It is in his prayer, in his relationship to the Father, that Jesus begins to understand more and more who he is and that to which he has been called. It is in his prayer that he begins to discover his own unique relationship to the Lord, that the God of Israel is indeed his Father, and that he is intimately related to the Father. It is also in his prayer that Jesus becomes aware of the generosity of the Father's love and the specific ministry to which he has been called, namely that of preaching the coming of his Father's Reign. And it is in prayer and in his relationship to the Father that Jesus becomes more conscious of the kind of Kingdom of Reign into which the Father invites us.

It will be helpful to consider this developing consciousness of Jesus. Jesus is a Jewish boy living at home in Nazareth with his family. He is not only a boy growing up in a Jewish home, however. He is reared with a religious consciousness and a love for the Hebrew Scriptures. He gives testimony to an extensive knowledge of, heart-felt appreciation for, and insight into, the Law and the Prophets. The time comes, however, when Jesus feels the need to leave his immediate family in Nazareth, to receive the baptism of his cousin John, and he leaves to be baptized by this ascetic prophet. It is in the experience of this baptism, a fundamental religious experience in the life of Jesus himself, that he becomes aware that he is being called to play a unique role in the history of Israel and in

God's plan for his people. Thus, immediately after that baptism, he goes into the wilderness, the desert, to search out the meaning of his own call and vocation more deeply. After a period of time—the Scriptures say forty days—he becomes more aware of who the Lord God of Israel is and that to which the Lord is calling him in particular. Thus he returns from that wilderness experience a wandering preacher whose mission is preaching and whose message is the Kingdom. The Father and his coming Kingdom are the two most central realities in the consciousness of the historical Jesus. In his ministry he is constantly aware of the coming of the Kingdom, his central concern; and in his prayer he is aware of the Father's love and his unique relationship with the Father.

When we realize the ministry and call of Jesus to preach, we are then forced to ask whether this ministry is in any sense unique to Jesus. Prior to Jesus, John the baptizer saw his ministry also as one of preaching and he also preached the message of the coming Reign of God. How then does Jesus' consciousness and preaching differ from that of John? There are many similarities, of course, between John and Jesus. They both preached the importance of baptism. They both emphasized the importance of repentance. John spoke about the coming of the Kingdom and even sees the Kingdom as close at hand, ready to break in. Jesus too realizes the imminence of the dawning reign of God. Yet there are at least three differences between John and Jesus that we need to understand.[8]

The first is Jesus' understanding of his own relationship to the Lord whose Kingdom is about to be more fully realized. Jesus realized that the Lord is not only the transcendent God of the chosen people of

Israel but that he is very personally One who calls on us to share in his life, that we are his sons and daughters, that the Lord God is *Abba,* our dad. Joachim Jeremias points out that this expression *Abba,* the Aramaic word for Father, is perhaps the single most important linguistic innovation on the part of Jesus.[9] Jesus teaches us to address the Lord as Father, teaches us to pray to our Father, and sends us the Spirit to enable us to pronounce the word *Abba.*[10] Jesus' understanding of who the Lord is surpasses the vision of John.

Jesus, moreover, is aware that the coming Reign is not only close but already breaking into history now.

Most significant for our purposes is a third point. This is that Jesus' preaching about the Kingdom differs from John the baptizer's in the broader way in which Jesus opens up the gates of the Kingdom. Jesus' preaching is always good news. Although it was not necessarily good news for many of the Pharisees or for some of the religious leaders of Israel, it was good news for the poor and the sinner. Jesus is aware of this. He chooses to read from the scroll of the prophet Isaiah when he first began to preach:

> The spirit of the Lord has been given to me,
> for he has anointed me.
> He has sent me to bring the good news to the poor,
> to proclaim liberty to captives
> and to the blind new sight,
> to set the downtrodden free,
> to proclaim the Lord's year of favor (Luke, 4:18).

Jesus' understanding of the Kingdom—which flowed from his understanding of who the Lord was, from his image of God—and his realization of the gratuitous generosity of the Father's love enabled him to under-

stand that the coming Reign or Kingdom of the Father
was for all, not just for those who were able to live up
to the demands of the Law as it had come to be interpreted by some of the Pharisees. Jesus spoke out
against the Pharisees' interpretation of the Law because
this interpretation was inimical to the very nature of
God. Jesus' message was grace; the Pharisees' message
was earned righteousness. The Pharisees were religious
men and Jesus saw goodness among them in someone
like Nicodemus, yet he realized that their teaching as
a form of self-justification was not the message of the
Lord. The message of God is that we are justified by
grace alone, by the Father alone, by the Father's generous and compassionate love alone. Thus Jesus realized that the gates of the Kingdom were open to all
those for whom the Pharisaic understanding of the
Law had not opened up the gates of heaven. Jesus had
love for tax collectors, sinners, drunkards, gluttons,
prostitutes, outcasts of society because he knew how
his Father loved them. Thus Jesus himself associated
with those with whom the Pharisees would not associate.

Jesus' preaching was indeed good news for the poor,
the captive, the blind, the outcast of society, the sinners, those who had no hope of salvation through the
Law. It is not that the Father's love did not also extend
to the religious leaders and the Pharisees, but these
did not fully know God as we can conclude from their
interpretation of the Law and the Prophets. Preaching
the Kingdom as being the good news of grace is central
to Jesus as a man for others.

Just as Jesus was called to preach, so each of us is
called through baptism to the ministry of preaching.
Not every Christian is called of course to preach in

every kind of way. The preaching of a bishop differs from the preaching of every other baptized Christian. Yet conveying the message of grace is a central part of everyone's Christian ministry. Just as each of us is called to love in five ways, just as each of us is called to love our neighbor and minister to those in need, so each is called to preach the good news of salvation by grace.

Now we will move to the second ministry of Jesus, the ministry of presence. An extremely important fact about Jesus' preaching is that his fundamental message was not only verbally articulated but actually lived. Jesus was what he preached. His integrity did not allow him to say one thing verbally and incarnate another reality nonverbally. Thus, Jesus' preaching in one sense encompassed all three elements of his ministry in such a way that Jesus as preacher could not be separated from Jesus as fellow-sufferer and Jesus as prophet. The ministry of presence implies the reality of simply being present to, present with, present there in the midst of, others.

We are probably often aware of situations in which we can do little or nothing to actually relieve the suffering of another. For instance, one of the most difficult ministries for many people, for many Christians who want to do something and to be of help, whose self-esteem is based almost exclusively on their capacity *to do something* for others, is that which confronts them with their own helplessness and powerlessness. Take as an example sitting on the corner of the hospital bed of a person dying of terminal cancer; both patient and visitor knowing that the end is not far off. The difficulty of ministry in that situation is that we know there is nothing that we can do other than simply be there. We cannot change the situation; we can only share it. Somehow the ministry of presence can be profound.

Jesus is one who not only preached good news for the poor but also made himself present and available to them. Even when there was nothing that he could do, he was still there with them. In fact we can interpret the entire incarnational understanding of Christ as the fact that God is present to his people, that the meaning of the Cross points to the extent to which he is willing to be present to them even though he might not be able to allow his Kingdom to be ushered in fully in the present. He can still reveal his love by being there with us on our journey. Jesus' preaching then becomes a presence. As a man for others he became a person present to others. This presence is exemplified in the references to Jesus as associating with the outcasts of the society. The message is not only good news for the economic poor, but for the poor in the widest sense: those who are socially and spiritually disadvantaged as well.

Here again is a contrast between John the baptizer and Jesus the preacher. We need read only a little further in Mark's Gospel to see this second ministry exemplified. Mark (2:15-18) writes: "When Jesus was at dinner in his house, a number of tax collectors and sinners were also sitting at the table with Jesus and his disciples; for there were many of them among his followers. When the scribes of the Pharisee party saw him eating with sinners and tax collectors, they said to his disciples, 'Why does he eat with tax collectors and sinners?' One day when John's disciples and the

Pharisees were fasting, some people came and said to him 'Why is it that John's disciples and the disciples of the Pharisees fast, but your disciples do not?' "

The evangelists tell of Jesus' presence to the outcast of society. One contrast between Jesus and John is that John was known for his asceticism and Jesus for his association with sinners. The people noted this. Luke (7:33-35) writes, "For John the Baptist comes, not eating bread, not drinking wine, and you say, 'He is possessed.' The Son of Man comes, eating and drinking, and you say, 'Look, a glutton and a drunkard, a friend of tax collectors and sinners.' " Jesus did not allow the threatening possibility of guilt by association to prevent him from making incarnate the Father's love for everyone, including the "unrighteous."

This kind of presence is so significant that it leads C. H. Dodd to point to this as the central characteristic of the Jesus of history. We know today how difficult it is to ascertain those elements in the Scriptures which definitely describe an historical Jesus as distinguished from the faith of the early Church. When, however, Joachim Jeremias speaks about the important linguistic innovation of Jesus in addressing the Lord as *Abba*, he signals an important historical event. Likewise C. H. Dodd writes in reference to Jesus' friendly attitude to the outcasts of society, "We may surely say on strictly critical grounds that we have here a well attested historical fact."[11] This is also the central thesis of Adoph Holl's book *Jesus In Bad Company*.[12] In addition to preaching, Jesus was present to people. His preaching flowed out of his life, out of his human as well as his divine relationships.

The third element in the mission of Jesus, the third way in which his love of neighbor is manifested, is his

prophetic mission, the ministry of justice and liberation. Not only did Jesus preach a message of justice
and freedom, not only was he present to the oppressed
whom society did not treat justly, but he acted on their
behalf and responded to their needs. If we could discuss here in more detail the developing consciousness
of Jesus, we would see the importance of his prophetic
awareness. Early in his life, according to Reginald
Fuller, Jesus saw himself in a prophetic role and it
was only gradually that he became more and more
aware that he would suffer and die.[13] Jesus saw himself
as a prophet, like a prophet of old, but not just one of
many prophets. He saw himself as the final prophet
to be sent to Israel. Understanding the prophetic tradition helps us to realize the importance of justice and
liberation in his message. If we continue with Mark's
Gospel we see this prophetic element.

In the first chapter of Mark we see Jesus' ministry
to others and his sense of being called to preach. In
the second chapter we read of his association with sinners and his presence to the outcasts. The last verses
of that second chapter, however, point to another element. Here Jesus allows his disciples to pick corn on
the Sabbath and Jesus defends the practice by saying
"The Sabbath was made for man, not man for the
Sabbath" (verse 27). Jesus strongly challenges traditional interpretation of religion, calling into question
hypocritical and formalized religion, religion which
is external and not of the heart, religion based on law
divorced from love.

This critique of traditional religion is found frequently in the classical period of Hebrew prophecy.
Amos, the prophet of social justice, clearly outlines the
desire of the Lord of Israel when he writes (4:1-2):

"Listen to this word, you cows of Bashan living in the mountains of Samaria, oppressing the needy, crushing the poor, saying to your husbands, 'Bring us something to drink!' "

Amos 5:11—Well then, since you have trampled on the poor man, extorting levies on his wheat—those houses you have built of dressed stone, you will never live in them; and those precious vineyards you have planted, you will never drink their wine."

Amos 5:21-24—"I hate and despise your feasts, I take no pleasure in your solemn festivals. When you offer me holocausts, I reject your oblations, and refuse to look at your sacrifices of fattened cattle. Let me have no more of the din of your chanting, no more of your strumming on harps. But let justice flow like water, and integrity like an unfailing stream."

Micah 6:8—"What is good has been explained to you, man; this is what Yahweh asks of you: only this, to act justly, to love tenderly and to walk humbly with your God."

Micah points out that the Lord longs for justice and the overcoming of oppression. Israelite religion, in its law of hospitality, was concerned for the stranger, the widow, the orphan, the poor, the needy, the oppressed, the outcasts of society. This prophetic consciousness emerges in Jesus' own teaching about the final judgment in Matthew 25, "I was hungry and you gave me to eat." Jesus' identity with the one who is in need and to whom we minister shows the centrality of the needy, the oppressed and the outcasts in the understanding of Jesus' gospel. Jesus not only preached, not only was present to God's people, but actually lived out as actively as he could the value system of his message. Human beings were more important than the Sabbath.

Compassion and hospitality and service and love were more important than the multiplication of prayers. Jesus, like the prophets, was not opposed to prayer, to worship, to the synagogue. They simply had to be put in their place. Authentic religion, however, realizes love of God cannot be divorced from love of neighbor. Thus Jesus' prophetic consciousness and his prophetic ministry led him to plead the cause of the needy, the outcasts, the sinner. His message liberated them; he spoke out against the fundamental form of oppression which was not that of the Roman Empire but that of the Pharisaic interpretation of religion. His desire for justice flowed from his understanding that we are justified through grace, and that grace demands openness to all people and an end to all self-righteousness.

We can see, therefore, that love of neighbor, that compassionate, hospitable, universal service to others, is a central Gospel value, a value incarnate in the life of Jesus who reveals that our Lord is God-with-us and God-for-us. We can model our own ministry on the ministry of Jesus. We too are called to preach the Good News of the Father's love. We too are called to be present to all those who are in need and especially to those alienated from church and society. We too are called to speak out and act on behalf of justice and liberation.

Theology, Justice, and Liberation

I make no pretense here of writing a theology of liberation nor even of reviewing the theologies of liberation already available to us. Nor can I develop completely a theology of justice or analyze the importance of justice for an adequate theology. Yet, we can hardly ignore the importance of these themes of justice and liberation for an understanding of love of neighbor and Christian spirituality. I shall single out, therefore, five points which can help us to become aware of the direction in which love of neighbor leads us.

1. James Cone, in his effort to construct a black theology of liberation, emphasizes that *liberation is God's work*.[14] We as Christians must constantly keep this understanding before us. We must discern which movement in history or what aspects of which movements come from God. Justice, liberation, and peace are God's concern. This is why anyone who says that he loves God but hates his neighbor is a liar. Seeking justice and liberation is central to love of neighbor.

Since the Second Vatican Council, Catholics like to speak in terms of the signs of the times. Undoubtedly one of the signs of our times is the liberation movements that have begun to develop in recent decades. These began with Black liberation, became highly influenced by Latin American liberation, and now manifest themselves in sexual liberation as well—both women's liberation and gay liberation. It is true that each of these movements is not without ambiguity. To support the move toward the liberation of human beings is not necessarily to accept every proposal or every agenda liberationists might proclaim. While the details are not always unambiguous, the call to liberation is; it is clearly the work of the Spirit at this time in history. God is on the side of human liberation.

To be with God, to grow in union with God, to act with God and to allow God to act through us is to place ourselves in the midst of that struggle for liberation. Christians must stand with clarity on the side of human liberation, and if there are aspects of any liberation movement with which they cannot agree they must still witness to God's liberating work on behalf of the outcast and oppressed. Christian responsibility is not resolved by supporting in the abstract and then being critical of liberation in the concrete. We must *be* liberators. This is the work of the Spirit.

2. Not only is justice and liberation an action of God, but *justice and liberation are intrinsic to the task of theology itself.* If theology is reflection on God and if God's act outside of himself is on behalf of justice and peace, then theology is directly concerned with justice, liberation and peace. Thus Gustavo Gutierrez points out that theology is critical reflection in the light of the Word on the presence of Christians in the world.[15] This reflection is for Gutierrez the prophetic function of theology. His concept should not be new or suprising to us as we more and more begin to see the counter-cultural character of Christian existence.

The Church, to whatever degree it is organized as religious activity or religious activity which goes beyond the borders of institutionalization, is counter-culture, a community of people of faith, attempting to live out a value system other than the value system of the culture or society in which we find ourselves. Counter-culture by no means implies a theology that is world negating and world rejecting. It means that Christians in the world will always provide a presence beyond that provided by the secular roots of a culture or society. Christians in the world will always be there with their roots in Christ, in the Word of God, and thus they witness God's promises for society in the midst of that society. If the Christian value system were already fully incarnate in society, there would be no need for Church. In fact, the Kingdom would already be here in its fullness. Eschatologically speaking, as the people of God we must help to realize God's presence in our society by pointing to his liberating activities in which all can participate, and also help to reveal the not-yet-ness of the fullness of God's Reign through our critique and denunciation of any form of oppressive existence. One task of the Church is to discern God's activity in our period of history and to point with clarity to where God is working: God is at work in the liberation movements of our day. Once we have realized this, theology provides a reflective consciousness-raising which enables Christians to participate in and not simply observe or reject that divine mission.

3. Dom Helder Camara has emphasized in his delineation of the main themes of liberation theology *the mission of the co-creator*.[16] A theology of liberation, then, begins with the theology of creation itself and with *our* role in that creative activity. Creation is one of the ministries to which we are called, and it flows from love of neighbor. To love one's neighbor is to go beyond one's personal response to those in need and to construct a universe so that the poor might find a more equitable and graceful world in which to celebrate God's gifts.

Creation comes forth from God as unfinished. It is a reality into which he invites us so that together we might prepare the way for the fullness of his Reign which we long for and which he has promised. Liberation is God's work; it is also our work. It is an activity which God has chosen to share with us, and is therefore a responsibility we must assume.

4. Liberation theologies can be placed within the evolutionary creation and evolutionary theology of Teilhard de Chardin. All of creation is a movement toward union with God, in which we participate, as

we build the earth, preparing the way so that God might be all in all. Marxists have affirmed the affinity between the Christian theology of Teilhard and their own world vision.[17] Liberation theology itself is also in a dialogical relationship with Marxist thought. Both approaches, that of liberation theology and that of Teilhard, have captured and included within their methodology a central aspect of the Gospel and of Marx, our responsibility for the world.

This is not to imply that the Kingdom will be built by us, that the Kingdom will be inaugurated and consummated by us. The Kingdom is and always will be the Reign of God. Yet, for Teilhard, our role in building the earth is a necessary precondition for some of God's acts. Just as God could not be proclaimed the messiah without a long history of messianic expectation, just as God could not bring forth a universe perfect from the beginning, so his Reign cannot be completed without our role of preparing the way. This is the lesson that comes to us from salvation history. Divine initiative incorporates human response and human response prepares the way of the Lord, prepares the way for his next innovative activity. Our role is to build the earth so that God might perform his next act on our behalf.

The Christian takes the world with ultimate seriousness because ultimately God loves the world; it is his creation. Even infected by sin, it is still his creation, his project, a labor of his love. Love of neighbor, then, in a post-Marxist era, is transformed into social and structural change as well; our consciousness is raised. As Teilhard writes, no longer can we think of charity in personal terms only. He does not deny the significance of personalism but it cannot be separated from universalism, from building the earth, from our responsibility for our world. Love of neighbor does have a socialist or social dimension to it.

5. This brings us to the relationship between justice and love, justice as a pre-condition for loving. The capacity to love is diminished by an overriding concern for survival. Such is the situation for those for whom the social situation does not meet basic human needs. Thus the Church seeks a just society in order that there be a loving society. Injustice prevents love. In another way, justice can be seen as an effect of love, as an effect of love of neighbor. If we love our neighbor, if we care for those who are in need, if our caring is active, loving leads to justice. Justice leads to love and love leads to justice.

Pointing to the contrast between justice and love, however, is not sufficient. As Christians we too readily separate the two. What is the relationship between love and love of self or self-esteem? What is the relationship between love and friendship? What is the relationship between love and community or fellowship? Also, what is the relationship between love and justice? The relationship is that justice is one form of love and one cannot love without acting justly. Tender love implies just action, liberating activity, thirsting for peace, elimination of whatever artificial barriers keep us apart, whether those be religious, sexist, racist, or nationalist. What is the relationship between love and friendship? Not all love is friendship but all friendship is love. Not all love is community or fellowship but community and fellowship are love. Similarly not all love is justice but all justice is love.

Just as we cannot say that we are called to love of friendship and not concern ourselves with love of God, just as we cannot say we are called to love of God and need not concern ourselves with love of neighbor, so no Christian can exclude justice as one of the ways in which he or she is called to love. We are all called to love ourselves, to love friends, to love brothers and sisters, to love those who are in need and to love the Lord our God. We cannot exempt ourselves from any of the ways of loving. Every Christian thirsts for justice, liberation, and peace. Love of neighbor must be put into effect, must be effective loving, active caring, participating in the work of the Spirit. Jesus exemplified this in his own life. As we see in his life friendship exemplified, fellowship personified, so ministry or love of neighbor is manifest in his preaching, in his presence to people, and in those prophetic actions which led to his suffering and death.

Play and Leisure

As the complement to a life of ministry dedicated to service, we need to consider the important role that play and leisure have in the life of a Christian. Play and leisure are one of the pillars of Christian spirituality. Although it is possible to play by oneself, we generally think of play as social interaction, more active than passive. Play suggests participation rather than observation. Leisure, on the other hand, is easily solitary, passive, and appreciative or responsive. Leisure and solitude have a close relationship.

I would like to state my own theology of play based upon play as realized eschatology. It is important for us as Christians to look at every reality in the light of the Kingdom, the Reign of God. The Scriptures provide an eschatological frame of reference for self-understanding as well as for understanding the world in which we live. Jewish eschatology influenced Jesus of Nazareth. For Jesus, the Kingdom of his Father was the primary concept in his consciousness. The proclamation that the Kingdom was in some measure already present but not fully so distinguished Jesus' preaching from that of his predecessors.

Since the Resurrection we have looked at reality from the viewpoint of the Risen Christ. We see all in the light of the Reign of God and our own resurrection. To look at something eschatologically, however, is to look at it from a two-fold perspective, the perspective of *the already* and the perspective of *the not yet,* the perspective of the present and the perspective of the future, because the Kingdom has already broken in within the ministry of Jesus, yet is still not here in its fullness, in its completeness, as it will be at Omega when God is all in all.

When we look at life from the viewpoint of God's Reign already present in our midst, when we talk about the present reality of the Kingdom, the present realization of God's presence, we are called upon to rejoice and to feast. When we look at reality, however, from the viewpoint of the Kingdom not yet fully established, we look at the not-yet-ness of that for which we long and wait and we call to mind the tragic side of our existence; we rely on the virtue of hope and witness to this not-yet-ness through a practice such as fasting. This is why the rhythm in Christian life is to feast and fast as Jesus himself said, "When the bridegroom is with us it is the time to feast."[18] God's presence in Christ means that the bridegroom has already come. In this sense play is realized eschatology, a sign that the Kingdom is already present in our midst. The realization that God acts in our midst enables us to play. To a great degree we can picture the Kingdom of heaven as simply being play.

When we get to heaven, there will be no work in the way we ordinarily think of work, that by means of which we earn our daily bread. Work will give way to the fullness of life and playful activity. In some ways, however, this is regrettable, given the fact that most of us when we grow up forget how to play. Many of us need to learn how to play as adults. Jesus tells us in Matthew 18:3 that unless we are like little children we will not enter into the Kingdom of heaven. Those of us who have lost the capacity to play, those who are too grown up to enter into what we consider childish activity, those who no longer feel comfortable playing, will not enjoy heaven. Heaven will be hell for them. Thus they are the ones for whom it can be said, "Go to hell; the gates of Gehenna have been prepared for the likes of you."

Those of us who have not developed the capacity to play will not be able to enter into heaven because we simply would not be able to enjoy life without burdens that we place upon ourselves. However "literal" this interpretation of heaven and however facetious some of these remarks, we need to understand that play, leisure, spontaneity, social activity, rest and humor all contribute to the Christian life. They are eschatological signs and give witness to the presence of God in our midst and are signs of what will be more fully in store for those who love God. This is understanding play eschatologically.

Classical as well as contemporary literature attests to the significance and the "seriousness" of play. Plato, Aristotle and Cicero all stress the importance of play and leisure, as does Thomas Aquinas. Huizinga in

Homo Ludens provides us a classic treatment as well.[19] Contemporary treatments can be found in Hugo Rahner's *Man At Play* and Jurgen Moltmann's *Theology of Play*.[20]

The words *play* and *leisure* cover a variety of forms. They include the world of literature, art, music, dance, painting, sculpture, the world of culture as well as the world of games and sports. Entertainment and other forms of relaxation are included in the definition of play. Play is enjoyment, purpose-free activity, entering into an activity for the sake of itself and not for some goal or purpose beyond itself. I point to this wide variety of forms because, in the Scriptures, it is important to be aware that various kinds of play are indicated. We find references to dance, even in a sacred context, when we see David and others dancing before the Ark of the Covenant (2 Sam. 6:5 and 21).

A particularly important reference is the book of the prophet Zechariah, 8:5. Zechariah provides an eschatological perspective similar to that developed above. He is concerned with providing a vision of the future. In chapter 8:3, Zechariah writes: "Yahweh Sabaoth says this. I am coming back to Zion and shall dwell in the middle of Jerusalem." Verses 4 and 5 then go on and present Zechariah's vision of that coming time. He writes: "Yahweh Sabaoth says this. Old men and old women will again sit down in the squares of Jerusalem; everyone of them staff in hand because of their great age. And the squares of the city will be full of boys and girls playing in the squares." His vision of the eschatological future depicts boys and girls at play.

Thomas Aquinas bases his reflections on the ethics of Aristotle. He is particularly concerned about the virtue of *eutrapelia*. In Aristotle, virtue is a mean between extremes. The man of virtue is a *eutrapelos,* but this *eutrapelos,* this playful man, mirthful man, is always seen as a balance between the *bomolochos* and the *agroikos.*[21] The *bomolochos,* a difficult word to translate, is the fool, and the *agroikos* is one who lacks humor, the bore. The virtue of *eutrapelia* then is a mean between the two extremes, the extreme of playing so much that play is almost the end of life while the other extreme is refusing to play enough so that life becomes burdensome and serious. In his commentary on Aristotle's ethics, Thomas writes: "Unmitigated seriousness betokens a lack of virtue because it wholly despises play which is as necessary for a good human life as rest is."[22]

Thomas treats this virtue of play also in the *Summa Theologiae.*[23] He raises the question whether there can be a virtue with respect to games or play. After responding affirmatively, he writes:

> Consequently the remedy for weariness of soul must consist in the acquisition of some pleasure by slackening the tension of a person's study. Thus in the conferences of the Fathers, it is related of John the Evangelist that when some people were scandalized on finding him playing together with his disciples he is said to have told one of them who carried a bow to shoot an arrow. And when the latter had done this several times he asked him whether he could do it indefinitely and the man answered that if he continued doing it the bow would break. Thence John drew the inference that in like manner man's mind would break if its tension were never relaxed.[24]

Thomas not only points to the virtue of play but to the qualifications that must exist for play to be proper; one cannot make play of an injurious or indecent deed, or at inappropriate times and places. There are qualifications about what the virtue of play consists in; yet play is a virtue, the virtue of wittiness or *eutrapelia.*

Thomas also raises the question of whether there is lack of virtue in excessive play and points out that there can be; he also raises the question whether there is lack of virtue in the lack of play and writes:

> In human affairs whatever is against reason is a sin. Now it is against reason for a person to be burdensome to others by offering no pleasure to others and by hindering their enjoyment. . . . Now a man who is without mirth not only is lacking in playful speech but is also burdensome to others since he is deaf to the moderate mirth of others. Consequently they are vicious and are said to be boorish or rude as the philosopher states.[25]

The Scriptures point to a relationship between play and dance. Hugo Rahner, in his book on play, writes in a similar vein, "Play and dance, therefore, when they genuinely succeed in expressing here on earth what is in the heart, are an anticipation of heavenly joy."[26] We see again the eschatological perspective that play and the arts provide. In a similar way Moltmann writes:

> Since about the sixth century Christian art has been acquainted with the type of dance called the *resurrection dance*. Here, in a spirally round dance, the elevated Christ draws the redeemed upward toward the Father with a sweep of his mantle. This represents an exact counter-image of the later medieval dances of death in which the sickle bearer is leading emperor, pope, noble, peasant and serf into the pit. The risen one, who opens up the eschatology of freedom, is himself the 'lead dancer in the mystical round,' as Hyppolitus has said, and the church is his 'bride who dances along.'[27]

Moltmann points out that the goals of games and the arts are the same, the construction of an anti-environment in McLuhan's sense or a counter-culture which opens up creative freedom.[28] Being able to move into another environment enables us to look at the environment of ordinary experience from a different point of view. In addition to the eschatological perspective, Moltmann also points out that "the glorification of God lies in the demonstrative joy of existence."[29] Play gives honor and glory to God as well.

The Christian can look at reality both from the viewpoint of the cross and the viewpoint of the resurrection, from the viewpoint of the present and the viewpoint of the future. We should see that both comedy and tragedy enter into the reality of life. An emphasis on one or the other alone would lead to one of the extremes that Aristotelian virtue avoids. Focusing only on the tragic side of life would lead one too quickly to be the *agroikos* or bore. Looking only at the comic side of life would lead one to be a *bomolochos* or fool. As I like to put it, the Christian is a person who can stand at the foot of the cross with tears in his eyes and a smile on his face because he faces the reality of the human situation and yet looks at it from the perspective of God's dawning Reign. Even those who serve the Lord and others through ministry must never turn ministry (which is love) into an unalleviated burden, a work so consuming that they lose touch with the joy of the resurrection and the beauty and delights of creation. Such unrelieved seriousness would scarcely give witness to the message we find in the ministry of Christ.

Chapter Six

PRAYER

The Meaning of Prayer

There is no way of talking adequately about prayer, no possibility of defining prayer appropriately. Yet prayer is so important a reality in the lives of human beings, in the lives of Christian men and women, that we must struggle to talk about it even though our language does not adequately reflect the reality of which we speak. The Scriptures attest to the centrality of prayer in the life of Jesus himself. The instructions which Jesus gave with regard to prayer were quite simple. We need not make our understanding necessarily complicated then. To give prayer the centrality which life demands, however, we must reflect upon this experience in our lives. We can consider prayer in six ways. All of them help us to understand that prayer is loving God and that the art of prayer is the art of loving God.

Praying is relating. The art of praying is simply the art of relating to the Lord, to God, to the Father, Son and Spirit. Within our human experience we have contact with what it means to relate to others. The other to whom we relate in prayer is one whose life, whose nature, is much fuller than our own. In prayer we relate not to one like ourselves as we do in human friendship but to one whose being transcends the kind of being that we ourselves are. We relate to a being whose life is full and more complete. To choose consciously to enter into a relationship with this transcendent friend is to choose to pray.

Traditionally prayer is spoken of as communication

with God. That is precisely what it is. There is no relationship without communication, whether that be verbal, nonverbal or both. To communicate is to open up the possibility for further and deeper bonding, relating, partnership. Prayer is simply the word that we use to describe our communication with the Lord. This art of relating, however, is in itself the art of loving. In fact, rather than speaking of prayer as relating one could speak of prayer as loving, actively loving God. Just as we actively love ourselves, our friends, our brothers and sisters and those who are in need, so we actively love the Lord, relate to the Lord, allow ourselves to reach out and embrace the Lord. The arts of relating and loving teach us much about how to relate to and love the Lord himself.

Although love is something that happens to us, it is also something to which we contribute. It is not simply a happening; it is also an activity which involves two sides. Loving is an active way of opening our lives, our hearts and our souls, to another, to the Lord. Although there are many ways of describing or defining love, one way is that loving is active caring. Caring actively might sometimes better communicate the Gospel message than the word love itself which is so readily distorted in different cultural and social situations. To love is to care. The heart of loving is caring, being concerned, allowing one's being to be affected by, being vulnerable to, choosing to risk sharing in the life of another.

Loving is caring, but any authentic caring is active, something to which we give ourselves, in which we choose to participate. Friendship is caring actively about those whom we allow into our lives on an intimate level. Community is caring actively about those who come together as brothers and sisters for the sake of fellowship. Ministry is caring actively about those who are in need and prayer is caring actively about God, about our relationship with God, desiring to nourish and nurture that relationship, to let it grow and deepen, making ourselves vulnerable to God. Prayer is caring for God, loving God because we know how he cares for and loves us. This first way of describing prayer, then, is simply to see praying as relating, consciously relating, actively caring and freely loving. Prayer, then, is simply friendship with God and praying is building that friendship actively so that it might grow and blossom rather than stagnate and be left unattended or taken for granted.

Praying is also listening. This is not in distinction from what has been said above. Indeed, much of relating is listening. In fact the art of relating is to a great degree the art of listening. Yet focusing our attention on this word can give us further insight into what praying is all about. If prayer begins the moment we are conscious of our relationship to God and if praying involves our consciousness of relating to God, praying will then involve listening as well.

Listening, however, is not something which comes easily to us. In our expanding technological world, listening is something which can be systematically destroyed. Few have the capacity even to listen to themselves because the social situations in which we frequently find ourselves provide distractions to enable us to avoid listening. There is always something else to which we can give our attention. Listening requires lengthening our attention span. Although we can give attention, our tendencies are to frequently move from one object of attentiveness to another. Listening im-

plies the capacity to sustain attention. Listening begins
by attending to the other, being attentive and waiting
upon the other. Listening is attending, but an attending which opens us and allows us to truly hear what the
other has to say.

There are three phases or dimensions to listening.
The first step in listening is giving attention, attending, being present to the other, making ourselves available to the other, letting ourselves be in the presence
of the other. This first task for one who wants to develop the art of listening is itself difficult. In the end
it means that we allow ourselves to be in the presence
of someone and to be in the presence for the purpose
of hearing. Hearing is the second task or activity involved in listening. Listening in that sense is active.
Active listening is hearing. It is not simply placing ourselves in the physical presence of the other but giving
our attention to the other in order that the other
might penetrate our being, communicate to us and be
heard. That which is heard might be communicated
verbally or nonverbally but the active listener is able to
hear what the other longs to express. Listening, however, is not only giving attention to and hearing the
word or words of the other. It eventually involves our
response. Responsiveness requires not only our hearing
but our acting upon what we hear in order to affirm,
confirm, or let ourselves, our being, be known in such
a way that communication is complete. We place ourselves in the presence of another and in turn communicate so that the other might hear us as well. Listening
is attentiveness, hearing and response.

Prayer, then, is listening to God, giving our attention to him, placing ourselves in his presence and
opening our being to him so that we might indeed hear

the Lord, experience his communication, and respond to him. Praying is listening to God, attending to him, hearing him, responding to him. The art of praying then is the art of relating and the art of listening. It is the art of friendship and communication.

One expression moves us to the next. Relating becomes listening, and listening becomes waiting. Praying is waiting. This is an extension of the art of relating. Actively caring eventually means developing the capacity to wait. Waiting is also an extension of the art of listening. The beginning of listening is attending and attending is waiting upon, waiting for, being there for the sake of another. It does not mean to program that which will follow. We who listen must learn to wait and we wait in order to listen and to hear.

Prayer is listening to and with the Lord. Likewise prayer is waiting with and for the Lord. It is not placing demands, not raising expectations, but simply being there for the sake of the other in order to be with the other.

Waiting is such a human experience that it might be beneficial for us at times to focus upon it in detail. So much of one's life involves waiting, whether that be waiting for a letter, waiting for the end of the day, waiting for graduation, waiting for a train, waiting for dinner, waiting for summer. To be human is to wait and yet as human beings we so frequently fail to develop the art of waiting. Waiting is difficult because it means allowing reality to be out of our control, being there for others rather than for ourselves. This is why waiting involves surrender. In fact, one of the best ways of understanding our relationship to God is through surrender to God. Surrender is not something God asks of us because he wants to teach us a lesson. Surrender is simply something we must learn as human beings if we are to love, to relate, to listen and to set aside our need to be in control. If the first two expressions mentioned above, relating and listening, point to an active role that we play in our lives, waiting begins to move us in the direction of a less active stance although it still points to our role, our way of being present. Waiting, however, must always imply being open to surrender, to not having our way, to having our will broken and our minds changed. To wait means to be attentive without prior agenda. It is not far removed from what Ignatius of Loyola means when he speaks of detachment which ultimately means freedom. To be able to wait means to be interiorly freed in such a way that I can be unburdened by my own demands so that I am free to be present, so loving and sharing can develop. The art of relating, the art of listening, cannot be sustained without developing the art of waiting, the openness to surrender. Surrender can be difficult to learn because it means the art of letting go of the controls, of our need to be in control. Prayer is waiting with God and surrender to God.

Prayer is relating, listening, waiting. It is also life giving. If, with the level *waiting,* we move from a more active to a less active mode of being, with *lifegiving* we find ourselves clearly in a recipient modality. Life is that which comes to us through relating, listening, waiting, and surrender, whether this be in human friendship or friendship with God. The difference is that life given us in our relationship with God and as a consequence of our surrender to God is unlimited life.

Life is most completely and most fully found in God himself. We can talk about the hierarchy of being or different levels of being from inorganic to organic to sensitive, psychic, and conscious being. In this hier-

DONALD GOERGEN

archy of being we notice at least three different degrees of life. A plant is alive but there is a way in which animals are even more fully alive. There is a degree or fullness of life which is not yet found in the vegetable or animal world. The consciousness, freedom, reflectivity found in human beings is a fuller way of being alive than is possible in the pre-human world. The fullness of life is not found with us, however, but beyond us. It is a beyond in which we can participate and for which we can prepare. This is the fundamental promise of Christ exemplified in the Gospel of John: I have come that you might have life and have it more abundantly (10:10). But we can close ourselves off from the fullness of life which is our inheritance. Prayer, in opening us to a relationship with God, allows God to enter into our lives. It is an entrance into the divine life, into the fullness of life. Prayer is the Lord's sharing his life with us and our sharing our lives with him. Prayer is that kind of mutual permeation or interpenetration which takes place between two who love. Prayer, relating to God, eventually places us in the recipient mode of receiving the life God has to give us. Prayer is lifegiving, a fuller way of being alive, a way of being alive to which faith is the access. Prayer is not only our actively caring, relating and listening and waiting. It is also receiving, receiving life which follows upon waiting for the Lord.

Prayer is sharing life, receiving life, becoming one, coming alive. Prayer then is also union with God. This is the fifth aspect to apply to prayer. Prayer at this level is no longer an art because it is no longer an activity. Once we focus on the recipient side of the relationship there is no art which can be developed beyond the arts of perseverance and surrender. Waiting is the last thing which we *do*. We can only wait in order that life might flow into us and we might become one with God himself.

It may help us to understand prayer if we realize the wisdom contained in the traditional way of speaking about the three stages or ages of interior life. Unfortunately we have sometimes considered these purgative, illuminative, and unitive phases as successive, believing that only after one has completed the purgative phase does one move into the illuminative phase. It is better to think of these three as realities that enter into every phase of relational life.

Anyone who has the experience of friendship knows that one does not develop such a relationship apart from pain and suffering. And a theology of suffering is central to the spiritual life and to the theology of prayer as well as to the theology of friendship, community and ministry. There is no growth without pain. This is simply a fundamental axiom of human existence. One does not learn to wait, to let go, to surrender, to allow a relationship to change without finding it difficult. Although growth might be desired and deeper union welcomed, union does not come without cost, the cost of friendship, the cost of discipleship, the cost of uprooting our selfishness. If we are to maintain our access to the life that God has to give us and sustain the union which that shared life brings us, prayer means suffering.

Not only does a willingness to suffer make union possible, so does the experience of insight, illumination, enlightenment. As one allows oneself to wait, to stand back, to stand under the relationship with reverence, one begins to understand. These flashes of enlightenment, revelation, intuition or wisdom may be few but they are central. They are keys which help us to understand the relationship in such a way that we do not destroy it. Relationships are a source of wisdom as well as a source of pain.

The purgative and illuminative counterparts of relating, however, find their fullest expression in the union into which we are drawn by the divine lover. God so loves us that he longs to share his life with us. Eventually prayer is no longer something we do but is experienced as grace. It is life given to us, life shared with us, life which makes us whole, uplifts, sanctifies. And this is the very definition of sanctifying grace—sharing in the divine life, partaking of the divine nature, realizing now that we too are divine, not by nature but through grace. We have become divinized because his life flows through our veins. It is now no longer I but he who lives in me.

Prayer is union with God, a highly enlightening union for which we have paid the price, which has come about because we have opened ourselves to the light which he longs to give us, for which life we have waited. That active relationship we began and in the midst of which we listened now finds us being there waiting and gradually or suddenly becoming conscious that new life is flowing into our veins and that we are now more than ourselves alone. We are new beings. Prayer is not static, not something that can be defined in one way once and for all, because it is a process of growing and deepening in our relationship with God. The way of best describing it at one stage in that relationship may not be the best way of describing it at another stage. All relationships change. We cannot describe our love for another human friend or person in simply one way because it is always undergoing change. The way to describe it now might not have been an accurate way of describing it two years ago nor the way we will describe it two years from now. When we realize that praying is relating and is then subject to change, we understand the variety of ways Christian men and women have continued to speak of prayer.

Prayer is mystery. Once we enter into a relationship and begin to share life with another, we find ourselves standing in awe before the other, before the mystery of the other, before the incommunicability of being into which we have penetrated and which penetrates us, the mystery of becoming one and yet remaining ourselves. Prayer is waiting. It is standing in the presence of mystery. It is letting ourselves be so that mystery might simply be, might be revelation which our previous inclination to control would have prevented. This is why prayer implies awe, reverence, worship. Prayer is awesome. It introduces us into the depths and heights, the pain and joys that any relationship can bring and that a relationship with God will inevitably bring. When we allow ourselves to be in the world in this way, we will stand with awe and respect before the mystery in which we now find ourselves, the mystery of another person's life and the life of one whose life transcends our total experience of living. Prayer is eventually an encounter with mystery, not something which can be grasped or defined, rather something that grasps us and defines us. When we first enter into this relationship with God, like all relationships, little did we know where it might lead. Now we find ourselves on the threshold of what we once thought we could grasp and we find ourselves in the face of an awesome mystery.

Prayer and Humor

Just as self-esteem needs to be balanced with self-denial, friendship by generativity, community by solitude, ministry by leisure and play, so prayer needs to be balanced by humor. A consideration of prayer without humor is to define prayer apart from its complement. In one sense, in this section, we move away from the sublime. In another sense, the comic brings us back to the divine. Comedy as well as tragedy, love of God as well as love of the world, laughing and crying are the accesses to the truth and the way to Divine Life. To laugh and to pray are the signs of the contemplative person. Thus I wish here to discuss this complement to prayer before completing our discussion of prayer.

Let me point to a biblical perspective in the story of Isaac. Isaac is a name which means laughter, or perhaps "God has smiled." It is difficult to translate *Isaac* exactly, but the story of Isaac is the story of that which his name represents and the story of Isaac is associated with laughter and playfulness.[1] Already in Genesis 17: 17, when it is first revealed that Abraham's wife Sarah will give birth to a son, we have a story that arouses laughter. Genesis 17:16-17 says:

> 'I will bless her and moreover give you a son by her. I will bless her and nations shall come out of her; kings of people shall descend from her.' Abraham bowed to the ground, and he laughed, thinking to himself, 'Is a child to be born to a man one hundred years old, and will Sarah have a child at the age of ninety?'

The humor might not be immediately apparent and yet the revelation of the birth of Isaac is accompanied by laughter. We almost have to picture the humor of the situation in order to appreciate it. We have an old couple, an old man and a woman beyond menopause, and God tells them that Sarah will conceive and bear a son. It sounds like a joke, sounds a little too playful on God's part. It cannot help but make Abraham smile and laugh. This perspective is carried further in the next chapter, 18:12. There we have the story of the three strangers who appear to Abraham at Mamre to whom Abraham responds hospitably, not yet knowing that the strangers are the Lord himself. Chapter 18:9 reads:

'Where is your wife Sarah?' they asked him. 'She is in the tent,' he replied. Then his guest said, 'I shall visit you again next year without fail, and your wife will then have a son.' Sarah was listening at the entrance of the tent behind him. Now Abraham and Sarah were old, well on in years, and Sarah had ceased to have her monthly periods. So Sarah laughed to herself, thinking, 'Now that I am past the age of childbearing, and my husband is an old man, is pleasure to come my way again!' But Yahweh asked Abraham, 'Why did Sarah laugh and say, Am I really going to have a child now that I am old? Is anything too wonderful for Yahweh?'

Here we have Sarah laughing. We can picture Sarah, beyond menopause, imagining to herself that Abraham and she are going to have the joy of making love and having sex, almost too humorous to be true. Sarah giggled. Isaac is the son of laughter. This play on the name of Isaac continues in Chapter 21. There we have the story of the birth of Isaac. It is reported in 21:5 and following: "Abraham was a hundred years old when his son Isaac was born to him. Then Sarah said, 'God has given me cause to laugh; all those who hear of it will laugh with me.'" Isaac is again the son of laughter, the laughter of Abraham and Sarah as God continues to work his will in history. Later in that same chapter we have another story in which there is a play or pun on the name of Isaac, but it does not come through in translation. It is the story of Isaac playing with the son of Hagar. The Scriptures read:

"The child grew and was weaned, and Abraham gave a great banquet on the day Isaac was weaned. Now Sarah watched the son that Hagar the Egyptian had borne to Abraham, playing with her son Isaac." What does not come through in the translation is the word *playing* which in Hebrew is a play on the word Isaac. If we could translate Isaac for a moment as laughter, it would be like saying "laughter was laughing with the son of Hagar" or "play was playing with the son of Hagar." This same play with words comes through in Chapter 26 where Isaac is at Gerar, the story of how Isaac concealed that Rebekah was his wife. The Scriptures (26:8) read: "When he had been there some time, Abimelech, the Philistine king, happened to look out of the window and saw Isaac fondling his wife Rebekah." Again play is playing with his wife. The entire story of Isaac is the story of the playfulness of God with his people.

Jürgen Moltman writes: "But can believers play, don't they have more important things to do? Games always presuppose innocence. Only the innocent, namely children, or those liberated from guilt, namely the beloved, are able to play. The guilty man is at odds with himself. He has lost his spontaneity and cannot play well."[2] This insight enables us to see the relationship between holiness and humor. Holiness is the capacity to laugh and to play, as well as to pray.

Christian humor is eschatological humor, looking back at life from a later perspective and seeing, from the viewpoint of distance, how one too readily makes what was penultimate into something ultimate. Eschatological humor is an ability to look at ourselves and laugh.

Only humor allows us to live in this world as though

it were not the whole world. Only humor allows us to live in this world from the perspective of that other world which we are building and for which we wait. Humor is an essential pillar in Christian spirituality, related to the perception of incongruity, flowing from and into contemplation. In contemplation we are in the presence of and in union with God; then we find ourselves back in the world: we can only laugh. The contemplative experience provides us the vantage point from which we can see the world from another perspective—the perspective of the coming Reign of God—and allows us to laugh. The perception of incongruity can be painful; it can also be fun. Prayer, as any friendship, is a source of joy; it is not all serious business.

Prayer and Friendship

An understanding and experience of friendship itself not only contributes to our human growth but also to our relationship with God. A basic principle of spiritual theology is that friendship with human beings is not totally different from friendship with God. In other words, what we learn in the school of human relationships can readily be applied to our relationship with God. This means that friendship itself is an important phase in the spiritual life contributing not simply to our own deepened capacity to love but contributing to our ultimate union with God himself. Only in an appreciation of friendship can one begin to fathom what it means for God to have called us into friendship with himself. Friendship with another person and friendship with God are analogous, and we need to give ourselves to one in order to grow in the other.

171

Dependency, for example, is central to friendship. Too often in Western thinking we consider independence as the goal of human maturity. It is difficult to imagine the United States making a "Declaration of Dependence." And yet dependent we are. We need to acknowledge and affirm our dependency as well as our need for autonomy. Interdependence is the Christian goal. Yet many of us are never able to achieve interdependence because we strive for independence and need to be in control. This desire prevents us from entering deeply into human relationships.

In human relationships we must at times sacrifice and surrender if we are to reach the depths of possible intimacy. This is true in our relationship with God as well. We can learn the meaning of dependency, open ourselves to dependency, allow ourselves to experience dependency, become dependent in human relationships and then know what it means to be dependent upon God. Dependence upon God is necessary before friendship with God can develop. Yet there must be that breaking of our self-sufficiency within human life if we are going to allow our self-sufficiency to be set aside in our relationship with God. For many of us, friendship with God is inhibited because we insist upon being in control of the relationship.

Another reality in human relationships is its developmental aspect. We can apply this to friendship with God. All of the phases in the development of a relationship—the ecstasies and dark nights, the honeymoons and the moments of hostility—can be found in our own deepening union with God himself. Even the force of ambivalence which we experience so readily in human relationships can lead us to understand the ambivalence we experience with God. There are times when we say to ourselves that we are going to give ourselves totally to God; we soon discover how inconstant we can be. We love God and we want to give ourselves to him and then we discover what it means to give ourselves to him and what he might be asking. Then we are no longer faithful. The longing and the fear, the moving toward and the moving away from, can be found in our relationship with God as Francis Thompson observed in "The Hound of Heaven."

> I fled Him, down the nights and down the days;
> I fled Him, down the arches of the years;
> I fled Him, down the labyrinthine ways
>   Of my own mind; and in the midst of tears
> I hid from Him, and under running laughter.

I recall once giving a talk to a group in Kentucky and someone telling me about a person I was going to meet shortly thereafter in the Boston area. I thought in the back of my mind, "Yes, I will be happy to meet her. I'm sure she is a good person. On the other hand, there are many good people you meet when you go places." In other words, I was not as enthusiastic about meeting her as I was supposed to be. Yet, when I found myself in Boston and did have the opportunity to spend a very brief time with her, I had to agree; she was someone with depth and this was revealed even in a twenty minute conversation. I was glad I had met her, and it occurred to me how different it is to hear about someone and to meet them.

We can apply this realization to our relationship with God. Many of us know much about God. How many of us have actually met God? How many have actually entered into a personal relationship with him? This is the problem in "God-talk." "Knowledge about" often falls short. Sometimes it even gets in the way. We have often had the experience of people who knew about us before they met us, and who allow that previous knowledge to prevent a genuine encounter with the persons we understand ourselves to be. The goal of communication with God is not to learn more *about* him but to enter into a relationship *with* him, with the Father through a relationship with Christ by means of the Spirit.

As we reflect upon relationships, however, we soon discover that the fullness of a relationship does not simply come with the first encounter or the first meeting. For this reason development within a relationship must consider three stages. The first stage is reflective. This is a period in which there is much verbal sharing. People get to know each other and become excited about sharing ideas, common visions, reflection together. This is usually the first encounter, listening to and speaking with the other. The same is true in our relationship with God. The first step in communication with God is reflective prayer, the stage in which we bring our concerns to God, our souls to God, our reflective and meditative praises to him.

We notice, in some relationships, a movement from the reflective level to the affective level. This begins when more emotion is involved and we begin to feel a need for the presence of the other. We begin to say to the other, "I love you." Now expressions of affection become a more valued aspect of the relationship than the shared reflections. This does not mean that reflections are no longer shared or prized, but now the heart and soul of the relationship seems to be affection. Verbal explanations of the relationship are now simplified. This corresponds to the second level of prayer, affective prayer. At this point we move out of the reflective meditation on God or conversations with God into more ejaculatory or mantric prayer. Now our love for God is felt. In other words, our relationship with God must move in the direction of affection which we experience for God and which we realize he has for us.

It is only by entering into this deepened aspect of human friendship that we can begin to discover what friendship with God has to offer. We would miss much if our friendships were all reflective, and many people miss much of what friendship with God has to offer because their prayer remains reflective and never becomes affective. Many people miss the heart of prayer by not allowing themselves to enter into the prayer of the heart. This is why emotional growth is central to the spiritual life. We cannot approach the spiritual life only on an intellectual level. Friendship with God—which is the depth of what life in Christ can be—only comes when one is opened emotionally to another.

Relationships do not stop after reflective and affective sharing. After three or four years of saying five or six hundred times "I love you" to someone whom we love, those words no longer convey the original meaning. In fact, those words cannot quite say anymore what we now want to convey. The relationship then moves to a level where the nonverbal communication becomes central and most profound. Words are, in fact, no longer necessary. An image would be two elderly people who have been married for forty or fifty years. Too often we lament that they no longer have anything to share because we do not see them talking to each other as previously. Yet the relationship is still being expressed in their presence to each other without words.

The "Song of Songs" expresses a love for which

words are ultimately inadequate. This is the contemplative phase in a relationship. It comes only after years of deepened sharing and affective growth. Understanding has been established and communication flows; now the greatest communication is simply being there in the presence of the other. This kind of presence corresponds to a level in our relationship with God which is often spoken of as placing ourselves in the presence of Christ, or the prayer of quiet, or contemplative prayer.

When we reach the contemplative level in prayer, we do not always experience the presence of the other, but sometimes the absence of the other. Absence from the other is now even more painful than before we loved to this extent. We need only be aware of—after a couple has lived together for years and given their lives to each other—the grief that ensues when one partner dies. The relationship has moved to that level where one can no longer be defined apart from the other. In our friendship with God we can no longer be defined apart from him, nor he apart from us. He is now my friend and I, his.

In short, there are three stages in the deepening of prayer and of friendship with God; reflective, affective, and contemplative prayer. Many of us miss the deep love that prayer can be because we remain at the reflective level or, indeed, at the level of knowledge and not encounter.

Growth in our human relationships can teach us what is most valuable about how to develop our relationship with God. Friendship with God can also teach us much that is applicable to the world of human relationships. In our relationship with God we experience the meaning of fidelity, the kind of fidelity that is not always our experience in human relationships. With God, before whom we are so frequently unfaithful, we can discover what constancy in a relationship can be, as he continually calls us to be with him, as he continually forgives us, as his love is always there growing strongly for us. Knowing his love, we can learn to love with constancy.

There is a dialectical growth between human friendship and divine friendship. Growth in human friendship allows us to deepen our relationship with God and deepening our relationship with God allows us to deepen our relationships with other human beings. Friendship with God is not unlike friendship with others and thus human friendship can be one of the greatest sources for growth in our relationship with God. Human friendship teaches us how to grow in divine friendship.

The Eucharist

No discussion of prayer is complete without a discussion of the Eucharist, the highest form of prayer into which we as Christians can enter. It is the highest expression of our love for God, the most holistic act of love for God we might experience. The Eucharist brings together all five loves of which we have previously spoken as well as God's love for us. Eucharistic prayer is not unrelated to ministry, community, friendship and self-esteem. In fact, it flows from them, integrates and perfects them.

We must see the Eucharist and all of liturgy as intrinsically related to mission if we are to have a proper understanding of sacramental theology. Here I distinguish mission and ministry although the two are closely related. Mission is the act of being sent. Ministry is being there for the sake of others, for the sake of service. In the Eucharist we are all commissioned and sent forth to be ministers, to serve. The universal priesthood of all, the vocation to ministry in which we all participate, the Gospel imperative that calls us forth to be servants, is rooted in the Eucharistic activity. Because we all share in the Eucharist, we all participate in the priesthood of Christ and are sent forth to do his work in the world. Mission and ministry are correlative. We are sent to serve. We are commissioned to minister.

The Eucharistic act itself concludes with this commission by pointing us to apostolic responsibility and raising our consciousnesses once again as to the reason we have actually come together. In worship we discover God's desire that we go forth to love one another, for the Eucharist exemplifies the close relationship between love of God and love of neighbor. The apostolic aspect is most clearly communicated at the close of the Eucharistic activity: "Ite, missa est." The commission is "Ite" or "go forth." *Missa est* comes from the Latin *mitto, mittere,* to send. "Go now," means "we are being sent." We have come together for our celebration, our fellowship, our worship. That in which we have involved ourselves here reminds us of our vocation to be servants in the world. The Eucharist then is not only an act of love of God but is also an act in which we are sent forth to love and serve our neighbor. The Eucharistic prayer incorporates and makes central love of the poor, the needy and the oppressed.

Our celebration of the Eucharist, as a Christian fellowship, cannot be separated from our work and vocation in the world. As is readily recognized today, what we celebrate in the Eucharist we are called upon to build and make manifest elsewhere. The community we experience in the Eucharist we are to build throughout the world. The union with God in the Eucharist is the source of divine energy through which we might accomplish in and for the world that which the Lord wants. In the end, as Teilhard de Chardin points out, the Eucharistic activity is cosmic in scope and significance.[3] It is the transubstantiation, transformation, or Eucharistisation of the universe. Eucharist can never be separated from mission.

This social, political, economic and worldly significance of our Eucharistic activity is exemplified in the significance of table fellowship itself and the part it played in the life of Jesus. As Joachim Jeremias points out, table fellowship was one of the crucial symbolic acts of Jesus; he was willing to break bread with sinners. That Jesus invited all to his banquet to share fellowship with him, to sit at the table with him, was a radical and revolutionary act in which he made concrete and manifest the kind of love that his Father is, generous and universal. No one is excluded. Insofar as we are also willing to break bread together as a fellowship in which status and artificial barriers are left unrecognized, we act in the name of Christ, continue his activity on earth, and continue a radical and revolutionary way of being in the world. When we come to that which matters, the table of the Lord, we are all one. We break bread together and we dine together because we all are sinners and we recognize the generous love of the Father. This social significance of table fellowship cannot be separated from the social mission to which we are sent when our Eucharistic activity has been completed. It would be hypocrisy as well as blasphemy to turn the Eucharist into an activity which does not have social, political, economic and worldly implications. This is why we must reconcile ourselves with our brothers or sisters before we bring gifts to the altar. The prophets readily challenge formalized worship as being hypocritical. We cannot worship Eucharistically, participate in the sign of fellowship and reconciliation, if we are unwilling to live accordingly. The Eucharist is an act in which we love our neighbor and are sent forth to continue that same love of neighbor once apart from that table fellowship.

The Eucharist is not only an act of prayer in which love of God and love of neighbor come together. It is a prayer in which love of God and the love of fellowship come together as well. This is more immediately obvious than what has been said above, for the Eucharist is a communal activity. The Eucharistic act is always an act of and for the sake of a community, a particular community which has come together precisely for the sake of worship. With the liturgical renewal following the Second Vatican Council, the concept of Eucharist as fellowship has become more obvious. This aspect of the Eucharistic activity is frequently preached, commented upon, and made central. The Eucharist is a fellowship, a sharing, a coming together of brothers and sisters, a manifestation of the kind of love that community is. The Eucharist is not only intrinsically related to ministry but is also intrinsically related to community. In fact, as we already discussed (Chapter Four), the fundamental meaning of *koinonia* for Paul is the Eucharistic fellowship. Fellowship for Christians is table fellowship, Eucharistic fellowship, a fellowship in which we share in the breaking of the bread. This is the fundamental meaning of community. Fellowship reaches its full significance in the Eucharistic community. The type of prayer that the Eucharist exemplifies is no longer a private prayer, an individual prayer, or even personal prayer. It is the prayer of a worshiping and ministering community. It is the coming together in the Lord out of love for God, love for neighbor, and love for our brothers and sisters.

Because we are always more complete in community than alone, the Eucharistic prayer is the highest form of prayer into which we have been invited and into which we enter. Communal prayer, liturgical prayer, which might not always reach the same level experientially that personal contemplation might, still perfects and completes us, because it makes our relational nature visible. Whatever it means to be human, as Christians we are not complete or fully human by ourselves. We are only complete in relationship to others. This theory of personality which sees the person as the center of a network of relationships is emphasized by both Teilhard de Chardin and other process thinkers.[4] Because individuality and sociality are correlative concepts, the perfection of ourselves as individuals takes place only as we come together in union with our brothers and sisters. Thus the possibilities within Eucharistic prayer extend beyond the possibilities that exist within an individual's prayer because it is the prayer of the community, the prayer of the body and the prayer of the world.

One can hardly overemphasize the centrality of this Eucharistic act as a form of prayer within Christian spirituality. It is a prayer into which Christians moved historically as soon as they were moved and guided by the Spirit. Christian identity revolves around the breaking of the bread. Long before the Scriptures were formulated, written, and developed into canonical writings, Christians had been coming together to celebrate the Eucharist as the heart and core of Christian life. Even in the age of martyrs, when martyrdom was respected as a supreme exemplification of radical response to Christ, the Eucharist equalled the act of martyrdom in its significance within the life of the Church.

The Eucharist is love of God and love of neighbor. It is brotherly, sisterly, communal fellowship. Community and ministry are central to the nature of Eucharistic activity. The Eucharist is also an act of friendship. The first sense in which it is an act of friendship is that it makes divine friendship concrete. In his last discourse, Jesus says to his disciples, "I do not call you servants but friends" (John 15:15) . One of the eventualities of friendship is friendship with God himself. Friendship is not only human sharing, but sharing with the Lord. What Jesus is saying when he invites us into friendship with God is that we are invited into a relationship in which there is equality and mutuality. The Eucharist is divine and human friendship in which we partake of the divine nature and in which Christ once again manifests how he shares our human nature. The union is complete. This equality into which we are invited is grace. It is not through our nature that we have either the right or the power to embrace such a relationship. The Lord himself elevates us in such a way that we might be one with him in friendship, that we might be equal through grace. Grace elevates us beyond what we can be through natural abilities alone. Indeed the Eucharist manifests not only human love, our love for God, but also divine love, his love for us. It is the supreme exemplification of the two loves and the way in which these two loves come together and become one.

Although the Eucharist as a celebration of friendship is best exemplified in God's relationship with us and our friendship with God, we can also say that human friendship enters into the reality of the Eucharistic celebration. Human friendship is by no means excluded and unacknowledged. We come together as friends many times to celebrate the Eucharist. We come together as a family. Conjugal friendship is frequently made public in the Church within the context of the Eucharistic setting. The Eucharist is an appropriate context in which to celebrate and make more visible our love as friends. Friends choose to share the Eucharist together because they wish to bring their human intimacy into contact with divine intimacy. Human intimacy is central to the Eucharistic celebration, and Eucharistic activity which leaves intimacy and its power unrecognized fails to achieve the fullness possible in worship. The Eucharist is a celebration of fellowship, of our love for God, our mission, but also of the gift of friendship which we have been given. The Eucharist is an act of thanksgiving by its very nature in which we thank God for his love and his gifts, and one of the important gifts that God has given us will always be the friends with whom he has united us. Thus we celebrate in the Eucharist not only our communal love and our apostolic love, but also our intimate love. It is there that we bring it into union with God.

The Eucharist, as a celebrative banquet of love, a feast of love, cannot be separated from love of God, love of neighbor, love of our brothers and sisters, love of friendship. Neither can it be separated from self-love, self-esteem, self-affirmation, self-actualization, self-transcendence. The personal self comes to its greatest realization in Eucharistic activity. In the Eucharist we are (at least potentially) most fully human and most fully divine. In the Eucharist we come to celebrate and recognize the fullness of life which has been given to us. Self-esteem is never achieved through isolation, for development of self is never something to which we come by ourselves alone. It is only in community, through ministry, with friends, and in union with God that the self becomes the Self that it can be. Thus self-realization, self-actualization, is most completed in Eucharistic activity. The Eucharist can never be expected to perform miracles which are supposed to be performed elsewhere. We can never substitute the Eucharist for friendship, nor for self-development, the arduous task by means of which we come to self-knowledge and self-acceptance. Yet, for the person who accepts himself or herself, the Eucharist is the context in which that self can be realized, completed and celebrated. Within the human potential, there is the capacity to become divine, to become one with God, to be a sacrament or manifestation of the kind of love that the Lord himself is. Within our human potential we can move out of ourselves, transcend ourselves, become ourselves by going beyond ourselves. It is precisely in the ecclesial context of the Eucharistic activity that self becomes Self. The Eucharistic act is diminished to the degree that self-love is diminished, our love for friends is ruptured or our response to need is neglected. In the Eucharist we are called upon to love ourselves with the highest kind of love possible, with the kind of love that the Spirit gives.

The Eucharist is love of neighbor and fellowship. Central to the Eucharistic celebration are also friendship and self-esteem. The Eucharist, however, is primarily prayer, love of God. It is adoration, worship, and it is precisely for the sake of worship that we come together. This is why the Eucharist is a supreme exemplification of prayer, of our love for God as well as his love for us.

I already said in Chapter One something which I will repeat again: we need to avoid the tendency to look at these five loves in terms of priority. We are all called to love in all five ways. I must insist upon that again since it is easy to make love of God so significant that we do the character of Christian love a disservice by separating rather than relating the different kinds of love, by seeing them as separate rather than as being one love.

When we are talking about love, we tend to think of love of God as more important than other loves. Wisdom, however, teaches us that love of God is inseparable from love of others. In fact, God is inseparable from others. We love God not only as he is in himself but as he is present in ourselves and others as well. Religion longs to relate us to God, yet God constantly escapes definition. The best way for Christians to talk about God is to see him as love, as the loveable One, as the One who by definition deserves to be loved. We do not deserve to be loved; we in fact are loved and loveable; yet, because of sin, this love of God for us is not something we deserve. It is, however, still ours through grace. God deserves to be loved, and adoration points to the degree to which human love can go. Although we are called to love ourselves and others, we are called upon to adore only God. The distinction between the other loves and adoration is not that adoration is more important. The word *adoration* points to the significance and importance of the object of this particular love, namely God. In the Eucharist then we come to worship but we come to worship as a community of men or women living in fellowship, we love ourselves and see our lives at the service of all God's people as well as of those friends with whom we have been gifted by God himself. We come together into a Eucharistic celebration as a whole people, a wholesome people, where we might stand in awe and love before our Father.

In the Eucharist we are called upon to open up the depths of ourselves before the Father; to express our reflective, affective and contemplative selves. In contemplation we come to the depths of our own personal relationship with God. Now, in the context of fellowship, we express the depths to which contemplative prayer has brought us and place ourselves in the context of community before the Father. Eucharistic prayer thus perfects contemplation. Contemplation leads us to the Eucharist and the Eucharist leads us to further contemplation, for the Eucharist is also contemplative activity.

The more contemplative one becomes, the more responsive, receptive, passive one is in prayer. Yet the love which has been given to us through waiting in personal prayer can now be brought forth and placed in the context of liturgical prayer. Personal prayer is not so much a contemplative activity as it is contemplative receptivity. In the Eucharist we are all celebrants; the contemplative presence to God is something we do together. In the Eucharist, we are active as well as receptive. Our activity is contemplative activity, whereas in personal prayer contemplation is contemplative receptivity. The mystical life culminates in the Eucharistic contemplative act.

The Eucharist is self-affirmation, friendship, community, mission and ministry, contemplative and celebrative prayer. At the same time, it is also a recognition of the presence of Christ in our midst. The Eucharist is that activity in which God, through the ministry of his Church, makes present once again, for the sake of worship, the body of his son. This is why there is a depth in the Eucharist to which all Christian love is drawn and where all five loves come together.

There are three fundamental ways in which the expression "Body of Christ" can be used.[5] The first of these is the body of Jesus of Nazareth, the Jesus in history, Jesus as his disciples and friends knew him, talked to him, experienced him. The second is the presence of Christ in the Eucharist, the presence of the Risen Lord, the same Jesus whom the disciples experienced in history now physically present to us in the breaking of the bread, under the appearances of bread and wine, yet Christ himself. The third is his presence in the poor and the needy, the hungry and the thirsty, those with whom he so strongly identified, his presence in those to whom we are called to minister, his presence in others and in the world, the total body whose Head he is. In the Eucharist, Christ becomes as tangible, as real, as present as he was in history. His Eucharistic presence continues to guide us just as his historical presence did.

The presences of Jesus should never be separated. They are the presence of the one Lord. Just as Christ is present in the Eucharist, so he is present in the human beings with whom he so strongly identified when he said "I was hungry and you gave me to eat." Thus, in the Eucharist, we come to a fuller appreciation of the body of Christ, and realize that the fullness of Christ is not in the historical Jesus alone nor in the Eucharistic act alone but in the Body of which he is the Head, the Body which is composed of us as the members. The Body of Christ made visible in the Eucharistic celebration is not only the individual Jesus. It is also the total Christ, Head and members. The act of worship once again returns us to ministry to the world.

Three Modes of Prayer

There are many ways in which one can talk about prayer, as many ways as one can pray. Prayer involves the very mystery of being, of love, of God. Thus there is no way in which it can be described completely or categorized neatly. We can, however, examine three aspects of the life of prayer.

The first of these is liturgical prayer, the prayer of the Church coming together as *ecclesia* so that together we might raise our hearts and minds to God. The supreme exemplification of liturgical prayer is the Eucharistic celebration about which we have already spoken, but the liturgical life of God's people extends beyond the Eucharistic act into other sacramental activities and into the liturgy of the hours. Liturgy is an act of love, a way of loving and an exemplification of love of God. Liturgical prayer is loving God and hearing his Word of love for us. Liturgy is love. This is why liturgy can never be separated from life, from mission, from community, from friendship, or from self-esteem.

Not all our prayer, however, is done together as a people. Just as some sacred dimensions of life involve others, so other sacred dimensions of life are encountered in solitude, in aloneness. In addition to liturgical prayer there is the prayer of solitude, personal prayer, the heartfelt expression of being in love on the part of one who comes to the presence of God. It is frequently alone with God that our encounter with God can be experienced most deeply. When alone, we can open our hearts to him most strongly. In solitude we allow ourselves to make love with him most vividly. Solitary prayer is also love of God. To a great degree reflective, affective and contemplative prayer develop because of the interpersonal character of our relationship with God, which grows more in private than in public. Like all relationships, our relationship with God needs both a public and a private dimension. Any human relationship that is never given privacy is prevented from reaching the depths to which it can go when two are alone together. Likewise any human relationship which never manifests publicly runs the risk of becoming privatized, isolated and anti-social. Thus we need to relate both privately and publicly as human beings in our interpersonal spheres. Prayer also is manifested in both private and liturgical modes. The prayer of solitude allows a depth which cannot be created when we are in public. Liturgical prayer allows a universalization of the self which cannot be accomplished in solitude.

In addition to the prayer of a community and the prayer of solitude, there is another kind of prayer. The first two kinds of prayer are examples of explicit prayer, conscious prayer, time purposely set aside for the sake of developing our relationship with the Lord. Our relationship with the Lord, however, does not develop only during those times which we consciously set aside to be with him, either in private or in public. Our relationship with the Lord develops continuously between those times set aside for prayer. This type of prayer is continuous prayer. Sometimes it is explicit, sometimes it is implicit, but it is a way of being which permits a person to be defined as one who is the beloved of the Lord, one whose style of life is always one which is explicated by the fact of being in relationship with the Lord. There is a sense in which we pray always as prayer begins to permeate our lives, as our relationship with God begins to permeate our lives. The time comes when we can no longer be defined apart from that relationship. It is not I, but the Lord who lives within me. In this way of speaking, we can see that prayer is life itself, or at least *a certain way of being alive*. This kind of prayer, however, is always developmental, in process, never finished. Continuous prayer is that way of being in which we are constantly in relationship with the Lord and allow ourselves to be defined by that relationship which continues to take greater and greater hold of who we are until we become fully his. It is a way of doing all that we do in the context of who we are in relationship to God, lovers of God and his beloved. In this sense ministry is a source of prayer and ministry is prayer. In this sense community is a source of prayer and community is prayer. Friendship is a source of prayer and so is the self. All we are and all we do can contribute to our love for God. Life becomes God made incarnate in our personal histories.

PART THREE

Divine Love

God our Father,
you send the power of the gospel into the
world as a life-giving leaven.
Fill with the Spirit of Christ
those whom you call to live in the midst
of the world and its concerns;
help them by their work on earth
to build up your eternal kingdom.

Opening Prayer
Mass for the Laity
The Sacramentary of the
Roman Missal

Chapter Seven

THE FATHER'S LOVE REVEALED

God's Creative Love

Few images are as important to Christian spirituality, even to personality itself, as our image of God. The God Scripture and tradition reveal is the God of love. God reveals himself to us as One who loves us, who cares for us, who cares actively for us, who acts on our behalf. Creation itself is a revelation of who God is. In understanding creation we see God as One who moves outside of the fullness of his own life in order to share his life with us, with creatures.

A theology of creation explores the nature of creaturely dependence upon God, the meaning of being limited by nature, the continuousness of divine creative activity, and the purpose of God. Creation helps us to understand who God is and the nature of his love, for creation implies a relationship between God and the world. If we follow the Teilhardian strand of process thought, this relationship is posed in christological terms, the relationship between Christ and creation, the complementarity and mutuality between Christ and creation, whereas in the Whiteheadian strand of process thought the discussion takes place within the context of the nature of God himself and the relationship between God and the world. In the context of process thought, we become aware that there is a mutuality between God and the world, between his Son and creation, that there is a way in which the world brings something to God or creation brings something to Christ.[1]

Process theology has challenged us to rethink the divine attributes and the meaning of divine perfection. We readily admit that God is perfect, but what perfection consists of is not immediately obvious. For some, perfection might be utter independence, self-sufficiency, or complete power. Even then, however, it must be asked what kind of power is the perfection of power. In what does perfect power consist? It is an assumption of process thinkers, whether Teilhardian or Whiteheadian, that the world brings something to God himself. Yet a traditional way of understanding perfection frequently suggests, whether explicitly or not, that God in no way needs the world in order to be complete, and that therefore the world is superfluous with respect to God's ultimate happiness and satisfaction. The universe could have remained uncreated, be completely annihilated, or humanity as a whole could go to hell, and God would still be all-perfect, all-loving, all-happy for all eternity. This is an image of God which can misinterpret the contingency of creation in such a way that creation lacks value for the life of the Lord himself.

Yet this is not the God which the Scriptures reveal. In the inspired texts, God is in love with the world. He cares about his world. It is created in his image and likeness. What the world brings to God may be different from what God brings to the world, yet there is complementarity between these two realities. God needs his world and Christ requires his members. In other words, God without the world and Christ without his body would not be the same, and would not be complete. This theology of the world points out the intrinsic value of creation because creation brings something of completion to the Lord himself.

This need not surprise us. The image of the Christian life so readily used by Paul is that of the Body of Christ. Just as the body would not be a body if it were all ear or only leg, so it would not be a body if it were only the head. In order to be the head of the body, Christ requires the other members. And, speaking in traditional terms, the glory of God or Reign of God is something other than just God in himself. God without his Reign or without glory is somehow not the same as God in his Kingdom with his glory manifest. Even in traditional Western thought, creation has been considered as bringing something to God: giving him glory. It allows his intrinsic perfection to be manifest.

We can also say that the freedom which God grants creation means that the shape which the future will take remains open. Although God creates his world, he does depend upon his creatures to give shape to that world. Which particular world of all possible worlds will finally come into existence depends not only upon God but upon us as well. Thus there are many ways in which creation completes God and completes his work.

The question of language is important. We are not saying that God needs the world in order to be *perfect*, only that he needs the world in order to be *complete*. In his own trinitarian life God is already the perfection of relational existence. Yet, although God is perfect, he is not complete; this "incompleteness" says something about his relationship to time and it is in his relationship to time that we can come to understand God better.

Consider the analogy of friendship. We readily affirm that God is love; yet many times our image of

God prevents God from being love for us. God calls us into existence to be friends with us and that we might be friends with him. In any such relationship of love, however, there is a sense in which the lover needs the response of the beloved so that love may be complete, not necessarily that love be perfect. Let us assume for the moment that God is perfect within himself in his own interior relational and trinitarian life. God does not need any others to be, to be in love, or to be loved. Yet God freely chooses to move outside of himself to enter into relationships with others whom he does not need for his nature, but whom he will now need because of his free decision to create. It is his freedom that is the root of God's incompleteness.

Friendship tells us that love seeks mutuality and reciprocity. In every human relationship, when we move out to another, we do so because of our own needs and deficiencies. God in no way needs others than himself because of deficiency in his nature. Yet, in any relationship based on love another need is created, not a need which flows from the nature or deficiency of the lover but one which is created by the love itself, the nature and character of love and not the nature or character of the person. It is the nature of love to long for the response of the beloved in such a way that reciprocity might complete that which the initial stirring of love began. If God is love, he too longs for the response of his beloved, his chosen people, his people. In this way his love is incomplete until it is reciprocated.

God's love is perfect because greater love there could not be. Yet God freely chooses to create, not because he needs us but because he loves us. Perfect love does not require reciprocity; love of enemies is a perfect manifestation of love. Reciprocal love is not necessarily more perfect as love but does bring completion to love. It makes the love of the lover not more profound or more perfect but more complete. In this sense God longs for the completion of his love.

I call into question here the distinction readily made between *agape* and *eros*. In many ways this is a false dichotomy not based on the Scriptures themselves. *Agape* describes divine love. In John's Gospel *agape* is interchangeable with *philia* as well.[2] *Agape* is also not so easily separated from *eros*. If we see *agape* as selfless loving and *eros* as loving based on need, there is *eros* in God and the Scriptures do picture God as such a jealous lover. The fact that we are surprised to think of *eros* in divine love is because we have associated the word *eros* too quickly with sin. God's love is selfless; it is also self-seeking, seeking its completion in the responsiveness of the Beloved.

Eros in God, however, does not flow from his nature but only from his free decision to create. God's freedom is the root of his dependency. He does not create us because he needs us due to any deficiency or lack. Yet God does "need" us. His "need" for our response, his dependency upon us so that his love might be reciprocal and complete, arises not out of any limitation or imperfection in his nature but out of the magnificence of his love, the altruism and generosity of his freedom.

God in no way needs to create us to be who he is, to be who he might be, or to be a perfect lover. He already is love as Father, Son and Holy Spirit. Yet, once he freely chooses to create, he freely chooses to become dependent. Once he freely chooses to create, he "needs" creation for his creative love to be complete. This is the mystery. He freely chose to create in the first place. The dependency which God has upon his creatures does not flow in any sense from a lack within his nature but is something which is chosen freely by God. Greater love than this no one has, not to be dependent and to choose freely to become so.

Is this not what takes place in any relationship? As we move out of ourselves, enter into a relationship with another, and say to someone, "I love you," we are also saying that we are willing to become dependent, to establish a relationship of mutuality and interdependence. To love includes to need, not necessarily that deficiencies might be remedied but at least that love might be reciprocated. Even perfect love longs for the response of the beloved. This is the character of love itself. *Love is freely chosen self-limitation.* Love is freely choosing to become limited, dependent, for the sake of the other. Love places the totality of self at the feet of the other.

God is love. He now exists for us. That is what he longs to reveal to us. He is a divine lover, infinitely capable of being for us. To be for us, he freely chooses to become dependent, to place himself, the perfect One, in a position of need. He freely chooses to need us. Not to respond to his love will forever leave the love of the lover incomplete, unsatisfied, although not less perfect as love. Yet unreciprocated love is not the goal for which the lover longs. God's *agape* creates *eros.* God's *agape,* his infinite love and complete freedom, allows him, frees him, to be *eros* as well. God's *eros,* however, is in no way selfish. It is totally altruistic. It is a willingness to change for our sakes, not only to be a lover in himself but also to be a lover outside of himself, *for* us.

This indeed raises the metaphysical problem of

whether, if God is love, he could refrain from creating. Given his nature as love could God not create? We are faced with mystery. Since God is absolutely free, there is no need to create. Since he is absolutely loving, however, there is no way in which he could not create. The best way of resolving the difficulties is to realize that God must "necessarily" create freely.[3] God creates freely but there is no way in which he would not or could not do so. He creates freely and he creates "necessarily" because he is love and because he is freedom. The type of necessity which we apply to God, however, is not the type of necessity which is attached to contingent creatures. We need God in order to be. God in no way needs us in order to be since he is being itself. Yet being love, there is no way in which God could freely choose to not create.

This would require our going further into the theology of freedom itself and we cannot adequately cover these topics here. All we can do is provide the avenue for understanding how God's creation is a revelatory action of who God is, that he is love. Yet we must call to mind that our understanding of freedom is often distorted. This is why it is so hard for us to see that God as love must "necessarily" create freely. We too often think of freedom as being able to love or not love. Is God able to, free to, not love? No, of course not. This would contradict his nature. This does not mean, however, that God is less free because he is unable to not love. The same can be said in discussion of the sinlessness of Christ. Is one less free if he is unable to sin? Being unable to sin or unable to love does not imply less freedom. There is, strictly speaking, no such thing as being free to sin. It is because of sin that we are unfree. Sin is unfreedom. Because we are sinners, we are not fully free. The degree to which we overcome sin, we are free, free to love but not free to sin. Freedom finds sin repugnant, finds sin as an enemy. If we were totally free, we would only love, but, because we are sinners, and partially unfree, we love faultingly. If we were totally free, however, we could only love. We would be free to love; we would "necessarily" love. Freedom means loving "necessarily." Not loving necessarily is a result of unfreedom. Thus God's perfect freedom means that he "necessarily" loves us.

Thus God "necessarily" chooses freely to create us. In this freedom, the root of his love can be found. Greater love than this no one has than to not need us in order to be or in order to be perfect and yet to choose freely to create us and thus become dependent upon us. God's "neediness" flows from his free decision. Our neediness flows from our insufficiency and finitude and nature and sin. God's neediness flows from his magnificence and sovereignity. Rather than this need making God less perfect, is this not that in which his perfection consists? The perfection of God is that he loves. It is only this image of God which can adequately convey who God is; that he loves us, cares about us, and longs for our response. He waits for us. But he needs us only because of who he freely chose to become for our sakes. Creation is the first act of God and the first act of grace. It reveals the nature of God as being grace. Creation is already grace, a manifestation of the gratuitous and magnificent love that God is. Creation is already grace and already revelation on God's part. God's love is freely given and we are freely created. Greater love than this no one has than to not need us and to freely choose to enter into a relationship with us in order that he might share his life with us. Who is God? The fact of creation itself reveals that God is love.

God's Incarnative Love

In looking at the creative act of God, we see that the creator is a lover. Greater love no one could have than to have freely chosen to create an other than himself and enter into a relationship with that other and thus choose to place his own future into the hands of the other—freely choose to become dependent. Unfathomable as it might seem to think that there is a greater love than that expressed in the creative activity of God, greater love than this our Lord is. He not only created us but chose to become one with us.

This is the meaning and significance of the Incarnation. This is the reason that the name to be given to the one for whom all of Hebrew history waited was Immanuel—God with us. Jesus of Nazareth is a supreme exemplification of God's incarnative love, his presence with us in history. Jesus continued the revelatory activity of God which had already begun in the creative activity. God does not create us for union with himself and then leave us to be ourselves. God cares too much about us to allow us to be by ourselves until union with him is eventually realized. Even before that union with him for which we have all been created is accomplished in its fullness, God chose to be present to his people. This is the image of God which breaks through in Hebrew history—our God is always a God who acts on behalf of his people. He acts in history; he is present in history; he calls people forth; he is here with us. We have not been left to our own resources.

Jesus of Nazareth, the Incarnate Word, is the supreme exemplification of God's presence in history. He manifests that God's love is not only creative but also incarnative. He not only calls us into being but becomes enfleshed with us, shares creaturehood with us, participates in our very nature so that we might participate in his. Jesus of Nazareth is a presence of God in history.

Jesus is man, one like us in every way, participating fully in the human condition. At the same time there is no contradiction in affirming God's presence in him, God present and active in history. To be human and to be divine is not a question of "either/or." The question is not how Jesus could be both, for in the revelatory character of the Christ event humanity and divinity are disclosed as being complementary rather than antagonistic. Jesus is fully human because he is fully united with his Father. Jesus is fully divine because God has fully emptied himself into his union with this man.

Biblical references abound which point to the full extent that Christ is one with us, that Jesus is totally one of us, that God totally empties himself in order to be in union with us. The author of the Epistle to the Hebrews states that Jesus was tempted as we are in every way (4:15). He was like us in every way although the category of sinner is not applicable to him as it is to us. Yet he struggled with his emotional life, with the limits of his own knowledge, with his own culture and tradition, with his own family and destiny, with his religious vocation. The second Epistle to the Corinthians testifies to this humanness to an even greater degree (5:21). Paul writes that the sinless one became sin for us. We see in this understanding the degree to which God loves us, the degree to which he goes on uniting us to himself. There is no limit placed upon his incarnation. He became fully one of us, entering into the midst of the human struggle and the limitations of the human condition. He took on the effects of the history of human sinfulness.

In the Epistle to the Philippians we read of this aspect of God's incarnate love: Divinity is not something to be clung to but rather something to be let go of that the incarnation might be complete (2:6-11). He did not cling to his divine status but became like us, obedient to the Father even unto the end, even unto his death on the cross. Divine incarnate love reveals God as self-giving, self-emptying, self-limiting, kenotic.

In the incarnation, therefore, God chooses to freely limit himself even further for our sakes. The incarnation is the completion of creation; it shows the extent to which God's creative love will go. He creates us and is with us, one of us. This is the reason why we can be assured of mercy, as the Epistle to the Hebrews states, when we find ourselves before the throne of grace (4:16). God knows what it is like to live the human life. We can be assured that we can count on his mercy when we stand before him.

Greater love than this no one can have than to choose freely to open his own future to a dependency upon us, to choose freely to share his freedom with us, and to choose to become totally one of us, confined within the human condition. The incarnation is the second stage of grace, the second revelatory act of God. It reveals that God is love and the extent to which that love is who he is. Greater love than this no one can have.

God's Redemptive Love

I have stated that there could not be a love greater than the love revealed by creation in which God calls others than himself into being in order to share his divine life and limits himself out of love for us. Yet greater love than this is the Lord; he not only chose to create but to share his life fully by sharing our life fully. He not only created us; he became one of us. His love was never only from the outside; it took on flesh and blood. Greater love than this there could not be. Yet greater love than this is the love of the Lord! God's love overflows into redemption. The redemptive activity of God shows the extent to which his incarnate and creative presence will go. He is not only with us; he is for us. There is no limit which he places on his love. He limits himself for our sake but never limits his love. Precisely because of the fullness of his love, He freely chooses self-limitation in order to be for the other. Thus the Lord does not simply choose to participate in human life but chooses to share in the struggle of human existence and the confinement of the human condition even if this means a love unto death. There is no limit to the extent to which he is willing to identify with the human condition for our sake. Jesus suffers and dies as well.

To speak of incarnative and redemptive love is to speak of Jesus of Nazareth, the historical man who lived and walked and preached in our midst. One significant aspect of the life story of this man is that it came to be interpreted as atoning for our history of irresponsibility, thus reconciling us to his Father by making us justified in his sight. An appropriate question, however, is how the life of one man could do that. How could the life and death of one person make up for the history of the sin of all people? How could the history of one overcome the history of all? In trying to understand this, we can learn to appreciate what it means to have been justified by Christ and to have been reconciled to the Father.

The book of Genesis gives us a context by which we can more easily understand what is being said in this interpretation of the life and death of Jesus as an atonement.

> The men left there and went to Sodom while Abraham remained standing before Yahweh. Approaching him he said, "Are you really going to destroy the just man with the sinner? Perhaps there are fifty just men in the town. Will you really overwhelm them, will you not spare the place for the fifty just men in it? Do not think of doing such a thing: to kill the just man with the sinner, treating just and sinner alike! Do not think of it! Will the judge of the whole earth not administer justice?" Yahweh replied, "If at Sodom I find fifty just men in the town, I will spare the whole place because of them."
>
> Abraham replied, "I am bold indeed to speak like this to my Lord, I who am dust and ashes. But perhaps the fifty just men lack five: will you destroy the whole city for five?" "No," he replied, "I will not destroy it if I find forty-five just men there." Again Abraham said to him, "Perhaps there will only be forty there." "I will not do it," he replied, "for the sake of the forty."
>
> Abraham said, "I trust my Lord will not be angry, but give me leave to speak: perhaps there will only be thirty there." "I will not do it," he replied, "if I find thirty there." He said, "I am bold indeed to speak like this, but perhaps there will only be twenty there." "I will not destroy it," he replied, "for the sake of the twenty." He said, "I trust my Lord will not be angry if I speak once more: perhaps there will only be ten." "I will not destroy it," he replied, "for the sake of the ten" (18:22-32).

This passage can be used in a spiritual sense to prefigure what occurred later in salvation history and can help us to understand the life of Jesus himself. Understanding Jesus helps us to understand the justice and mercy and hence the love of God as well. What is being revealed here is that the justice of God is different from the justice of human beings. Here we see Abraham bargaining for the people. If there are fifty just people, will the Lord save the city? If there are forty-five, or thirty, or ten, will he? One can carry this account to its logical conclusion and hear God saying that he will not destroy the city if there is one just person. For the sake of the one, he will save the many.

This justice of God is unlike our own. Our tendency is to punish the many in order that a guilty one might not escape. Divine justice is willing to set free the many in order that the innocent one might not be punished. We, of course, would take no such chances. Incomprehensible though this may sound, divine justice is, in fact, mercy. It is incomprehensible to us because of our sense of justice, yet divine justice requires treating all as if they were innocent—that is, if there is any one at all innocent. Jesus of Nazareth is the fulfillment of this Old Testament story. God will save the entire city if there is one good man. God will save all of human history, all people, if there is but one good person. But there has been and is one good person, namely Jesus of Nazareth. Because of the goodness of this one, we are all saved, all pleasing in the sight of the Lord.

This is behind Paul's attempt to articulate this mystery to the Romans. Just as through one man sin entered the world, so through one man we have all been reconciled to God. Jesus of Nazareth was good, holy, just and righteous. Because of the goodness and righteousness of this man, we are not separated from God.

The goodness of that one man makes us pleasing in the Lord's sight, justifies us before our creator, makes up for the entire history of human sinfulness.

And it is not as if this relationship between Jesus and ourselves is simply an extrinsic one. It is not as if God simply forgets or forgives because one man has succeeded. As head of our body, Jesus of Nazareth is intrinsically related to who we are. The organic solidarity which exists between Jesus and all of us can never be severed. We are in Christ and he is in us. Thus mankind itself is good because this one man is good. God does not simply overlook the faults of the rest of human history. God realizes that human history is also good as it has come to be manifest, exemplified and completed in the life and death of this one. Because of this man human history has been intrinsically justified, from within. God's justice is mercy and his mercy is love. His justice is love in the sense that he does not treat us according to what we deserve but according to how we as a human, organic, solidified people have come to respond to him together. He does not punish us for our faults. He saves us because of our goodness.

In Jesus of Nazareth, however, we not only have the goodness of one who repairs the irresponsibility of human history by bringing us into relationship with God. Jesus of Nazareth also witnesses to the degree to which he himself, as God's Son, is willing to go personally in order to accomplish what he accomplishes, in order to be faithful to his own self and his own call. The life and ministry and death of Jesus is constantly seen as one of obedience to the Father. The life of Jesus is a life of obedience, a life understood in terms of its relationship to the Father. Jesus is one whose prayer is always to the Father whose Kingdom he preaches, one whose entire life is seen *ad patrem*. Jesus is not only a good person, he is an obedient person and his obedience is always a surrender to the Father.

Jesus' obedience points to the extent to which the love of Jesus will go. He is obedient even unto death. He does not falter in the mission for which he has been sent, the ministry to which he has given himself, the love which he longs to reveal. That love leads to his death, but there is no holding back in his revealing the love of a Father for his people, a love that he has come to understand through his own relationship with the Father. Jesus is a man who struggled to be righteous in the midst of a sinful world and was faithful to that struggle and obedient to his Father, not counting the cost.

In seeing the extent to which Jesus is willing to go, the love of the Lord takes on flesh, becomes incarnate, is revealed and made apparent once and for all. The Father is indeed love. The degree to which he cares! He cares actively and passionately. The cross reveals to us that God himself is willing to open himself to suffering that his life might be fully shared. The way and the degree in which the Lord suffers is not something to explore here. Yet the suffering of Christ and the meaning of the cross help us to appreciate that God is revealing to us how he patiently awaits our response. Love freely chooses to suffer—not manipulative self-pity—for Jesus' suffering is self-limitation *for our sakes*.

The suffering that is inevitably part of human life and thus is inevitably part of the life of Christ as he chooses to share in the human condition is inevitably a part of the life of God himself as he chooses to make our story his story.[4] Suffering need not be self-defeating; it can be potential energy. God longs to reveal to us that he is not only with us but that he is for us as well. We have every reason to hope that even suffering can be utilized for creative advantage, that it can transform us and our sinful world, that death can give birth to new life, and that the dead can be raised. God is willing to suffer that we might live. His love is redemptive. This means that it is active, counteracting the power of evil, turning evil into good whenever it can.

The faith, hope and love of Jesus reveal the degree to which the Father can be trusted, the degree to which the Father can be the basis for our hope, the degree to which the Father is love. The story of God which is revealed in the story of the Hebrew people as well as in creation as a whole is a love story, the story of the extent to which love is willing to go, the limitations which love is willing to choose, the degree to which love is willing to define itself with reference to the other. The story of God eventually includes the story of Jesus. Our God is the God and Father of Jesus of Nazareth. Our God would not be our God apart from Jesus, for our God is always Jesus' God and Jesus is always Son of God. To know the Father is to know the Son and to know the Son is to know the Father.

To get caught up in the story of Jesus, however, is to find ourself caught in the story of the Son of God, in the story of God himself which is to realize that one's own life is now enmeshed in the most tremendous love story that has ever been. There was no way in which God could communicate to his creatures the extent of his love more appropriately than to be completely and unconditionally with us and for us. Just as God's creative act already manifested his inner life, so his incarnative act was the second manifestation of the drama of grace. His redemptive suffering also reveals the extent to which he is willing to identify himself with our plight. This is the third revelatory act of God as grace. Love is *agape* but an *agape* that longs for a reciprocity without which it will not be complete but without which it is willing to live for our sakes. God's love may forever be unreciprocated on our parts—but that is love, the willingness to risk one's own self.

God's Transforming Love

We call into play a number of adjectives to describe divine love. The Father's love is *creative, free,* and sustained in an *everlasting* way. His creativity, freedom, and everlasting fidelity describe who he is and his way of loving. We can also see God's love as *effective* insofar as it recreates and transforms those whom he loves. Divine love is a transforming love; it changes those who are called into a relationship with God as they are given the capacity to love God in return.

The beginning of our inquiry into the love of God revealed, in his free decision to create, a love greater than anything we could imagine. God's free decision to allow his divine nature to become incarnate revealed even more of his love. Meditation on the meaning of the incarnation, however, leads us to the degree to which God is willing to be with us. Over and over again we find ourselves saying with surprise that greater love than this there could not be and yet greater love than this there always is. Thus we are surprised, after the redemptive activity of his Son, that the love of God does not cease. God not only shares his Son with us; he shares the Spirit as well. As we begin to talk about the effectiveness of divine love, our own transformation, the story of God leads us into the story of the Holy Spirit.

If we could pursue the story of Jesus further, we would not only grow in our appreciation of the significance of the totality of his life, of his total involvement with history, of his willingness to remain obedient to the call of the Father as it was actively manifested in his own life and experience, but we would come to the death and resurrection of Jesus and the experience in which the Son sends us another advocate, the Spirit. This sending of the divine advocate is, in many ways, the culminating event in the story of Jesus. The meaning of the resurrection and ascension points out that divine love does not cease with the death of the historical Jesus. That story which Jesus himself embodied continues as Jesus is raised, is still present to us as risen Lord, is still with us in the presence of his Spirit, is still with us because of the gift of the Spirit which he both promised and sent. The story of divine love involves now not only a christology but a pneumatology as well. Christ and his Spirit are inseparable from the story of God's self-revelation.

In many ways we are familiar with this story; in other ways we are quite unfamiliar with it. Too often this story remains at the level of the God story rather than at the level of *our* story, at the level of our experience. That which Jesus left incomplete becomes completed in the activity of the divine Spirit, the holy breath.[5] It is through the power of the Spirit that we ourselves finally become temples of the Holy Spirit, temples of the triune God. We are drawn into the indwelling, sanctifying and transforming love of the Father. The story of the Spirit tells us that God re-

mains with us; he never leaves. He never departs. We
are never alone, even in the midst of felt absence. With
the coming of the Spirit we realize the magnificence
of the divine gift.

God gave us himself in the incarnation of his son.
God continues to give us himself through the presence
of his Spirit. God also sends with the Spirit the manifold gifts that the Spirit brings. The risen Christ continues to be with us as well within the Eucharistic
activity of his people. Divine transcendence and divine
omnipresence become fully revealed even if not fully
grasped. We gradually and hesitantly become aware
of what God is telling us: there is no limit to the extent to which he is willing to go because he is our God
and we are his people. We begin to realize that there is
no end to his love for us. Finally we get the point.
There is no end, no limit, to the degree to which he is
willing to limit himself for our sakes. There is no
limit to God's love. It is unbounded, unlimited, without end, lasting forever, inexhaustible. We are caught
up in the mystery of that which is both immanent and
transcendent, the mystery of a love so immanent because it is love and reaches the depths and recesses of
the most intimate aspects of our lives. It seeps into
every nook and cranny of our being; it cuts more finely
than any two-edged sword. Divine love permeates who
we are, and at the same time that it permeates us it is
more than who we are. It is like nothing else which
we have experienced. It is inexhaustible. It is communicable but incomprehensible. All we can say, standing
in awe at the mystery which has been revealed to us,
is that we are loved, we are loved by a powerful love,
a power beyond all power. We stand in awe before

the mystery of love, before one whose very nature is to love, whose perfection exists in the ability to love, whose infinitude points only to the unlimited capacity to love. We find ourselves embraced, grasped, by what we had hoped to fathom and control.

We are willing finally to let ourselves be, to accept our inability to define God, for to define would be to confine and that is precisely who and what God is not. He is the One who cannot be defined because he is the One who cannot be confined; he is the One without *finis*, without limit, the undefinable and unlimited One. Yet we long to express the meaning of this mystery in the grips of which we find ourselves, the meaning which has now so impressed itself upon us, the meaning apart from which there can be no understanding. Therefore, we go on describing divine love for ever and ever.

Divine love is unfathomable mystery, unlimited self-limitation, free grace and gracious freedom, sustained promises, surprisingly creative and creatively surprising, an effective and transforming power, the power of transformation itself. This is the power of God and this is the power which has been given to us. This is the power in which we share and participate as we are called to share the divine life.

The Holy Spirit has the capacity to transform us. We are gods by grace, gods by participation, not gods by nature but created gods, human beings finally having achieved that to which we are called through grace, human beings in union with their Maker, the Lover, the Father.[6] We have been transformed into being lovers in return. This process of personal transformation, however, is still incomplete. We find in our experience that we are not yet fully who we are called to be; we have not yet owned the fact that we too are divine. God shares completely and everlastingly the fullness of His life with us. He is the only One who is totally for others, whose very being is being for others.

Chapter Eight

THE MISSION OF JESUS

Jesus of Nazareth, as we discovered in the previous chapter, is the supreme self-communication and self-revelation, the supreme Word of the Father. He is the Word Incarnate. As we look at that Word in history, we ask ourselves why that Word was spoken to us. What was the mission on which Jesus was sent?

We are not considering here the consciousness of Jesus as a christological problem, but we must consider the consciousness of Jesus of Nazareth in a specific way as mission consciousness, a consciousness of being sent for the sake of service or ministry.[1] This consciousness of mission is manifested early in his life when Jesus chooses to leave his home to receive the baptism of his cousin John, after a number of years of living in Nazareth, long beyond what would generally be considered the marriageable age for Jewish men. It is in the religious experience of his own baptism that he becomes more clearly aware that he has been called by the Father to play a special role in the history of God's people. He has been called; he has been chosen. His consciousness is one of vocation, and one's vocation is always mission.

Once we realize the call, the question arises: where are we to go? Leaving Nazareth, receiving the baptism of John, experiencing the presence of his Father, all deepened the conviction of vocation and mission within Jesus. As the Scriptures develop the story, Jesus goes to the wilderness for at least forty days in order to sort through the meaning of that call, to clarify his mission for himself. In this ordeal he surrenders to the Father.[2] The words which sum up his life point out the thrust of his whole life as well, "Not my will, but thine be done."

Within the wilderness experience (which need not be seen as a geographical location), a second dimension in the consciousness of Jesus manifests itself strongly, namely that of prayer. Just as vocation (*having been called*), mission (*having been sent*), and ministry (*going*) all sum up the first pole within the rhythm of the life of Jesus, so his turning to the Father provides the other pole in terms of which we can understand how he understood himself. Alone in the wilderness, in the midst of temptation, opening himself to the Father, placing himself at his service, Jesus turns to his Father and places himself completely in his hands.

Jesus' prayer is the ultimate source of his consciousness of mission. To understand Jesus of Nazareth, we need to understand not only the culture or milieu of which he was a part but also the life which his Father shared with him. Jesus' life comes from the Father as he senses vocation and mission, and his life is referred to the Father as he surrenders himself in constant prayer and fasting. The prayer of Jesus had been all along the source for his sense of vocation, for his sense of mission, and it provides the ultimate source for the direction which he will pursue faithfully through life, always returning to his Father for guidance and for direction as he continues to understand more and more deeply the full sense of the mission on which he had been sent, to which he had been called.

For the Christian, putting on Christ means putting on the consciousness of Christ, which is always *ad*

Patrem. Christ can only be understood in relationship to the Father, the referent in terms of which he is defined is always the Father. In his prayer, Jesus comes ultimately to the awareness of who he is, namely Son. This relationship defined Jesus of Nazareth. Jesus of Nazareth relationally understood, relationally defined, is that particular relationship, sonship, to which he invites us as well.

Jesus then always understood himself in relationship to the Father as the Father's person, the Father's man, the one called by the Father, the one sent by the Father, the one whose whole life is lived in service to the will of the Father, whose will was that he go forth and minister to his Father's people. In that sense, then, ministry and prayer provide the two poles in terms of which the consciousness of Jesus develops. His is to be a life of ministry and a life of prayer and it is the notion of vocation or mission which mediates these two poles. His vocation is always from the Father. His mission is always one on which the Father sends him. But that vocation and that mission send him to the people, to God's chosen people, to his beloved people, into ministry. Vocation and mission mediate prayer and ministry as the two poles in terms of which Christ's consciousness developed and they permeate our consciousness as well. To live in Christ is to see the totality of our existence *ad Patrem,* as mediated between prayer and ministry, which mediation is effected by a sense of vocation and mission. The rhythm flows forth from prayer (existence *ad Patrem*) to vocation to mission to ministry (existence *ad alios*) and back again.

In his experience of the Baptism and in his ordeal in the wilderness, Jesus allows himself to be defined by the Father, to be defined as one whose life comes from the Father and whose life is to be given, according to the will of his Father, to others. This consciousness can be further described in terms of prophecy, eschatology, and servanthood.

During the years within which Jesus lived at home in Nazareth, he studied and prayed the Hebrew Scriptures. He allowed those Scriptures, God's Word, to permeate him and to become part of him. There is no question that the early consciousness of Jesus as he came out of the wilderness was prophetic. He saw himself like the prophets of old, in an even more final way than the prophets of old but still within a prophetic role, having experienced a prophetic call and possibly sensing a prophetic destiny. He was called to preach. This was the mission of the prophet and this was the mission on which Jesus was sent as well. Jesus was called to preach, to preach the coming Reign of the Father, and to give witness to the universal and generous character of that Reign, having come to the realization in the wilderness experience that his Father was life, generosity, grace, and that there were no limits which could be placed upon the extent to which the Father's love would go. Even sin could not bar one from that Kingdom. Only self-righteousness could possibly exclude anyone, and that is self-exclusion, never the exclusion willed by the Father.

His Father's Kingdom is a universal Reign into which all are invited and into which all are welcomed. In the midst of his own prayer in the wilderness Jesus discovered this insight which contributed to his uniqueness, his understanding of God as Father, the new image of God with which he came out of the wilderness: God is unlimited love. It was this which drove him, which he preached, and which eventually got him into trouble. It is a message too preposterous to bear, yet it was the message which shaped the life of Jesus of Nazareth, a prophetic message because it is being spoken on behalf of God, because it is God's Word, and is preached to God's people, because it is a word in terms of which judgment will come. Judgment, however, is now pronounced upon self-righteousness, rather than the failure to observe the Law.

Christ's prophetic consciousness led him not only to preach but to live the message which he was called to proclaim. In fact, it was his life, his action, which preached the Word, and destined him for rejection and assassination: his open traffic with sinners and those in disreputable professions, his willingness to associate with the outcasts of society which then included all those who had been cast out and rejected by the religious establishment. He refused to accept the human barriers which had been constructed in the midst of God's people, which defined those people in terms of the righteous and the sinful, "us and them." It was this false barrier which the life of Jesus threatened and a barrier on which so much of established religion had been built. Jesus' life was an attack on the very character of religion itself as it was then preached and known by many. There were not two divisions within the human family, the righteous and sinful. There was only one group of people; all were sinners. Yet, all had been saved, not because of their sin or lack of sin, but only because of the nature of God himself, that God is love. In the midst of these sinful people, however, some twisted the doctrine so as to be able to speak in terms of their own righteousness. Thus, there were the sinners and the self-righteous. All were sinners, all were loved, but those labeled as sinners were the beloved of the Father because they could hear his Word, a Word which the self-righteous would never hear. Jesus was opposed to a particular current within first century Pharisaism, which was not necessarily the perspective of every Pharisee or scribe or devout Jew. Yet this current was not able to tolerate the threat that Jesus was.

The tables had been turned; those who were righteous would not be saved, those who were sinful would be saved. What a scandal manifested itself. This "scandal" became incarnate in the very life of Jesus of Nazareth as he associated with sinners, went to parties with gluttons, refused to condemn the adulteress and made friends with the prostitute. He risked his own reputation because he had his own source of inner strength, the Father's love. The prophetic consciousness of Jesus was not only a preached word but an incarnate word, a word which he put into effect within his own life. It was that incarnational preaching which made the point so strongly, so effectively, that it meant in effect that those who stood for another interpretation, whose image of God was different, would have to get rid of him eventually. There was no way in which this new word could be tolerated.

The consciousness of Jesus, however, was not simply prophetic as the classical prophets of the 8th and 7th centuries before him had been. In this period of Judaism, his consciousness could not escape being eschatological as well, pointing toward the future and seeing his message in the light of a more definitive reality: the coming Reign of the Father which was close at hand. In that sense, the consciousness of Jesus was the consciousness of the coming Reign of God. Jesus did not attempt to understand himself in terms of traditional roles. His consciousness was permeated by that coming Reign for the sake of which he lived his life, a Reign understood as gathering together the two poles in the consciousness of Jesus to which we have already referred, the Father and the Father's people. The Reign would bring these together. The Father would be all in all.

This eschatological consciousness continued to develop within the ministry of Jesus as he saw that ministry first as one to the house of Israel alone. He gradually realized that he had been sent not only to the lost sheep of the house of Israel but to all nations and all peoples. This eschatological consciousness manifested itself as the prophetic consciousness did in a twofold way. As the prophetic consciousness led Jesus to proclaim the word and also to make that word incarnate, so his eschatological consciousness led him to an inner freedom and an inner expectation. *Freedom* and *expectation* provided the poles in terms of which his eschatology developed.

Expectation in Jesus' developing eschatology meant that the coming Reign was not yet here. It was something for which he still had to wait, anticipate it insofar as he could, hope for it and pray for it. He could not, however, establish it definitely once and for all through his own power. Jesus waited for the Father. He waited in the midst of his prayer that the Kingdom might come, prayer which led to the expectation that the Kingdom was not far off.

Freedom was part of Jesus' developing eschatology insofar as he could let the Father be, let the Father decide when all was to be accomplished. This inner detachment or freedom allowed Jesus to gradually realize that his own prophetic role would not be that role alone in terms of which the Reign of God would come. He could let God be God and thus manifest that love is a question of being present, being at the service of the other, and letting the other be. It takes interior freedom to let the other be free as well. Our own selfishness limits our ability to respect the freedom of the other; our own self-centeredness limits our capacity to let others be. The love of Jesus, however, was not only a desire for union but a desire based upon mutual freedom. This inner freedom did not demand that the Kingdom come. Jesus' eschatology, so influenced by apocalyptic thought of his day, deviated from that thought precisely at this point—for no one knows the day or the hour except the Father, not even the Son. This lack of knowledge on the part of Jesus himself required a tremendous detachment, freedom, and surrender to live his whole life in terms of that coming Kingdom and yet to let that Kingdom be in his Father's hands.

It is this freedom which allowed the Reign to break in within the life of Jesus himself. To demand that we bring on the Kingdom, that we build the Kingdom, is precisely that which can prevent the coming of the Kingdom. Yet, the Kingdom does come through us and is built through us if we let God be God and if we let God act in us. It is not we who determine God's activity but God's activity which determines us. Jesus' eschatological consciousness, in terms of which he lived for the sake of the Father's Reign, led him to wait in prayer for his Father and in ministry to allow his Father's Reign to break through in his own life so that the signs of that life were already present. Signs could only be manifest insofar as Jesus allowed himself to be a channel of divine love, an incarnation of his Father's love. Again, Jesus' eschatology is *ad patrem* and *ad alios*. He continued to live for the sake of others in accord with his Father's will, constantly hoping for the coming of that Kingdom which he could leave in his Father's hands—even if it meant not seeing it in his own lifetime and even if it meant his own death.

Ad patrem, but also, *ad alios.* This second phrase is equally important in understanding Jesus of Nazareth, for his prophetic and eschatological awareness by which he allowed the Father to be God led him to a sonship which was servanthood. It eventually meant that he, as son of the Father, would be the servant of the Lord. This developing prophetic consciousness led him to realize more and more that his mission would involve suffering and rejection. His understanding of the servant tradition could have helped him to solidify his own awareness as his preaching began to reflect more and more a realization that the eschatological figure would in fact suffer and die. It is clear that Jesus saw himself as one totally for others; not only was he God's man, but he was—and is—man for others. He was the Father's son who was called to give up his life for others. It was only the interior freedom which became perfected within Jesus that allowed him to assume the fullness of this concept of servanthood. Yes, Jesus means freedom.[3] Jesus also means servant. This servanthood meant a willingness to eventually set aside any clinging to his own particular eschatological perspectives and set aside all consciousness of self as well as any fear about what his message would lead to in terms of his own personal future. His life was at that point completely in the Father's hands. He trusted the Father. The Father would some day raise him from the dead. In the meantime, however, his life was to do the will of his Father. This meant that he live for the sake of others. His servanthood meant that the revelation of the Father's love would be complete.

In his role as servant Jesus shows us the power of *freely chosen self-limitation*. As servant, Jesus most visibly exemplifies his Father's love. The love of the Father became incarnate. It is now complete. Jesus is now Lord, and as soon as he was raised from the dead, he was proclaimed Lord, mediator between heaven and earth. Yet this Lordship, which was his by nature, to which he had a right, was never something to which he clung. The Epistles to the Hebrews and to the Philippians both indicate that the Lordship of Christ was— and is—his servanthood. His Lordship was one of service and not status. He did not consider status something to be clung to, as the author of the Epistle to the Philippians states (2:6-11). Nor was his Lordship, or his priesthood, one of dignity in the ordinary ways of the world. It was not one of status, not one of prestige, not one which one welcomes, which one longs to put on. It was one of humiliation and kenosis, self-limitation, servanthood. As the author of the Epistle to the Hebrews states, "this is how we know that we shall receive mercy when we stand before the throne of grace, for the Lord knows what it is like to live the life to which we have been called" (4:16).

Jesus so totally immersed himself within our condition as to experience with us what it means to be human. The dignity of human life most manifests itself in the vocation to service and servanthood. It was this for which Jesus was highly exalted. It was this which gave him the name above every name. He is indeed the servant of servants. This was a new Lordship, a new priesthood, not like the ones of old. It is

DONALD GOERGEN

one which comes from total self-surrender and total willingness to die, one which does not count the cost.

Traditionally, Jesus has been described as prophet, priest and king. This threefold way of understanding the mission of Jesus can be helpful if properly understood. Too often, however, we apply our preconceptions about prophecy, priesthood and kingship to Jesus and then interpret him in the light of these preconceived notions, rather than allowing his life and death and resurrection to determine the content of these concepts for us. With Jesus of Nazareth no preconception about prophet, priest, or king was operative. Only the Father determined the new meaning of these roles into which his son was sent.

To be prophet is to preach the Word and to allow that Word to become incarnate in such a way that we do not shape the Word but the Word shapes us. To be prophet is to be God's Word for God's people. It is to be God's Word Incarnate.

To be priest is to be servant, to be first only because we are willing to be last, to be strong only because we are willing to be weak, to live our total life as generosity, the generosity that the Father himself is, to live our total life for the sake of others, to choose freely to limit ourselves in order to be totally defined as being for others. Self-limitation is chosen so that self-definition might come from being for others alone. To be priest is to be the servant of all, to choose to be with and for all, to be at the service of the Father that we might be placed at the service of his people, at the service of his world, at the service of his Reign, so that his Reign might indeed break in. The high priesthood of Christ is the complete servanthood which was manifest by the incarnation. The servanthood of Jesus was symbolically acted out as the Lord of heaven and earth washed the feet of his disciples at their last banquet together. His Lordship is not status; his priesthood is *diakonia.*

His kingship is that eschatological consciousness in terms of which messiahship had come to be understood. At one time in Israel's history, "messiah" meant anyone anointed by the Lord to act on behalf of the Lord for the people. This notion of messiah, however, gradually became an eschatological notion and referred to the one who was to come, the one who eventually would be anointed to restore Israel and to save the people.[4] This eschatological expectation manifested itself in a wide variety of ways: as a longing for the political messiah from the house of David, or a prophet like Moses, or one like a son of man to descend on the clouds of heaven, the expectation that Elijah would return, that Michael would blow his trumpet. Jesus' kingship merely means that he was the one whom the Father sent, that no fuller revelation can now be made manifest, for all had been revealed—namely that the Father is love. There is no other word that can be spoken, other than the word that Jesus of Nazareth is. Jesus as king, as God's anointed one, as the messiah, as the eschatological figure, means that Jesus is not only proclaimer of the Word, servant of the people, but the final mediator of the Father. He is the one in whom and through whom and for whom we can now live so that we too might be completely *ad patrem* and *ad alios.* Jesus' kingship is not one of power in the coercive sense but one whose power is the power of love.

It is in the good news of the mission of Jesus that the love of God is totally revealed. It is in the missionary gospel and the mystery of that mission that revelation takes place. Jesus' love is the same as the Father's love, and the Father's love is divine. Jesus and the Father share the same nature. Jesus is love and we realize that his love is an unlimited self-limitation for our sakes. How does this, however, relate to the previous loves of which we have spoken, in terms of which we model our lives, and which we saw as gifts of the Holy Spirit?

In all that we have said, Jesus remains the supreme model of self-esteem or of a love of self which is central to the Hebrew tradition. It was only in accepting himself that Jesus could accept his mission. Only in accepting himself could he accept that he had been called. An inability to own himself would have been detrimental to his sense of vocation and his sense of mission. It was only because he loved himself that he was able to accept the unconditional and total love of the Father. The importance of self-love is not to center us on ourselves alone. It is precisely to excentrate ourselves to love others and supercentrate ourselves to love God.[5] As Teilhard de Chardin says, before one can be for others, one must first of all be. We must have a sense of self to be a self for others, to surrender ourselves to the Father. Jesus loved himself and thus was able to accept the Father's love for him, was able to accept the mission on which he was sent, and eventually able to persevere in that mission even unto death. It was because Jesus loved himself that he was able to die for others. Those who are not able to give completely to others are not yet able to love themselves. A life of total service then does not rule out or make inferior the value of self-esteem. Jesus valued self, his own self, or there would have been no way for him to accept the role to which he had been called. He could not have allowed himself to be Son, to be servant, if he had not first accepted who he was.

Jesus not only manifested self-acceptance, he also manifested fidelity to friends. Just as self-esteem played a role in the life of Jesus, so did friendship. In fact, the *ad alios* includes *philia*. Jesus loved friends with a special love, and his mission did not exclude loving them in a particular way because he was called to love all in a universal way. Love never excludes love. *Diakonia* will never exclude *philia*. Jesus not only models self-love and love of friendship but also fellowship or community. He created community; he saw himself as brother. He leaves healed rather than broken relationships behind him. He reaches out to all. He creates *koinonia*. Through him we all become one. Because he reaches out to all of us, we become brothers and sisters. The *ad alios* includes not only *philia* but also *koinonia*. Jesus' life was for others, for friends, for all his brothers and sisters who are called into relationship and sonship with the Father, to all those who are in need. Thus Jesus is a model of *philia, koinonia* and *diakonia,* all manifestations of love of others, the others in terms of which Jesus understood his life, the others to whom he had been sent, the others who were his Father's children, whom he invites into a relationship with him so that they too might be one with the Father. Thus love of self, love of others, and love of the Father all took on flesh in the life of Jesus. These three foci in terms of which love can be understood are the poles in terms of which Jesus of Nazareth reveals to us the meaning of love.

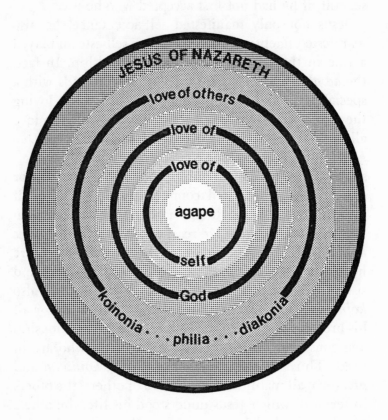

These three poles of self, others and the Father are the starting points in terms of which we can understand Jesus of Nazareth. The more deeply Jesus became self-aware, the more un-self-conscious he became. This is why the entire question of the consciousness of Jesus can sometimes be wrongly posed. Jesus did not think of himself; he thought only of his Father and his Father's Reign and the people to whom he had been sent. Jesus' consciousness was not self-consciousness but consciousness of others. This does not mean that Jesus' self-esteem is not one pole in terms of which he needs to be understood. It simply means that his self was so strong that he could let go of it and not be preoccupied with it. His source of life was so strong that he could let go of his life for the sake of others. Jesus knew himself, he knew himself to be the Father's son. But the three poles of consciousness dissolved themselves into two, love of others and love of the Father, as Jesus saw more and more who he was: one called by the Father for the sake of others. Jesus is the supreme example of the one who lets go of himself in order to become himself, the one of final mediation between the Father and us.

Jesus then is a man who is most truly himself, and at the same time most completely for the Father, and yet becomes the one for others. This is indeed revelation par excellence. This is also who the Father is. The Father is the one for others. Love is *being for others*. Jesus is being for others. This kind of being, being for others, is the kind of being that God is, the kind of being which we are to become, and which is incarnate in Jesus of Nazareth. *Philia, koinonia* and *diakonia* are all manifestations of this being for others. Yet, *diakonia* most clearly shows the extent

to which each of these loves can and will go. *Philia,* a
supreme exemplification of love, manifests most clearly
the kind of love that God is when it is for another and
not only for ourselves alone. Likewise, *koinonia* is most
a manifestation of the kind of love that God is when
we are for one another and not for ourselves alone.
Thus, *diakonia* has the power to speak very clearly
that love is being for others. Jesus' own self-consciousness led him to summarize the Law as love of neighbor
and love of God, although his love of neighbor always
included loving our neighbor as ourselves. These three
poles which get focused on the two poles eventually
become focused on *diakonia* as that which speaks the
Gospel message most strongly because diakonia most
clearly points to the degree which love is able to go.

Although we are not considering love of enemies as
a distinguishable love, we should realize that such love
is not so much another kind of love but points to the
extent to which love of neighbor will go. It is in love
of enemies that being for others most clearly manifests itself. This does not make any of the five loves
inferior to *diakonia;* it simply points out that love of
enemies clarifies the true character or shape or Christian dimension of all the loves, namely that love is
agape. Agape is the form that Christian love takes. *Agape*
is the kind of love that the Father is. *Agape* is the kind
of love that Jesus is. And *agape* is the kind of love that
the Spirit brings into our lives, the kind of love into
which we are molded in order that we might love even
as the Father loves. *Agape* then is Christian love, the
form of love, the shape of all the loves if they are truly
Christian. Love of self, friendship, community, ministry and prayer are all *agape.* They are all shaped by
the Spirit, all self-giving and all seen as being for

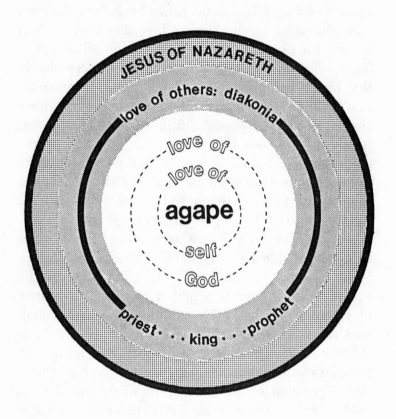

others. *Agape* is freely chosen self-limitation for the sake of others. Love is *agape*. *Agape* is the most powerful love. *Agape* is God and *agape* is in us.

Too frequently within the Christian tradition we attempt to distinguish *agape* and *eros,* setting these two loves over against each other, again in the manner of an "either/or" type of thinking. Here we do not define *agape* over against or exclusive of *eros.* The relationship between the two is something to which further consideration will be given in appendix 2. *Agape* is the soul of love, the heart of all the loves. God gives us himself, his very self, so that we too become gods. It is the divine life we share, the divine nature in which we participate. It is God, and it is in us. It is a creative, free, incarnative, redemptive, transforming being whose sole reality is existence for others; self-limitation for the sake of others. *Agape* is *kenosis*[6] and it is *kenosis* that is the form or soul of self-esteem, friendship, community, ministry, and prayer. All these are love, *kenosis, agape,* the Word of the Father, that which Jesus makes incarnate, that which the Spirit gives to each of us.

Chapter Nine

THE POWER OF THE SPIRIT

The Power of Sin

We cannot discuss the power of love without considering the power of sin as well, for sin and grace provide the context within which we understand and live our Christian lives. We often fail to see sin as a power in the way Paul did when he wrote, "What I want to do I do not do, and what I do not want to do I do" (Romans 7:15). Many times our experience is that it is now not we ourselves but sin within us that is responsible for who we are and what we do. We need to take seriously the character of sin because its effects are so manifest. In fact, from an empirical point of view, we would have to say that the power of sin seems more powerful than the power of love, for the effects of sin are so apparent—in diverse ways, prejudice, genocide, injustice, loneliness, and human suffering of every kind.

To understand sin appropriately it is helpful to distinguish between the concept of sin (in the singular) and sins (in the plural). We frequently begin a discussion of sin with a consideration of our own individual acts, which we or others judge to be immoral, and which we associate with personal guilt, at least if we have sufficient knowledge and sufficient freedom with respect to those acts. From a biblical point of view this is not, however, the starting point for a theology of sin.[1]

Rather we need to begin with a notion of sin in the singular. This means we must first consider the power of sin, a condition of sin, the sin of the world, a history of human irresponsibility which precedes all of our individual activities. Our first emphasis, then, must be placed upon sin as a reality which affects us rather than on sins which we commit. The notion of sin in the singular is a collective reality which preexists us, which manifests itself as a power in our lives and in our world, and is more closely associated with the traditional concept of original sin. It is, in fact, original sin as much as personal sin which is the focus of the Scriptures, although original sin is not so labeled in the Scriptures. Yet, even in our discussion of original sin, we often reduce it to the personal or actual sin of Adam. Traditionally, however, original sin was seen in a twofold way: *passive original sin,* or the so-called effects of sin, the human condition, and *active original sin,* the cause of the corrupted environment within which we find ourselves. Passive original sin should be our starting point.

Sin can be considered on four levels: victimization, internalization, manifestation, and ratification. Only the fourth and final stage refers to personal guilt. A discussion of sin should not be immediately associated with the theology of guilt.

The first aspect of sin is that you and I are victims. To face the reality of sin means to face the reality that we are victims of sin. This is the meaning behind much of the conceptualization of the sin which is with us from our origins. "Original sin" as an expression does not mean the original actual sin, the sin of Adam. Rather it refers to that sin which is with us *ab origine,* from the beginning, from our origins, that which is present in the world before we are born into the world. Sin in this sense refers more to the environment, to the world, into which we are born. The environment is corrupted, perverted, and consists of manifold forms of unfreedom, whether these be cultural, social or psychological.

From the moment of our conception, from the moment of our birth, we enter into a world which perpetuates corruption and evil. We are and will be the victims of that environment. This is not to say that the power of sin is the only reality present in our environment. God is also active in our environment and in the world. Grace is present there, too. Since the redemptive activity of God in Christ we can also talk about Christ's presence in the world. At the same time we cannot dismiss the fact that our environment is "full of evil" as well. The world of sin and the world of grace is the world into which we are born, and sin begins to do its work from the very first moments of an individual's conception. Thus to be a sinner means first to be affected by the sin of others. To be born into the world is to be a victim of the power of sin which is loose in the world.[2] Sin means victimization and a victimizing environment.

Sin does not remain, however, outside of us, within the environment alone. We are aware today of the close interdependence between person and environment. There is no way in which we develop apart from the culture, society, or world of which we are a part. Enculturation and socialization are facts of life. Thus victimization is almost immediately followed by internalization. The corruption that is outside us enters into us, flows into us and becomes part of us. This happens prior to any consciousness or ratification on our part.

This is not hard to understand. A good example of

how environment affects us is our becoming aware of linguistic differences such as accent between subgroups within a particular society. We move into a different environment where there is a different accent spoken and soon that accent begins to affect our speech as well. Environment inevitably is internalized and becomes a part of those people who enter into it.

Evil is a power in the face of which we are weak. It exercises a force. It infects the world, is contagious and overtakes us. We can see how we become sinners simply by our being born into the world. But we must realize that the first fact about our being sinners is that we are first of all victims. We are victimized and we too become sinners. Sin enters into the very makeup of who we are.

At this second level, however, it may not be immediately apparent that sin manifests itself in our thoughts or behavior. Yet it does not take long before that which has become internalized manifests itself externally. The corruption which became part of us through the process of internalization soon makes itself recognized. This third level is a level of actual sinning, although an actual sinning of which we are not wholly aware, an unconscious sinning, a sin which we might describe as the power of sin objectively making its destruction felt even prior to our being conscious of it or freely participating in it. In other words, there is much evil which we have done without our being aware of its extent. This is one of the effects of consciousness raising; we become aware of the evil which we have already perpetuated and of which we have not previously been aware prior to our consciousness being altered. Sin has a hold on the environment, enters into the very structure of our personality, and soon manifests itself within our own lives without our knowing the evil we do. Sin manifests itself in our lives even before we are responsible, before we are guilty.

This unconscious sinning, however, at some point in life enters into our awareness and is influenced by our freedom. Even after reaching a certain level of consciousness and with a certain degree of interior freedom, we still do not withdraw ourselves from the process of actual sinning, so great is the hold sin has on us. We continue to perpetuate it and we ratify what before manifested itself in an unconscious way. We now freely and consciously contribute to the vicious circle that sin is. We continue the process of corrupting our environment, our relationships, our world, and continue to perpetuate an atmosphere which will victimize us, others and those still to enter into our world. This level can most appropriately be described as personal or actual sin and is the level at which we must assume responsibility for the sin in our world.

Our fight against sin must be a fight against sin at all four of these levels. We begin with the last level first as we attempt to uproot our personal sinning; as we accept forgiveness which leads to conversion, as we proclaim and experience reconciliation, as we assume responsibility for what we do in an appropriate theological sense. This can then lead to changed behavior. At the same time, we refuse to involve ourselves in the complacency of psychological guilt which "atones" for sin without doing anything about it.

We cannot be satisfied, however, with assuming responsibility and attempting reconciliation. We must attack not only the conscious personal sinning in our lives but the unconscious sinning as well. There is no attack on sin which does not eventually move into consciousness-raising. To attack only the fourth level of sinfulness is treating the symptoms, but never attempting to cure the disease. Unless we eventually get to the very root of sin, it will continue to overpower us. Eventually we must attack the unconscious sinning through consciousness-raising. The more conscious we are, the easier it is to assume responsibility. One of the major effects of sin is precisely that it weakens our desire to assume responsibility. We will do almost anything rather than accept responsibility for what we do and who we are.

The Church, in its concern for preaching, must undertake an effort at consciousness-raising so that we become more and more deeply aware of the roots of our sinfulness. Eventually this consciousness-raising must enable us to see within ourselves the roots of that power which has planted itself in our lives. We can use as an image the example of a tree, a tree which can manifest life but which also can manifest death. Sin is like a tree which roots itself in the core of our interior being. Our attack must be not only on the fruit which that tree bears. The fruit is corrupt, but picking the corrupt fruit will in no way get us to the source of that corruption. Eventually the very roots of sin need to be destroyed. We need to become aware of the source of sinfulness in our lives so that we get to the roots of the power of sin rather than to its manifestations only.

In the end, however, no attack on sin will be successful unless it gets at the source of the victimization itself, to that first level in which we find corruption and perversion perpetuated within the environment. Eventually to strike out at sin is to strike at the economic, political and social conditions which are at the heart of the environment in which we find ourselves. To be concerned about sin, responsibility, reconciliation and offense against God without an attack on the exploitative, manipulative, depersonalizing and victimizing aspects of the world is to fail to take sin seriously. Too often moral theology deals only with sin as unethical acts rather than with the origins of sin and the sin of the world. Also, a faulty sacramental theology of reconciliation concerns itself only with sin at the surface level rather than with sin at its roots.

There are many ways in which we can talk about the mystery of sin, the power of sin, which is experienced in different ways by different people. Yet sin is very much associated with the notion of alienation. We can see that one of the effects of sin is that we ourselves become instruments of alienation rather than instruments of reconciliation and love. Alienation is an unhealthy and unacceptable form of distantiation. Alienation can manifest itself as self-alienation, as alienation from others or as alienation from God. We can even speak of an alienation from nature in the context of the ecological crisis.

Self-alienation is a process by which we become distanced from ourselves and develop two selves. The true self and the false self, the authentic self and pseudo self, the graced and the sinful selves, the healthy self-centered self and the selfish self. Self-alienation manifests itself as the refusal to grow, to become, to be on the move. It is a rejection of who we are. It is disowning parts of ourselves. It is also the refusal to accept and act with and through our own divinity. We too are called to be divine. The difference between Jesus of Nazareth and ourselves is not that he was divine and we are not. We too partake of the divine nature through grace. The refusal to acknowledge and accept our divinity, however, is one form that self-alienation takes.

When we are alienated from ourselves, without self-esteem, we create masked forms of self-worth. Then we not only refuse to love ourselves but we also refuse to love others. We find ourselves estranged from others. The other is alien, frightening, threatening, an enemy. We set up barriers: the in-group and the out-group, we and they, the touchable and the untouchable. Sometimes these barriers flow from false religion which leads to self-righteousness or from sexism, classism, racism, or nationalism—whatever enables us to bolster our own inner insecurity in the face of the others.

Just as self-alienation can exist on unconscious as well as conscious levels when we refuse to be in touch with ourselves, to own ourselves and to grow, so can estrangement from others. It manifests itself without our being conscious of what we are doing. We refuse to enter into the demands of interpersonal life or collective life. We act on the basis of fear within friendship; we withdraw from the demands of ministry; we are unwilling to create a world in which fellowship is possible. The other, rather than becoming a part of us, is seen precisely as other, totally other. The other is turned into enemy, thing, object, rather than person who participates in the very makeup of who we are.

But the forces of alienation affect our very relationship with God as well and this is when the tragedy of sin makes itself most manifest. We can point to the initial sense of distance between God and ourselves, our ignorance of God, the lack of experience we have of God, the numbers in the world who have never met

God, those who have never heard the message of Christ. Sin places distance between God and us, so much so that there are many who have never heard his name, many who have never heard him called by his *proper* name: Love. Even those who have heard have readily neglected their relationship with God and are unwilling to manifest dependence and vulnerability. They are unwilling to surrender to him.

We can see the effects of sin in the life of our world. It places obstacles before our capacity to love ourselves. It is the fundamental internal opposition to self-esteem. It is the force which prevents friendship from taking place as constantly and as frequently as God truly wants this gift for his people. It prevents the building of community and fellowship in our world. As a result people cannot become whole. They cannot reach out; they cannot love. It prevents us from being able to reach out to those in need and, rather than realizing that they, like us, are all victims of a reality which precedes us, we alienate them and cast them out. We then create a rationale for rejecting the outcasts rather than responding to them in love. Sin also prevents us from growing in our relationship with God and excuses us for leaving that relationship undeveloped. We take God for granted.

Sin is the enemy of love. It weakens our capacity to love. Sometimes it inflicts minor wounds but sometimes it can be more deadly. The one who seeks to grow in love, however, cannot be naive in dismissing this power of sin too quickly. Yet, neither can we become obsessed with the power of sin, for we realize in the Good News that the power of sin, as enormous as it is, has itself been weakened and will ultimately be destroyed.

Theology and Power

Some reflections on the nature of power itself are appropriate in this context. Christians too quickly think of power in a negative way. Power is not simply a destructive, negative reality in our lives. There is still too much manichaeism among Christians when they look at realities like sexuality, materiality, the world, and power—too much hesitancy and suspicion. We associate power too readily with force, the ability to get what we want or do what we want, having our own way. We associate all power with its destructive and unhealthy manifestations.

Power, finite power, as a part of creation, needs to be understood within the context of the goodness of creation. It is a gift which the Lord has given to us for our own good. In fact, God has not only given us finite powers but has also shared with us his own life, his own power, in which we participate. He has given us the gift of his Spirit and the power that his Spirit brings. Power for Christians is a good, positive, and necessary reality in life.

Another way of realizing the goodness within power is to explore the notion of the power of being itself. Paul Tillich, in *Courage To Be,* makes a point similar to one made by Rollo May in *Power and Innocence.* May talks about five different levels of power.[3] The first is simply the power to be, which is followed by the power to affirm and finally the power to assert self. There is a way in which the capacity to affirm oneself, the capacity to assert oneself, to stand out in the presence of others and be there either with or for them, all flow from whether or not we are willing to own the value of power. Being itself is a power. In classical philosophy being is good and being is already a manifestation of power. We cannot develop our capacity to love, whether that be the capacity to love ourselves or others, if we are totally unwilling to own the power to do so. Hence we need to realize that power is good.

Rollo May speaks about five kinds of power which we will enumerate here because they will help us to realize that power can manifest itself in both constructive and destructive modes. Rollo May speaks of exploitative, manipulative, competitive, nutritive, and integrative power.

Exploitation and manipulation are shallow, destructive forms of power, power which is more or less identified with force and manifested over and against another person. Exploitation and manipulation together could be conceived as coercive power, although this is not Rollo May's expression. Coercive power is the enemy of life in Christ, the misuse of what God gives us. Yet, power is not simply coercion.[4]

Competition, for Rollo May, is not necessarily either destructive or constructive. It can be either. Sometimes competition is destructive of human values or human persons and at other times it can provide motivation and zest for deepend life.

The two higher forms of power, however, point to the other side of the coin. Here we have forms of power which manifest themselves as being *for* others or *with* others. Nutritive power enables us to be for the other, such as the power which a parent has with respect to children, the power which comes from care for others, the power which manifests itself in teaching, in preaching, those helping professions where help is not seen paternalistically. Integrative power is shared power, power that comes from empowering others, as well as spiritual forms of power such as the power of love or the power of non-violence or the power of moral clarity. We can group these two manifestations together under the notion of the power of love. We can then see that there are two extremes in terms of which we can view power, the power of coercion and the power of love; we can also see how opposed these two manifestations are and that one is hostile to Christian life and the other at the very heart of Christian life. Power then is central to what it means to be a Christian.

Power can be a positive reality in Christian life. In fact, the power of love is that around which the Christian life organizes itself. Yet, we cannot be naive in our discussion of power, for we see quite apparent misuses in our world. We see the evil to which coercive manifestations of power can lead. Hence, while power is intrinsically good, it is existentially ambiguous, manifesting itself in both distorted and constructive ways. Sin in the world distorts power. The forms of power we frequently seek are not those which come from life in Christ. Not all that passes for power is good since many times that which passes for power enables us to define ourselves over and against others rather than in relationship to others and on behalf of others. We need to recognize both the good and the ambiguous aspects of power.

In this sense, at the same time that we develop a positive theology of power, we need to develop a capacity to be critical of the ways in which power manifests itself. We need to realize that power, while being a Christian value, is a relative value. It is not the summation of life. It does not provide the meaning and purpose for which life is lived. Yet it is a value which we can put at the service of our life in Christ. Just as sexual pleasure or the material world, as goods in themselves, can become demonic and overtake the human person in such a way that we pursue these alone and find our sources of meaning within them, so too the same can be said of power.[5] To seek power for its own sake is to begin gradually to distort the nature of what power is. When power, material comfort, sexual pleasure become ends in themselves, they become distorted. When they are put at the service of love, their beauty is manifest.

Relativized power helps us to realize that the sources of power available to us are meant to be at the service of other values such as faith, hope and love. Our critique of power should call to mind our need to develop noncoercive forms of courage and strength. This means realizing that control and self-sufficiency are not Christian values. In fact, life in Christ, as well as human relationality itself, means developing the capacity to let go, the capacity to let go of our need to be in control and to develop the interdependent mode of being rather than one which finds its satisfaction in self-sufficiency. At the same time, however, we cannot forget that power is a created good in itself, one which God wants for us in order that we might deepen our life. We all should be a power-seeking and power-hungry people—if, by power, we have the Christian concept of power in mind.

Power in itself is not evil and powerlessness is not good. As Christians, we need to confront this issue of power and powerlessness more and more. We need a theology of power beyond what is developed here. The insight of Rollo May provides a starting point, but we need to carry his psychological insights into theology.

How we integrate powerlessness into our lives is

crucial. Our ability to face our own limitations, our own weaknesses, our vulnerability will determine to a great degree whether we actualize coercive forms of power or Christian forms of power. As Christians, we recognize not only the value of power but the fact that we are not and never will be the only sources of power. By ourselves alone we will never be all-powerful. Often, however, there is a psychological striving for omnipotence. Again we can see the basic role that self-esteem plays in the Christian life. If, in fact, we are not by ourselves all-powerful, then we need to own the sources of power available to us as well as the powerlessness which will always be a part of who we are. We must recognize that we are both powerful and powerless, and we need to actualize our power, Christian power, at the same time that we accept our limitations, so that we might freely choose limitation for the sake of others.

Love as a freely chosen self-limitation begins to make sense when we develop an appropriate attitude towards weakness and vulnerability. Paul is enunciating common sense when he writes that, when he is weak, he is strong (2 Cor. 12:10). He is speaking neither a contradiction nor a paradox. He realizes that strength comes in the midst of weakness. A society based upon certain masculine value systems, and therefore a masculine understanding of power, which usually sees power in terms of domination and submission, has a hard time recognizing the power of vulnerability and the value of weakness. In a society built on the notion of maturity as self-sufficiency, weakness will always strike us as too feminine. Yet, unless we face powerlessness in a constructive way, it will do us a tremendous disservice. It will, as Rollo May says, break out in violence.

One of the more common destructive manifestations of unintegrated powerlessness within Christian men and women is the way in which we continue to perpetuate psychological guilt in others. Guilt is an important moral and theological reality. It is also healthy psychologically, if what we mean by guilt is an acceptance of responsibility. If by guilt, however, we mean feeling bad about ourselves, we are then talking not about moral responsibility but a destructive emotion. Many times, because we are unable to accept our own powerlessness, we strike out against others in a psychologically violent way. We lay our guilt on others.* This guilt flows from our own inability and limitedness which we have not yet accepted. We sometimes hear this when others call us to justice in the world. Once—and perhaps still—it was sexual guilt that was imposed from the pulpit. Now it is frequently "social" guilt. Christians are frustrated by their incapacity to create a just society because we have not yet owned our power and responsibility for a just society or accepted limitations and powerlessness within which we need to work to create a just society. We inflict on others the anger which flows from our inner frustrations and we make them feel guilty, although they are frequently as helpless as we are. This is a self-defeating, destructive, and an unhealthy manifestation of powerlessness. In it we can begin to see our need to face squarely the Christian meaning of power.

We are discussing power because we must realize that *love is a power,* that it partakes of the character of power, that it has strength. We should not shy away from the power that love is because power is good. If we continue to think of power negatively, what can we then say of the power of God, or the

THE POWER OF THE SPIRIT

power of the Spirit, or the power of love? Our image of God is important. Do we think of God as one who is coercive or caring? We see God as full of power, but if our image of power is coercive, we see God as coercive rather than loving. We begin to define our relationship with the Lord himself in terms of dominance and submission, and, within that definition, there is no route to follow in relating to him other than one of submissiveness. This image of God, however, derived from this theology of power, is not the Father of Christ. God is indeed powerful, but his power is the power of love.

Just as both coercion and sin are manifestations of power, so are love and grace. We can speak of the power of sin; we must also speak of the power of grace. Those who thirst for justice, for the fullness of life and for union with God also thirst for power. It is only power which will enable us to be, to live, to live more fully, to live for others, to create a just society and to bring us to union with God. We must assert ourselves (self-esteem) to be with (friendship and community) and for others (ministry).

We can ask ourselves whether the power of God is more or less powerful than the power of evil. Many religions, Zoroastrianism, gnosticism and others, have included the belief in two gods, the power of light and the power of darkness, the god of good and the god of evil, but that religious tendency has always been rejected within the Judaeo-Christian-Islamic traditions of the West. Gnosticism and manicheism have been and continue to be opposed to the Christian concept of power. In the end the power of God is more powerful than evil. This is what God longs to reveal and made manifest in the life of Christ. Death, where is your victory? Sin, where is your power? We need not be naive; there is no question that sin is a power. However we must be Christian. We must realize that the power of sin has been manifested as weaker than the power of God.

The question then is whether we believe in the power of love. If so, we must realize that the power of love is a power more powerful than any other power, more powerful than the power of sin or the power of evil. Do we believe this? Many of us, if we are honest, will in fact have to say no. We do not believe in the power of love. That is why we must once again capture the notion of love as powerful. Love is nothing other than the power of God himself, the gift of *agape* which the Son reveals and the Spirit gives us.

The Power of Love

Sin coerces; the Spirit frees. All that has been said in this book can be seen as a theology of the Holy Spirit, the Comforter, the Advocate, the Gift Giver. The Holy Spirit dwells within us and brings with her many gifts, among which are faith, hope and love. The Spirit gives us the gift of love which allows us to break through sin and reach out to ourselves, friends, brothers and sisters in Christ, those in need, and the Father himself. The Holy Spirit is the source of the spiritual life, the source of the Christian life, the one who roots us in Christ, and through Christ to the Father. It is the power of the Holy Spirit which does this. Thus Christians often pray in the name of Jesus and through the power of the Holy Spirit. The Holy Spirit is not only God; she is also appropriately and personally called love; she is power.

The Holy Spirit is indeed love, is indeed God. As

St. John writes, God himself is love (1 John 4:7-8). It is the nature of divinity to love. Divine nature is love. Jesus of Nazareth is love incarnate. The Holy Spirit is the gift of love. As Paul writes to the Romans, "The love of God has been poured into our hearts by the Holy Spirit which has been given to us" (5:5). Thomas Aquinas writes, "Of course, every beloved is in a lover. By the Holy Spirit, therefore, not only is God in us, but we also are in God."[6]

According to Aquinas, love is the proper name of the Holy Spirit. "The name Love in God can be taken essentially and personally. If taken personally, it is the proper name of the Holy Spirit as Word is the proper name of the Son."[7] God's essence is love. The Father, the Son, and the Spirit are love. Yet the Spirit is appropriately designated as love when we address the Lord personally as Father, Son or Spirit. Thomas also writes, "The love by which we love God is properly representative of the Holy Spirit. And thus the love which is in us, although it is an effect of the Father, the Son and the Holy Spirit, is nonetheless for a special sort of reason said to be in us through the Holy Spirit."[8] The Holy Spirit gives us the power to love. The Holy Spirit is within us as the source of love. It is through the Holy Spirit that we are brought into union with the fullness of the Triune God. God is in us and we are in God through the Holy Spirit. Love is in us and we are in love through the power of the Holy Spirit, the Spirit of love. Power is in us and we are in power through the love of the Holy Spirit, the power of love. Love is a gift God gives to us, a gift given to us through the Holy Spirit, the gift of the Holy Spirit herself.

God is not only love. God is also power. Correspondingly we can say that the Holy Spirit is not only love.

The Holy Spirit is power. In fact, the Holy Spirit reveals to us the true and authentic character of power. The Lord himself in that sense is the supreme exemplification of power. Sin, then, is revealed as not being true power but false power, being forceful but not powerful, not truly power at all if we understand the character of power itself. Sin is coercive; it is lacking in power. Power can be patient, kind and can endure all things, precisely because it is powerful. It can wait. It can persuade. It can respect. It can permit freedom. Coercion can never tolerate freedom. Power can. Christian theology has always seen power as most appropriately applied to God. Hence, Aquinas can also write, "The power of the Father, and of the Son, and of the Holy Spirit is identical just as the essence is, necessarily whatever God effects in us must be . . . simultaneously from the Father and the Son and the Holy Spirit."[9]

Although power is frequently attributed to the Holy Spirit, it is proper to the divine nature and thus essentially belongs to God, Father, Son, and Holy Spirit. We frequently intercede to God through the power of the Holy Spirit. In our Creed we confess that God became man through the power of the Holy Spirit. In Romans, Paul pictured the Spirit as coming to us in our weakness and empowering us to pray, empowering us to invoke the Lord as *Abba*, empowering us to love (Romans 8:14-30). In fact, for Paul, it is when he is weak that he is strong because it is when he is weakest that the power of the Spirit comes to his aid. In the midst of our own weakness, we become most powerful because then we are most in touch with the most tremendous source of power available to us. When we are strong, we are living in illusion and not powerful at all.

The Judaeo-Christian Scriptures, the history of Christian theology and revelation as God's self-communication all tell us that love is power and power is love. Love in fact is a power more powerful than any coercive force might be. There is no power more powerful than the power of love. No other power has the courage to risk freedom. The power of love is sufficient to let go of control, the power to let the other be while at the same time it offers union. The power of love is more powerful than any other power which we can conceive; it is the power of God himself, the power of the Spirit. This power of love is the essence of divine nature itself and has been made available to us through the gift of the Spirit, the Advocate sent to us by the Christ who was sent into the world by the Father. This is the mystery of life, of love, of power. The Father sent his Son into the world to be with us and for us and to send us the gift of his Spirit who can then give to us the gift of his own life and make us partakers in the divine nature, the power of love. Thus it is the very power of God, the power of love, which is made available to us in choosing to live life in Christ. It is the power of love which we long to develop and which we long to make available so that we and our whole world might be transformed through the power of the Spirit.

"Hence, since the love by which we love God is in us by the Holy Spirit, the Holy Spirit herself must also be in us, so long as the love is in us . . . since we are made lovers of God by the Holy Spirit, and every beloved is in the lover as such, by the Holy Spirit necessarily the Father and the Son dwell in us also."[10] This is fullness of life, living in union with the Father, Son and Holy Spirit. We are in God and God is in us. Through grace we are powerful, through sin we lose all power. The Christian life is the story and the theology of the power of God, what God can do in us, through us, and for us, as he recreates us in his image, in the image of life, making us lovers even as He is lover, freeing us to break out of our false selves, out of our sinful selves, to become ourselves and to reach forth in love to ourselves, others and even the Lord, so that all might be one as the Lord himself is one and as we are one with him.

Lord, that we might all be one, you in us and we in you, becoming one, united with you while still being ourselves, which is what your power to love can effect. Oh, that we might believe, that we might believe in this power, that we might believe that you have given us this power, so that we might continue to hope, to know that you are with us uniting all to yourself, so that we might love you and serve you all the days of our lives.

The Presence of the Spirit in the World

What does it mean to live out what we have discussed? The Christian life is only lived because the Spirit is at work in the world, because the Spirit is at work in us, because we have become temples of that Spirit, because that Spirit enables us to address the Lord as Father, as *Abba*. If we situate our lives, we situate our living in history. We are historical beings; we each have a history, but we also participate in a history, a story that transcends us, that has roots which go farther back than we ourselves do. And it is precisely this history out of which we come and of which we are a part where the Spirit of the Lord is at work.

The world has a history to it and it is the field of divine activity. We too readily limit the activity of the

Spirit to churchly functions. Our temptation as religious people is to believe that God is on our side. Yet our particular expression of religion at any particular moment in history cannot be a limitation of the activity of God. God's activity is not confined to the Church, not confined to ecclesial actions proper.[11] This in no way means that the function of the Church or the role of the *ecclesia* is unimportant. It just means that we must begin on a broader basis.

God is active, dynamic, active in creation and acting in Abraham and Sarah, in Isaac and Rebecca and in Jacob and Rachel, making himself present in the Temple. The supreme exemplification of God's activity comes with Jesus of Nazareth. We want to bring that closer to home and to talk about God's activity in us. He is active in the world, especially active in Israel, supremely exemplified in Jesus of Nazareth; but, just as God created in the past, continues to create in the present and will create in the future, so we can say that he acts not only in Israel, not only in Jesus, but in the new people of God, in the apostolic and postapostolic communities which trace their origins to his act in Jesus of Nazareth.[12]

The world in which we find ourselves, a secular world which has an *ecclesia* within it, is the milieu of which we are a part, in which we too must act. This is the history which brought us to our own day and to which we must contribute. How are we as Christians then to understand the historical character of our lives if we believe that the Spirit is at work everywhere in the world, attempting to defeat the rise of sin.

For Christians, *history* is closely associated with another word, *eschatology*. The Christian attempts to understand everything in the light of the eschaton.

History is not simply a series of past events that we can study scientifically, not simply the story out of which we come and which contributes to our self-understanding. History is where God acts and God is acting there for a particular purpose. In the Biblical version, history is eschatological—goal-oriented. John speaks about alpha and omega and Paul, in 1 Corinthians 15, talks about the end times, when the end will come and all enemies will be destroyed and Christ will be supreme. Christ will have subjected all to himself and then he will hand everything over to the Father; God will be all in all. This is Paul's panentheistic vision.

We all have different ways of looking toward this final consummation. The Scriptures themselves use different words, *pleroma*, the Greek word for fullness, *parousia* which means presence, when the presence of God is complete. In the Synoptic Gospels the expression used is the Reign of God. These are the words which express the end times.

Yet the relationship between history and eschatology is problematic. Does history have a necessary role to play in such a way that there are some things that must be done before that goal can be accomplished? Could God theoretically bring on the fullness of his Reign tomorrow? In other words, what is our role? Are we necessary to the Lord that his goals might be accomplished? If we say yes, does this limit God?

Furthermore, we often speak eschatologically in temporal terms, which is easy when we speak developmentally or processively. But is that the eschaton God has in mind or is the eschaton something which has already been accomplished, is already here? It seems apparent in the teaching of Jesus that the Reign of God has already come, not something for which we wait. Yet there is certainly evidence for a future aspect in the Scriptures as well. It cannot be disregarded. No matter what Jesus of Nazareth accomplished in history, we still have to say that not all has been accomplished yet. In other words, there is still something for which we wait. But it is not as if we are only waiting for the future. The presence of God has already to a great degree become a fact of history. If we are truly in touch with the Lord, we are aware that he is already present and we can celebrate the presence of the Lord now.

Eschatology does not turn our gaze away from the present and focus on the future alone; eschatology sees the value of the future *and* the value of the present. Both have arisen out of our history because it is history that has disclosed to us this presence of God. History is a basis for faith and hope. The expression *inaugurated eschatology,* used by John A. T. Robinson, corresponds to the Teilhardian understanding of the universe: All has been inaugurated, initiated, begun, although not all has yet been brought to completion.[13] The Reign of God has been inaugurated but is not yet complete. Eschatology then is concerned with the notion of the Reign of God, a notion which has sometimes been lost in preaching because we thought of eschatology only in terms of death, judgment, heaven and hell, a way of thinking that is individualistic, concerned with the moment of my death, the salvation of my soul and my particular judgment.

The primary Christian ethical responsibility in such preaching was saving our souls. For Jesus of Nazareth, however, the eschatological reality was his Father's Reign. This Reign is the reality within which the Christian lives his or her life. What do we do in this interim, this "little while," knowing that there may well be thousands or millions of years involved before that Reign has been once and for all established definitively? Christians in the past have frequently thought of living for another world, as if we were putting in time on earth in order to be tested. But what is the relationship between heaven and earth? Between the coming Reign of God and the history in which we are immersed? Is there any value to this earth? Is there any value to this history or is it simply where we wait? How do we live out the gifts which have been given to us?

One way is to make our lives an expression of gratitude. Whatever we do, whatever kind of life we live, it is not to earn salvation, nor to seek reward, not even to save our souls. Once we grasp what God has done for us, how creation has manifested his love, how the incarnation has even more deeply manifested that love, how the life of Christ, his death and his redemptive activity have manifested love, once we grasp the love of the Father, we live our lives only as an expression of gratitude. We do not live a moral life in order to be saved. We live a moral life in order to make visible our gratitude at having been saved. Thus, what is our role? Our role is sacramental, making visible our response to the grace of God. Ingratitude is a primary sin.

But, is there anything else? Yes, there is another factor in the relationship of history to eschatology, emphasized clearly by Teilhard de Chardin. What we *do* is significant. We cannot accomplish anything apart from God, but what we do is a necessary precondition for God effecting his final triumph. In other words, there are some limitations or conditions within which

God does act. There are some things necessary for other things to be accomplished. If history is going to have the birth of a messiah, it must have the expectation of and preparation for that messiah ahead of time. Hebrew history prepares the way for an even more significant act of God to take place. We could not have the prophetic tradition if there had been no Abraham. There are some traditions which are necessary for other actions to take place.

For God to act in Jesus required God's acting in John the Baptizer, which required God's acting in Abraham. God was continually acting, but we still needed Abraham's response. People had to cooperate so that God might continue to act in even more significant kinds of ways. In that sense, then, Teilhard would say that what we do today in history is of this sort. We must continue to respond to God's activity and God's will at this time in history so that we might prepare the way, set the stage, make the next move forward so that God's act might continue to take place with even greater grandeur. For Teilhard, the Kingdom of God, the Reign of God, that final supreme act of God cannot take place unless we now prepare the way. In other words, God could not bring forth his fullness and his Kingdom apart from us. But our role is more like that of John the Baptizer. What we do inevitably prepares the way so that God might act. First, we are called upon to live a life of gratitude for what God has done for us and continues to do within us. Secondly, we are called upon to live in a way that helps build those structures which can make an even greater or different act of God possible in the future, because the future will only be built on the basis of what we do now just as the present only emerged out of our history and the past. So our work is an expression of gratitude, but it is also a preparation or condition for God's act.

Thirdly, there is a medium ground between simply waiting and actually expecting; that middle ground is hope. We do not have the expectation that all will be accomplished in our lifetimes. It does not make a difference. Our work is aimed toward approximation. It is not as if our work will bring on the fullness of the Kingdom. Yet, we can live our lives to approximate the Kingdom; we can live as if the Kingdom were here. This is what the Gospels and Scriptures call us to—to live in the light of the Kingdom, which does not mean that the Kingdom will be here tomorrow or that we will be disillusioned because it is not here in all fullness now, but we can come close to it. We can live an ethic based on love; we can build community in our midst; we can break down barriers which keep people apart. It does not have to be a question of all or nothing.

If we look at the liberation movements today, Black liberation, Latin American liberation, women's liberation, gay liberation, we cannot say that any group will be fully liberated by what we do today but we can still approximate the liberation for which we still long. What we do is an expression of gratitude for what God has already done, an expression of gratitude that can actually prepare the way and build up the world so that it might provide the conditions for God to act on our behalf to an even greater degree, and this preparation might indeed be an approximation of the fullness of the Kingdom. We at least have signs, sacraments, visible manifestations in our midst that nourish and support our life of hope. Hope then is that medium between history and eschatology. We live in hope that what we are doing will prepare the way of the Lord and make more manifest in our midst his Kingdom and make it more possible that his Reign will come in its fullness soon.

A fourth dimension of our life flows from our freedom. The choices I make do determine to a great degree the character, the nature of that final Reign of the Lord. If we look at our own lives, we realize that there are many possible lives we could or could have lived. What I as husband might be or as father or as chemist or as a secondary school Latin teacher, all of these are or were my potential lives. Each of us has many potential lives but only one actual life. Come Omega, come the Kingdom, God will never Reign over what I was not but could have been. In other words, those possibilities, because of my freedom, will never be actualized. The decisions we make will actually determine the character of that final Reign. We do play a vital role in determining the universe over which the Lord will Reign.

In the beginning, the Lord created the heavens and the earth. But the new heaven and the new earth will be what we create together, with faith, in hope, and through the power of his love in us.

A Concluding Reflection

In one sense enough has been said. In another sense it is as if we are just ready to begin, as if we are just beginning to grasp what love is all about. Love is a mystery, the articulation of which never exhausts the reality. While love is mystery, it is also power, the very power of God, the power of Being itself. Love is the inner nature of God.

Being is love. To be is to love. To love is to share in the divine nature. To love is to participate in the power of God. Love is not only mystery, not only power, and not only God. Love is also that which God has freely chosen to share with us. Love is a gift in which God gives himself to us. A gift of the Spirit who is his gift to us. Love, God's gift, the gift of his Spirit, is given to us to dwell within us, transforming us into the very likeness of God himself.

This gift is also life, the mystery of life. The mystery is that we have been created in the image of God and called to share in the fullness of his life, that life which he has promised. This is the story of his life, a life of love with no limit. It is the story of how he sent his Son into our midst, whose unlimited love called him to die, and to send us his Spirit. The Spirit of love has been with us ever since. She is the giver of all God's gifts, especially those gifts of faith, hope and love.

In faith we trust in God. In hope we are confident in the future of his promises. In love we open ourselves to being for others, to being as God is.

Theology is our faith seeking to understand itself, our hope longing to know itself more clearly, and our love struggling to disclose itself. The understanding to which love comes through faith is that it is *kenosis, agape, gratia.* Love is kenotic, self-emptying, self-giving, self-limiting for the sake of others. Love is an outpouring which is ineffably undescribable. It, among other things, is creative, incarnative, redemptive, transforming, constant, generous, compassionate, active, and free. Love is grace alone, God alone, overflowing life which has been given to us. Love is not our nature but our true life, a supernatural life. It is the fullness of life.

This divine life of grace and love which is God has been given to us through the power of the Spirit. Divine love is infused into our finite beings and we are recreated as new creatures. It is this *agape,* this divinity, which has been given to us. Human love mirrors divine love and manifests itself in manifold ways, five of which we have developed in greater detail in this book.

God is *agape. Agape* is also a gift of the Spirit to the new creature. It enables us to break through sin in order to reach out and embrace ourselves, others, and the Author of our life. Authentic self-love is not ours by nature. It is a gift of God. It is a self-denying self-esteem, a gift of the Spirit in which God empowers us to love ourselves. Self-love is a gift of God, a gift in which God enables us to reach out and embrace ourselves, to accept ourselves. Christian self-esteem is *agape* and *grace.*

So too is love of others in its threefold manifestation. *Philia* is *agape; koinonia* is *agape; diakonia* is *agape.* All three express *kenosis.* All three are gifts of God's grace. They are not human accomplishments. Just as we can never love ourselves by our power alone, so we can never love others by our power alone. Only God empowers us to do this. Friendship, community, and ministry are all freely choosing self-limitation for the sake of others, whether they be others who enter our lives with particular affection, out of interest in a common adventure or faith, or out of their own needs due to the situation of the world in which they find themselves. These others we embrace and love because God is with us.

And God is with us even to the point of enabling us to love himself and be one with him. Prayer too is *agape.*

Love is both particular and universal, both personal and social, both affective and steadfast, both creative and redemptive, both free and necessary. It manifests itself in self-acceptance and self-denial, in intimacy and generativity, in community and solitude, in ministry and play, in humor and prayer. Love is a movement of the Spirit. Love is God. Paul already captured the indescribability of love in his own Song of Songs:

> If I have all the eloquence of men or of angels, but speak without love, I am simply a gong booming or a cymbal clashing. If I have the gift of prophecy, understanding all the mysteries there are, and knowing everything, and if I have faith in all its fullness, to move mountains, but without love, it will do me no good whatever.

> Love is always patient and kind; it is never jealous; love is never boastful or conceited; it is never rude or selfish; it does not take offence, and is not resentful. Love takes no pleasure in other people's sins but delights in the truth; it is always ready to excuse, to trust, to hope, and to endure whatever comes.

> Love does not come to an end. But if there are gifts of prophecy, the time will come when they must fail; or the gift of languages, it will not continue for ever; and knowledge—for this, too, the time will come when it must fail. For our knowledge is imperfect and our prophesying is imperfect; but once perfection comes, all imperfect things will disappear. When I was a child, I used to talk like a child, and think like a child, and argue like a child, but now I am a man, all childish ways are put behind me. Now we are seeing a dim reflection in the mirror; but then we shall be seeing face to face. The knowledge that I have now is imperfect; but then I shall know as fully as I am known.

> In short, there are three things that last: faith, hope and love; and the greatest of these is love (1 Cor. 13:1-13).

Love is one and love is many. There is only one
God, one Lord, one faith, one Son, one hope, one
Spirit, one love, one life, and manifold expressions
thereof.

God is:
Father
Son
SPIRIT.
The SPIRIT brings:
faith
hope
LOVE.
LOVE empowers us to reach out to:
God
self
OTHERS.
We are with and for OTHERS in:
friendship
community
ministry.

God is *agape*, is *diakonia*, is servanthood, is Lordship.

There is a unity and a diversity to love. There is no
need to ask for a hierarchy. To seek a hierarchy is to
fail to have understood. Which is more important,
Father, Son, or Spirit? Faith, hope, or love? Love of
God, love of self, or love of others? *Philia, Koinonia,*
or *Diakonia?*

The five loves of which we have spoken are but
manifestations of the one love God is. The ten pillars
of the Christian life are but a way of talking about life
in Christ. There are many other ways. What is important is: we love Christ and he loves us. No one
theology fully captures the mystery he reveals. No one
spirituality contains the fullness of his Spirit. What

we have discussed here is but one facet of one spiritual theology, one among many. It is neither the best nor the worst but one with which we can all identify because there is one Lord, the Father of Christ, the Father of Abraham, the Father of Mohammed, the Father of the Buddha, one Living God who longs for us all to be one as he is one. Both married people and single people can come to these ten pillars and find nourishment. Nations, races, sexes, and creeds can feel the vibrations of these five loves. And secular philosophers can perceive the wisdom of this Way which speaks of a life of true self-knowledge (humility), true friendship (fidelity), true brotherhood and sisterhood (generosity), true neighborliness (compassion), and a right relation with God (gratitude). And these five loves, humility, fidelity, generosity, compassion, and gratitude are still only one more way of speaking about our God whom we love, but who first loved us, who loved us into existence, whose love transforms our existence, whose love is all in all.

Praise and glory and honor to that Name, that Word, that Spirit in whom we all are.

APPENDICES

APPENDIX I

Relational Thinking

As I stated in the first chapter, the common Western way of thinking for centuries is what I would call thinking in terms of "either/or." This is a categorical, discursive, logical and rational mode of thought. It is satisfying to the intellect which searches for clarity because its tendency to categorize and, therefore, to dichotomoize helps us to establish clear and distinct ideas. One can already see the triumph of this way of thinking within the philosophy of Descartes.[1] In this form of discursive and rational thought we define one reality over against another, in opposition to another, in distinction from another.

Placing realities in contradictory opposition to each other when this opposition is unnecessary frequently means that to affirm something, we must deny something else. Is there no way in which both realities might be affirmed, a way in which we can think in terms of "both/and" rather than "either/or?" It is interesting to note that the rise of existential philosophy in the West was in fact in opposition to the prevalent monopoly exercised by rationalism. At the same time, however, Kierkegaard, one of the fathers of existential philosophy, because of his own intrapsychic and subjective swings of mood, entitled his first classical, aesthetic, and philosophical work *Either/Or*.[2] Thus the existential rebellion against rationalism does not necessarily escape this mode of conceptualization.

The dominance of rationalism in thinking can also be associated with masculinity in Western culture. The esteem with which this mode of thinking has been respected and trusted is related to the ways in which masculinity has been esteemed more than femininity.

There is no way in which we can reduce the history of Western philosophy, ideas, and culture to one modality. Indeed, the history of Western art and literature would show the falsity of this. At the same time, however, we cannot underestimate the power that this mode of conceptualization exercises, a method which eventually finds its epitome in applied science and technology. Here again, rationalism and empiricism are but two modes of the same reality although it might strike us that they make strange partners. The rise of empiricism, however, is simply one more manifestation of this trend in Western thought and it is no surprise that the glamour and esteem with which the scientific method is held is a natural outflow of the history of the West. And, as C. P. Snow pointed out, it is no surprise that the tendency of the one to deny the validity of the other has led to two cultures and a communication gap.[3] Of the two cultures, there is no question about which one, through most of Western history, has tyrannically reigned and which one has to beg for its rights.

With the dawn of a new consciousness, new developments and new knowledge in the nineteenth and twentieth centuries has come the demand for a new logic, a new way of conceptualizing, a new way of articulating ourselves which does justice to the developmental, interrelated, holistic, and organic character of reality. In order to articulate his grasp of the real, Hegel was led to the development of a new logic and Teilhard de Chardin was led to the creation of new words. The traditional categories provided by dualism and rationalism no longer served their purpose: they did not do justice to the character of reality. Hegel, a rationalist in his own idealistic way, is one of the first to move in a new direction and holds up for us the possibility of another way of thinking, namely thinking dialectically rather than rationalistically. Rationalist though he may have been and an enemy of the existential philosopher, he tried in his own way to escape the limitations which had developed in Western thinking.

Georg Wilhelm Friedrich Hegel (1770-1831) in German philosophy, Henri Bergson (1859-1944) and Pierre Teilhard de Chadrin (1881-1955) in French philosophy, and Alfred North Whitehead (1861-1947) in Anglo-American philosophy, all in their own ways struggled with the aftermath of Cartesianism. Some thinkers moved into areas other than philosophy to cope with the same problem, with the hope that a more mystical approach could achieve what philosophy could not. We see in our own day a return to mystical theology and spirituality, both Western and Eastern. Our era is comparable in that sense to the fourteenth century.[4] Psychology, for example, studied the problems of complementarity and paradox and gestalt. A new attack on the age-old problem of the one and the many has taken place as the unity and diversity of reality impressed itself on the modern consciousness and we moved beyond age-old splits and false oppositions.

Hegel was only one for whom there was a need for more synthetic thinking. His dialectical method was his approach to overcoming opposites. We continue to be indebted to him and he continues to influence us whether we are Hegelian or not. His legacy is in the air and we can no longer breath intellectually as we did before. Dialectical thinking opposed the rigidity of concepts which stand eternally over against each other; it was an effort to penetrate more deeply into reality, into the unity of reality and into the possible synthesis of seemingly or actually opposed realities. These oppositions are simply complementary moments within a higher synthesis. At one level of rational thought A and B are opposed. Upon deeper penetration, at a deeper level of understanding (Vernunft), a synthesis unites them without annulling their differences. Fredriçk Copleston describes this tremendous philosophical endeavor of Hegel:

> The fundamental purpose of philosophy, Hegel maintains, is that of overcoming oppositions and divisions. 'Division [Entzwiung] is the source of the *need of philosophy*.' In the world of experience the mind finds differences, oppositions, apparent contradictions, and it seeks to construct a unified whole, to overcome the splintered harmony, as Hegel puts it. True, division and opposition present themselves to the mind in different forms in different cultural epochs. And this helps to explain the peculiar characteristics of different systems. At one time the mind is confronted, for instance, with the problem of the division and opposition between soul and body, while at another time the same sort of problem presents itself as that of the relation between subject and object, intelligence and Nature. But in whatever particular way or ways the problem may present itself, the fundamental interest of reason (Vernunft) is the same, namely to attain a unified synthesis.[5]

One of Hegel's first tasks was the creation of a new logic. We can disagree with Hegel's idealistic rationalism, his conjunction of logic and metaphysics. Yet, we can sympathize with him on the magnitude of his task and find his effort a way of providing for contrasts without leaving them in total opposition.

Another representative of this contemporary quest for truth and understanding is Jacob Bronowski. Heidegger's influence in philosophy as well as the emergence of Lonergan's method in theology both point to the search for an understanding which stands under and deeper than what rational categorization alone might achieve. Although our purpose here is not to survey recent intellectual history in this regard, Bronowski is helpful. He affirms the reliable, or adequate, but limited character of human knowledge. In other words, our knowledge is both adequate and inadequate. One can immediately see that understanding the truth of this statement requires that we move beyond thinking in terms of "either/or." Adequacy and inadequacy need not be mutually exclusive in reference to a particular reality although they may be mutually exclusive in reference to certain aspects of that reality. An assumption of Bronowski's, and an assumption in much of modern thought, is the total connectedness of reality. Here we begin to see the relationship between the issue which we have posed and the issue of reality itself, the relationship between thought and reality, between logic and metaphysics. We can understand the validity of Hegel's attempt to redefine that relationship, even if his redefinition was inadequate. Yet, we can rightly pose the question whether our way of conceptualizing the universe determines our understanding of that universe or whether the character of reality itself must somehow be disclosed to us in such a way that we can know what mode of grasping or conceptualizing is going to be most adequate in order to deal with that disclosure. Does some decision about reality or metaphysics precede or follow one's decision about how to think about it?

In an "either/or" frame of reference, we would find ourselves in an insoluble dilemma and forced to make an unnecessary choice. Neither logic alone nor meta-physics alone should shape our conceptual structure. How we think is as important as the nature of that about which we think. There are ways of entering into an understanding of the nature of reality which allows that reality to disclose itself to us at the same time we attempt to grasp it with those modes of intellectuality which might appear to be more immediately natural to our cognitive ability. Yet, both manifest truth and it is only in the complementarity of both modes of apprehension that we will find the truth. There is a relationship between reality and the way we think about it. Some ways of thinking are more adequate to understanding than others, given the character of reality. This means that some prior understanding must exist first about the character of reality itself, and one of those prior understandings or presuppositions for many is the total connectedness of the universe.

Bronowski writes, "I believe that the world is totally connected: that is to say, that there are no events any-where in the universe which are not tied to every other event in the universe."[6] If this be true, it says much about our intellectual quest and methodologies. Be-cause of its total connectivity, nature is not capable of being finally formulated in reflective categories once and for all. This does not mean that our tentative formulations are inadequate to the task. Our knowl-edge of the outside world does depend upon our mode of perception. There are available to us, however, a variety of modes of perception which permit us reli-able, if never finished, knowledge. If the universe in fact is totally interdependent or connected, "then we should prefer those languages or systems which show the highest connection, not because they do in fact show the connections in nature, but because they are coming closest to it."[7] If our intuition, perception or preunderstanding is accurate with reference to the connectedness of the universe (which is also the conclusion of much modern scientific inquiry since Einstein) then we have to say that this fact itself means human knowledge must search for the connectivity, the synthesis, the unity of reality and not simply its dichotomies, its oppositions and its categories. This does not mean that the "either/or" way of thinking might not be more appropriate to some problems than to others. In fact, its supremacy in so much of science indicates that in our effort to understand the most material aspect of our world it is often adequate and appropriate, but not all of the time. The rise of rationalism is not unrelated to the rise of materialism.

As we move up the evolutionary scale, we become more removed from the simplest levels of material organization. The analytical/discursive mode of conceptualization becomes less adequate to our task. We need to prefer those ways of thinking or methodologies which not only give us division but synthesis, not only specialization but integration, not only proper understandings of realities in themselves but understanding of those realities in their relationships to other realities. In other words, we come to the principle of complementarity and relational thinking: nothing can be understood in terms of itself alone—because of the character of reality itself which forces upon us the need to reconsider the ways in which we think. Our search for truth means a search for connectivity. This is the very character of reality—a search for wholeness, ideas which might be distinguishable but not always expressive of intrinsically separable realities. The nature of reality is that one thing is part of another thing. Ultimately, reality is not discrete particles. Our method of thinking must do justice to this nature of reality.

Thinking in terms of complementarity should not be identified with the dialectical thinking of Hegel. Hegel simply represents a move in this direction. There are other examples, one of which is the mode of thinking in the East in contrast to that of the West. Eastern thought is exemplified in Chinese philosophy especially, where understanding means grasping both the *yin* and the *yang*, the complementarity.[8] Eastern thought can be denigrated by Westerners precisely because we do not recognize the importance and validity of another way of thinking. Not only Eastern philosophy, however, but Western mysticism represents this complementary mode of thinking. The tendency of mystical thinking is to perceive connectedness, unity. Its tendency toward panentheistic (and pantheistic) directions exemplifies another counter-current within the West in contrast to rationalism. Much mystical or religious thought discovers that the rational way of thinking is inadequate to articulate its own experience or understanding of reality. Thus mystics search for other models which always appear to be less precise to the rationalist although, for the mystic, they are more true.

In contemporary behavioral science, the Gestalt movement represents a similar effort toward synthesis, toward seeing the unity between form and background —interrelatedness. This effort is also found early in the depth psychology of Jung who represents more complementary, dialectical and Eastern thinking, whereas Freudian thought represents more rational and Western thought.

One of the current movements in Western philosophy which is attempting to grapple with this same question is process philosophy. A central affirmation of Whitehead's philosophy is the vector character of existence, the fact that something which is there can also be here, that prehension is an integrative factor in reality and that each entity or occasion is both subject and object, both cause and effect.[9] We also see in the work of Teilhard de Chardin that the search for unification is the prevailing metaphysical problem. Unification, however, does not deny diversification or differentiation. Union differentiates. That is, unification leads to a higher individualization. Although convergence is central to Teilhard's universe, he clearly distinguishes the principle of identification from the principle of unification: these are two converse forms of spirit. Much rejection of Teilhardian thought is based upon this misunderstanding in which his principle of unification is seen as one of identification.[10]

Complementarity does not deny the principle of identity; it simply wishes to pose the principle of noncontradiction in such a way that all reality is not seen to be ultimately discrete, substantial, and in opposition.

The work of Bernard Meland is significant in this regard as well. In *Fallible Forms and Symbols* he brings together *logos* and *mythos* as two modes or structures for coming to meaning.[11] It is the split between these two that "both/and" thinking wants to overcome. You can't have one without the other. The rationalization of *logos* and its separation from *mythos* has also led to the return to the importance of myth and symbol in our day. For Meland, it is necessary to rethink reason and its relation to myths—poetic participation. We will not live by logic alone. No one model of disclosure can be absolutized.

In a kindred spirit to the way in which I have spoken, Jonas Salk has written, "In an attempt to state concisely the difference between the recent past in human history and what is imagined for the future, . . . the difference is essentially between a philosophy, or attitude described by the word *"or,"* for the past, and the word *"and,"* for the future."[12] And also,

> The object is to offer a way of looking at problems and conceivable solutions in the human or metabiological realm in both intellectually *and* intuitively satisfying ways. A large part of the difficulty of the human condition is due to a disassociation between intellect and intuition, a division that has been greatly exaggerated as knowledge has increased and earlier beliefs have been brought into question. A new and consciously attained system of balanced use of the brain's two aspects—the imaginative and the cognitive—is vitally necessary today.[13]

Henri Bergson, the father of much processive thinking, sees this complementarity both in reality and in thought. He discusses "the divergent results of evolution not as presenting analogies but as themselves mutually complementary."[14] This complementarity, a part of reality which reflects the divergent tendencies within reality itself, divergent tendencies which complement each other, manifest themselves at higher levels of reality in the contrast between instinct and intelligence, realities which manifest how thought is eventually affected by the complementary character of reality itself. Instinct and intelligence, however, are not dichotomous. They interpenetrate, although they are distinguishable. Bergson writes,

> Let us say at the outset that the distinction we are going to make will be too sharply drawn, just because we wish

> to define in instinct what is instinctive and in intelligence what is intelligent, whereas all concrete instinct is mingled with intelligence, as all real intelligence is penetrated by instinct. Moreover, neither intelligence nor instinct lends itself to rigid definition; they are tendencies, and not things.[15]

We can see that when we are dealing with things, brute matter, the more sharply defined and clearly distinguished approach to conceptualization can be adequate. When, however, we go beyond that level of reality, "either/or" modes of conceptualization (what Bergson would describe as intellect) are less adequate.

Instinct and intelligence interpenetrate. "In reality, they accompany each other only because they are complementary, and they are complementary only because they are different, what is instinctive in instinct being opposite to what is intelligent in intelligence."[16] Yet, we can begin to see that instinct and intelligence must be understood in terms of their complementarity (if they are to be fully understood) and not only in terms of their distinctiveness. Complementarity does not deny distinctiveness for Bergson nor differences for Teilhard. Distinctions and differences need to be grasped in order for reality to be understood. When, however, those differences are grasped, we understand only half of the reality which can be understood unless we also understand how those differences are complementary. This is why, for Bergson, intuition and intellect (the two words he prefers to use to describe two modes of thinking) represent a needed complementarity.

> A complete and perfect humanity would be that in which these two forms of conscious activity should attain their full development. And, between this humanity and ours,

we may conceive any number of possible stages, corresponding to all the degrees imaginable of intelligence and of intuition. In this lies the part of contingency in the mental structure of our species. A different evolution might have led to a humanity either more intellectual still or more intuitive. In the humanity of which we are a part, intuition is in fact, almost completely sacrificed to intellect.[17]

There is no need to pursue the epistemology of Bergson here. We need only remind ourselves that the complementarity which he perceives in reality must also manifest itself in our way of attempting to grasp that reality.

Other examples will help us to understand this tendency in Western thought. For example, we make easy distinctions between masculine and feminine, defining masculinity over and against femininity. The more masculine one is the less feminine one is and vice versa. Although that mode of thinking is appropriate the more material, and perhaps also biological, a reality is, it is not necessarily appropriate at every level of reality. Thus at the biological level it is certainly true to say that we are either male or female (although even then that is not always clearly the case). Yet, generally speaking, material and biological realities can be fairly well grasped by "either/or" ways of thinking. The higher up the evolutionary scale we move, however, such as into the psychological realms beyond biology, the more we see that this mode of grasping reality is less adequate. Realities which are either male or female need not be either exclusively masculine or exclusively feminine. It is possible to be both and the two need not be defined over against each other.

We dichotomize also the intellectual life and the emotional life. The more intellectual we are, the less emotional we will be, and the more emphasis we give to emotion, the less we are likely to give to intellect. This dichotomy flows from our way of thinking, an unnecessary and inadequate way of thinking, also evident in the traditional Western relationship between mysticism and rationalism. In the East, the history of philosophy includes much of what we in the West include within the history of religion, namely mystical development. It is, however, our Western tendency again to define the two over and against each other rather than seeing the way in which, although distinct, mysticism and rationalism, religion and philosophy mutually relate to and support each other.

One could pursue these issues further. I only wish to present some representative thinkers to provide a more complete background to my discussion on complementarity in Chapter One. To discuss more adequately this question here would take us too far into the history of consciousness and into epistemology.[18]

APPENDIX II

Sexual Love

Eros is one topic which has not been considered at length in this book but will be briefly examined here. *Eros* has been omitted because it is not as such a particularly biblical or Gospel love. There is a difference between my presentation of the loves and the four loves of C. S. Lewis: affection, friendship, *eros,* and charity.[1] Rollo May talks about the differences among lust, *eros, philia,* and *agape.*[2] These are valid ways of speaking and are very helpful, as many would attest, myself included. Yet they do not arise out of the way in which the Bible speaks. Actually, the only one lacking in my treatment here has been *eros.* This is because I do not see it as another love but as an aspect of some love.

Perhaps the best way of expressing this point is to provide a contrast between my opinion and that of Anders Nygren whose classic discussion in *Agape and Eros*[3] will certainly continue to be recognized as one of theological accomplishments of the twentieth century. Nygren's work is a significant treatment, clearly written, and an excellent exemplification of motif research.[4] Yet, as much as I respect it, I disagree with it. I am willing to affirm one of his central theses, that love is the center of Christianity, that Christian love is *agape,* and that *agape* is grace. But his contrast between *agape* and *eros* reflects a completely "either/or" methodology in which they become mutually exclusive. This is a central thesis of his book which does not do justice to the biblical material, to the ambiguous character of human existence, or to the true nature of God's love. Although *agape* and *eros* are different motifs,

distinguishable motifs, they are not completely separable. *Agape* and *eros* need not be enemies; they can
be friends—unless one rules this out at the outset. The
problem is not, as Nygren affirms, that Christian tradition went too far in effecting a synthesis between the
two. The problem is that Christian tradition has not
yet gone far enough in the direction of such a synthesis.

Nygren's "either/or" approach to these two fundamental motifs is obvious: "There cannot actually be
any doubt that *eros* and *agape* belong originally to
two entirely separate spiritual worlds, between which
no direct communication is possible" (p. 31). "The
right answer to the question of the relation between
eros and *agape* . . . might very well be that there is
no relation between them at all" (p. 34).

For Nygren, "*agape* is Christianity's own original
basic conception" (p. 48). This is true enough but it
does not necessarily mean that it is totally incompatible
with *eros*. Can *agape* not appropriate and transform
eros? Are all forms of self-love and selfless love inevitably opposed? Is there not a truly spiritual and Christian self-love as well as a sinful form of self-love? Is it
not too simplistic to oppose the egocentric side of *eros*
against the theocentic side of *agape?* In the end, even
Nygren's human love of God is not what his *agape* is
about. It is not theocentric in terms of its object. Love
of neighbor is the supreme manifestation of *agape*.[5]

Nygren's *agape* is theocentric in the sense that its
subject is God, it comes from God, it is gift, grace.
This is true. But can this gift of the Spirit not enable
me to love myself as well as others?[6] Does God's *agape*
working within me allow me to love only others, never
myself, and allow others to love me and never themselves? To consider *eros,* whether heavenly *eros,* sen-

sual *eros,* or self-love as being completely egocentric is wrong. To make *agape* completely unmotivated is equally false. Ceslaus Spicq has pointed this out,[7] Christian tradition testifies to this, and God himself reveals it.

The *agape* that is God does not exclude the *eros* that he also is. God *longs* for our salvation, *desires* the response of his Chosen Ones, and *seeks* to make his glory manifest. The *agape* of God is that he is willing to risk his own completion for our sake. He is not willing, however, to set aside the desire for reciprocity on our parts. God's *agape* is too erotic for that. His *eros* is too self-sacrificing to be labeled unworthy of him. God's *eros* is a manifestation of *agape*—greater love than this there could not be than to freely involve himself in our lives so that we are now truly bound to each other.

Nygren rightly points out the distinction in Platonic love between earthly, sensual, vulgar *eros* and heavenly, spiritual *eros,* as is found in Platonic dualism, a higher love and a lower love (pp. 50-51). It is strange that we so often think of *eros* as sensual love when for Plato it was instead a sublimation of sensual love and a striving toward union with the Good.[8] Nygren is critical of any attempt to synthesize the *eros* and *agape* motifs: one is Greek and the other is Christian. Therefore they are irreconcilable. Hence his criticism of the Augustinian and other Christian syntheses of *agape* and *eros* in the *caritas* motif. For Nygren, Augustine and all the *caritas* theologies have already gone too far. For me, they have not gone far enough.

Nygren writes, "Between Vulgar *Eros* and Christian *Agape* there is no relation at all" (p. 51). *Caritas* attempts to synthesize only *agape* and heavenly *eros.*

This is true. This is also where the synthesis needs to be carried further today. The earlier *caritas* syntheses reflect their pagan (Platonic, Neo-Platonic, Manichaean) background. Sensual *eros,* however, is not inimical to *agape*. The *caritas* syntheses take *eros* seriously, but not all of *eros*. For sensual and sexual love have roots in Judaism as well as in Christianity.[9] The effect of the *caritas* syntheses (unavoidably) is to cut *agape* off from its earthy (erotic) roots, its Jewish roots, as it became transplanted in Greek soil. Christian *agape* is capable of more *eros* than Christian tradition has generally affirmed. Not all sensual *eros* is lust.[10]

To enter a more detailed discussion here would go beyond our purposes. I simply point out why the five loves of which I speak do not include *eros* and *agape* in a somewhat traditional fashion. These are not two different kinds of love as portrayed in the Scriptures. At least we can see that the problem is too large to be quickly resolved. I have not explicitly included sexual or sensual love as one of the loves because there is no need to. It is included everywhere. It is not less love and therefore less *agape* because it is sensual, sexual, earthy, or erotic. Not all sensuality is love or *agape,* but *agape* can manifest itself in sensual and erotic forms. But, as I have said, this is a separate problem— the history of the concept of love and its origins within and outside Christianity.

Eros and *agape* are not mutually exclusive in Scripture. Hence *agape* can be erotic, whether we consider it in a more earthy, sensual way or the more heavenly, platonic way. Thus there was no need for me to include *eros* because it was never excluded. *Eros* can be agapic, Christian, full of grace. I, however, did not choose to deal with that question here. It is not, as

I have said, that Christian tradition has made too much of *eros*. Rather, we have not made enough of it. Employing a Platonic way of speaking we have only made something of "the higher eros" and not "the lower". Only the higher *eros* was sufficiently integrated into Christian theologies of *agape*. The time has come now to do the same with sensual *eros* and sexual love. For it is here that the bias of Christian tradition manifests itself. This negativity toward sexuality shows the neo-Platonic, Platonic, and Manichaean roots of much in Christian tradition. Sexual love can indeed be love, *agape*, *philia*. It is not necessarily concupiscence. Genital love can be love, *agape*. Affective love can be *agape*, and in fact *agape* is affective in much of the Scriptures. *Agape* is a *felt* love. And *agape*, grace, a gift of the Spirit, manifests itself within us as love of self, *philia, koinonia, diakonia,* as well as love of God. *Diakonia* includes love of enemies. *Philia* may or may not be erotic or genital. All the loves, however, are *agape* and *agape* is also *kenosis*.

FOOTNOTES

DONALD GOERGEN

Footnotes to Chapter One

1. Especially important in this regard is Gerard Gilleman, *The Primacy of Charity in Moral Theology* (Westminster, Md.: Newman Press, 1961).
2. C. S. Lewis, *The Four Loves* (London: Collins Press, 1965) is a classical, important, and highly popular discussion of affection, friendship, *eros,* and charity. I recommend it highly. Yet my approach is different and, I believe, more biblical. Although I do not consider *eros* as such, I do bring it into the discussion in appendix 2.
3. The relation between *agape* and *philia* in John is a much discussed question. E.g. see Raymond Brown, *The Gospel According to John XIII-XXI* (Garden City: Doubleday; 1970), pp. 1102-1112.
4. E.g., *The Cloud of Unknowing* (Garden City: Doubleday Image, 1973), Chapter 8, pp. 17-23.
5. See *The Sexual Celibate,* pp. 98-99. Also Aristotle, *Politics,* 1, 3. Aquinas, *Summa Theologica,* I-II, q. 56, a. 4, ad 3.

Footnotes to Chapter Two

1. *The Sexual Celibate,* pp. 46-51 ff.
2. Ibid., 59-64. Also see Abraham Maslow, *Motivation and Personality* (New York: Harper and Row, 1970), esp. chapters 3-4. And Frank Goble, *The Third Force: The Psychology of Abraham Maslow* (New York: Grossman Publishers, 1970).
3. *Motivation and Personality,* p. 38.
4. Ibid., pp. 43-45.
5. Ibid., p. 45.
6. See Alfred Adler's *Superiority and Social Interest* (Evanston: Northwestern University Press, 1964) and the introduction to it by Heinz Ansbacher. Also *The Sexual Celibate,* pp. 47-49.
7. *Motivation and Personality,* p. 46.
8. Ibid.
9. Nathaniel Branden, *The Psychology of Self-Esteem* (New York: Bantam Books, Inc., 1971), p. 109.
10. Ibid., p. 110.

11. Nathaniel Branden, *The Disowned Self* (New York: Bantam Books, 1973), p. 3.
12. Ibid., p. 9.
13. Ibid., p. 23.
14. Ibid., p. 72.
15. Rollo May, *Love and Will* (New York: W. W. Norton and Co., 1969), p. 155.
16. Ibid., p. 157.
17. Ibid., p. 167.
18. *The Psychology of Self-Esteem*, p. 133.
19. Viktor Frankl, *Man's Search for Meaning* (New York: Washington Square Press, 1965), p. 176.
20. Ibid., pp. 178-183.
21. Ibid., pp. 187-188.
22. Teilhard de Chardin, *The Divine Milieu* (New York: Harper and Row, 1960), pp. 70-71.
23. Ibid., p. 70.
24. Ibid., pp. 73-74.
25. E.g., Eric Berne's *Principles of Group Treatment* (New York: Oxford University Press, 1969), chapters 10-12. Or Thomas Harris' *I'm OK—You're OK: A Practical Guide to Transactional Analysis* (New York: Harper and Row, 1969).
26. Edrita Fried, *Active-Passive* (New York: Harper and Row, 1971).
27. A practical guide to assertive behavior would be *Your Perfect Right* by Alberti and Emmons (San Luis Obispo: Import, 1974). An important work on assertiveness and aggressiveness in Rollo May's *Power and Innocence* (New York: W. W. Norton and Co., 1972).
28. E.g., Robert White, "Competence and the Psycho-Sexual Stages of Development," *Nebraska Symposium on Motivation,* vol. 8, (Lincoln: University of Nebraska Press, 1960), pp. 97-141.
29. E.g., see E. F. Schumacher, *Small Is Beautiful: Economics As If People Mattered* (New York: Harper and Row, 1973).
30. George Bach and Peter Wyden, *The Intimate Enemy* (New York: Wm. Morrow and Co., 1969). Leo Madow, *Anger* (New York: Charles Scribner's Sons, 1972).
31. I take this topic up again in Chapter Nine.

DONALD GOERGEN

32. *The Divine Milieu,* pp. 73-76.
33. This is reflected in Merton's spirituality. E.g., see John Higgins, *Merton's Theology of Prayer* (Spencer: Cistercian Publications, 1971). Also Dennis McInerny, *Thomas Merton: The Man and His Work* (Washington, D.C.: Consortium Press, 1974).

Footnotes to Chapter Three

1. See Don Goergen, *Personality-in-Process and Teilhard de Chardin* (Dubuque: Aquinas Institute of Theology, 1971), unpublished.
2. See *The Sexual Celibate,* pp. 14-16, for my discussion of the Yahwist's theology of sexuality. Also pp. 160-174 for a biblical and historical treatment of friendship.
3. Ibid., pp. 166-170. Also Aelred of Rievaulx, *On Spiritual Friendship* (Washington, D.C.: Cistercian Publications, 1974.)
4. Aelred of Rievaulx, op. cit., p. 73.
5. Ibid., p. 71.
6. Gregory Nazianzen, "Epistola 103 ad Palladium," *Patrologia Graeca,* vol. 37, 201-202.
7. John Chrysostom, "Homilies on Timothy, Homily 2," *The Nicene and Post Nicene Fathers, First Series* (New York: Christian Literature Co., 1889), vol. 13, p. 412.
8. Pierre Pourrat, *Christian Spirituality* (Westminster: Newman Press, 1955), vol. 4, p. 489.
9. Aelred of Rievaulx, op. cit., pp. 72, 103.
10. *Confessions of St. Augustine* (Garden City: Doubleday, 1960), pp. 97-100, Book 4, Chapters 4-6.
11. Aelred of Rievaulx, op. cit., p. 65.
12. *The Dialogue of St. Catherine of Siena* (Westminster, Md.: Newman, 1950), p. 110.
13. Paul Hinnebusch, *Friendship in the Lord* (Notre Dame: Ave Maria Press, 1974), p. 78.
14. *The Sexual Celibate,* pp. 146-160.
15. Ibid., pp. 64-72, 77-87.
16. Ibid., pp. 51-58. Also see Sively and Cecco, "Components of Sexual Identity," *Journal of Homosexuality,* vol. 3 (1977), pp. 41-48.

17. Paul Hinnebusch, op. cit., pp. 58ff.
18. Aelred of Rievaulx, op. cit., pp. 93ff.
19. More and more research is available on adult development. E.g., Daniel Levinson, *The Seasons of a Man's Life* (New York: Alfred Knopf, 1978).
20. Thomas Aquinas, *Summa Contra Gentiles,* III, chapter 124, section 5.
21. Aristotle, *Nicomachean Ethics,* Book VIII, chapter 6 (1158ª 10).
22. See *The Sexual Celibate,* p. 161. John 15:6.
23. See Galatians 5:19-23, 1 Cor. 12:10. Also *Discernment of Spirits* by Malatesta et al., (Collegeville: Liturgical Press, 1970).
24. See Donald Goergen's "Separation Anxiety and Celibate Friendship," *Review for Religious,* vol. 35 (1976), pp. 256-264.
25. Don Browning, *Generative Man* (New York: Dell Publishing Co., 1975).
26. Ibid., p. 145.
27. Ibid., p. 146.
28. Erik Erikson, *Childhood and Society* (New York: W. W. Norton and Co., 1963), pp. 247-274.
29. Don Browning, op. cit., p. 163. Also Erik Erikson, *Insight and Responsibility,* p. 130.

Footnotes to Chapter Four

1. Rosabeth Kanter's *Commitment and Community* (Cambridge: Harvard University Press, 1974) is an excellent sociological analysis of communes and utopian communities with insights into the causes of failure or success.
2. See Kittel, *Theological Dictionary of the New Testament* (Grand Rapids: Wm. B. Eerdmans, 1965), vol. 3, pp. 789-809, especially 804-809, for a discussion of *Koinonia.*
3. John A. T. Robinson, *The Body: A Study in Pauline Theology* (London: SCM Press, 1963), especially pp. 49-55.
4. See Teilhard de Chardin's "Cosmic Life," *Writings in Time of War* (New York: Harper and Row, 1968), p. 45; "Sketch of a Personalistic Universe," *Human Energy* (New York: Harcourt Brace Jovanovich, 1969), p. 60; "Some

Reflections on the Rights of Man," *Future of Man* (New York: Harper and Row, 1964), p. 194; *The Divine Milieu* (New York: Harper and Row, 1960), p. 122.

5. Teilhard de Chardin, *The Divine Milieu*, p. 122.

6. Teilhard de Chardin, "The Grand Option," *Future of Man*, p. 54.

7. Teilhard de Chardin, *The Phenomenon of Man* (New York: Harper and Row, 1959), p. 237.

8. Teilhard de Chardin, "Sketch of a Personalistic Universe," *Human Energy*, p. 62.

9. "Some Reflections on the Rights of Man," *Future of Man*, p. 195.

10. *The Phenomenon of Man*, pp. 256-257.

11. *The Divine Milieu*, p. 93.

12. As alpha or the starting point of personality development, individuality could move in different directions. Individualism or egoism is a possible path that it could follow. Thus we must look to the significance of its direction or goal as well as to its significance as the starting point of growth. Personality then is more than the given individuality of the person and Teilhard sets out to discuss what else is included. Thus he always distinguishes between individuality and personality. Julian Huxley writes in the introduction to *The Phenomenon of Man* (Harper Torchbook Edition) that man is a person, an organism which has transcended individuality in personality, commenting on Teilhard's reference in the text that egoism's mistake is to "confuse individuality with personality" (PM, 263). *In Science and Christ* (New York: Harper and Row 1969), 139, he speaks of confusing individualism and personalism. In *Human Energy*, 64, he writes, "The cause of our dislike of collectivity lies in the illusion which makes us stubbornly identify 'personal' with 'individual'."

13. "The Grand Option," *The Future of Man*, p. 46.

14. *The Phenomenon of Man*, p. 263.

15. "Sketch of a Personalistic Universe," *Human Energy*, p. 64.

16. *The Phenomenon of Man*, p. 244.

17. Ibid., p. 263.

18. Ibid., p. 246.

19. Ibid., p. 172.
20. Ibid., p. 262. There are numerous references in his writings to this thesis. Among them are *The Future of Man*, p. 55 and 302, *Human Energy*, p. 149 and 152, *Science and Christ*, p. 184. He writes in *The Future of Man*, p. 53, "True union (that is to say, synthesis) does not confound; it differentiates."
21. "Life and the Planets," *The Future of Man*, p. 119.
22. "The Salvation of Mankind," *Science and Christ*, pp. 136-137.
23. "My Universe," *Science and Christ*, pp. 45-46.
24. *The Phenomenon of Man*, p. 265.
25. "Super-Humanity, Super-Christ, Super-Charity," *Science and Christ*, p. 160.
26. "The New Spirit," *The Future of Man*, pp. 91-92.
27. "The Grand Option," *The Future of Man*, p. 55.
28. "Some Reflections on Progress," *The Future of Man*, p. 72. See also: "Life has an objective; and that objective is a summit; and this summit, towards which all our striving must be directed, can only be attained by our drawing together, all of us, more and more closely and in every sense —individually, socially, nationally, and racially." "The New Spirit," *The Future of Man*, p. 91.
29. *The Phenomenon of Man*, p. 266.
30. Ibid., p. 172.
31. Ibid., p. 246.
32. Dietrich Bonhoeffer, *Life Together* (New York: Harper and Row, 1954), p. 78.
33. Soren Kierkegaard, "The Rotation Method," *Either/Or* (Princeton: Princeton University Press, 1971), vol. I, pp. 281-282 ff.

Footnotes to Chapter Five

1. Note my comment on compassion in *The Sexual Celibate*, pp. 26-27.
2. Abraham Maslow, *The Farther Reaches of Human Nature* (New York: The Viking Press, 1972), pp. 160-162.
3. Consider S. R. Driver, *The Book of Genesis*, Westminster Commentaries (London: Methuen and Co., 1907) pp. 191

ff.; E. A. Speiser, *Genesis,* The Anchor Bible (Garden City: Doubleday and Co., 1964), pp. 128 ff.; Gerhard von Rad, *Genesis* (Philadelphia: The Westminster Press, 1961), pp. 199 ff.; and *Jerome Biblical Commentary* (Englewood Cliffs, N.J.: Prentice-Hall, 1968), pp. 20 ff.

4. R. A. F. MacKenzie, "Job," *Jerome Biblical Commentary,* p. 528, comment on 31:31-32.

5. Henri Nouwen, *Reaching Out* (Garden City: Doubleday and Co., 1975), p. 51.

6. See Louis Bouyer's History of Christian Spirituality, vol. 1, *The Spirituality of the New Testament and the Fathers* (New York: Seabury Press, 1963), pp. 190-210.

7. The discussion includes, among others: Oscar Cullmann, *The Christology of the New Testament* (Philadelphia: Westminster Press, 1963); Reginald Fuller, *The Foundations of New Testament Christology* (New York: Charles Scribner's Sons, 1965); Jacques Guillet, *The Consciousness of Jesus* (New York: Newman Press, 1971); Walter Kasper, *Jesus the Christ* (New York: Paulist Press, 1976); Jon Sobrino, *Christology at the Crossroads* (Maryknoll: Orbis Books, 1978); Bruce Vawter, *The Man Jesus* (Garden City: Doubleday and Co., 1973).

8. See Joachim Jeremias, *The Theology of the New Testament* (New York: Charles Scribner's Sons, 1971), pp. 43-49, 108-121.

9. Ibid., pp. 36-37, 67-68.

10. Matthew 6:7-15; Luke 24:44-49; John 16; Acts 1:6-8; Romans 8:14-17.

11. C. H. Dodd, *History and the Gospel* (London: Nisbet and Co., 1960), p. 94.

12. Adolf Holl, *Jesus in Bad Company* (New York: Holt, Rinehart and Winston, 1972).

13. *The Foundations of New Testament Christology,* pp. 102-141.

14. James Cone, *A Black Theology of Liberation* (Philadelphia: J. B. Lippincott Co., 1970), pp. 24 and 33.

15. Gustavo Gutierrez, *A Theology of Liberation* (Maryknoll: Orbis Books, 1973), esp. pp. 11-13, 145. Also see Juan Luis Segundo, *The Liberation of Theology* (Maryknoll: Orbis Books, 1976).

16. Helder Camara, "Principle Themes of a Theology of Lib-

eration," unpublished lecture delivered at the Padres Retreat in Tucson, April 24-27, 1973.

17. E.g., Roger Garaudy, *From Anathema to Dialogue* (New York: Herder and Herder, 1966).

18. Matt. 9:14-17; Mark 2:18-22; Luke 5:33-39.

19. Huizinga, *Homo Ludens* (Boston: Beacon Press, 1955).

20. Jurgen Moltmann, *Theology of Play* (New York: Harper and Row, 1972).

21. Aristotle, *Nicomachean Ethics*, Bk IV, 8 (1128).

22. See Thomas' commentary on Aristotle's *Ethics*, IV, 8.

23. Thomas Aquinas, *ST*, II/II, q. 168.

24. *ST.*, q. 168, a. 2.

25. *ST.*, q. 168, a. 4.

26. Hugo Rahner, *Man At Play* (N.Y.: Herder and Herder, 1967), 8.

27. Jurgen Moltmann, *Theology of Play,* pp. 35-36.

28. See Allen Maruyama's *Marshall McLuhan's New Man of the Electric Age,* unpublished doctoral dissertation, Aquinas Institute of Theology, Dubuque, Iowa, especially pp. 231-240.

29. Moltmann, *Theology of Play,* p. 21.

Footnotes to Chapter Six

1. Note commentaries on these texts. E.g. Eugene Maly, "Genesis," *Jerome Biblical Commentary,* esp. p. 20, comment on Genesis 17:15-16. Also see "Isaac" in dictionaries of the Bible.

2. Jurgen Moltmann, *Theology of Play,* p. 31.

3. Donald Goergen, "The Eucharistic Presence: A Process Perspective," *The Teilhard Review,* IX (1974), pp. 16-23.

4. Donald Goergen, *Personality-in-Process and Teilhard de Chardin,* unpublished doctoral dissertation, 1971, Aquinas Institute, Dubuque, Iowa.

5. I referred to this in Chapter Five. See John A. T. Robinson, *The Body,* p. 51.

Footnotes to Chapter Seven

1. The discussion of the relationship between God and the world, between Christ and creation, is related to develop-

ments within process theology. For further reading on Teilhard one could consider Robert Faricy's *Teilhard de Chardin's Theology of the Christian in the World* (New York: Sheed and Ward, 1967); and Christopher Mooney's *Teilhard de Chardin and the Mystery of Christ* (New York: Harper and Row, 1966). For Whiteheadian process perspectives, consider John Cobb's *God and the World* (Philadelphia: Westminster Press, 1969); John Cobb and David Griffin, *Process Theology—An Introductory Exposition* (Philadelphia: Westminster Press, 1976). The perspective I take in this chapter is my own reflection, but one stimulated by process theology, both Teilhardian and Whiteheadian.

2. The relationship between *agape, philia,* and *eros* presents a special theological problem. I have previously maintained that *agape* and *philia* are used interchangeably in John's Gospel. See *The Sexual Celibate,* p. 165. The even deeper issue is the relationship between *agape* and *eros.* Anders Nygren in *Agape and Eros* (Philadelphia: Westminster Press, 1953) lucidly presents the issues but approaches *agape* and *eros* in a completely either/or framework with which I disagree. Ceslaus Spicq's *Agape in the New Testament,* 3 vols. (St. Louis: B. Herder Book Co., 1966) includes significant research. This is a problem to which I wish to return in appendix 2.

3. Like other issues which I raise in this chapter (e.g., the interdependence between God and the world, the relationship between *agape* and *eros,* and the suffering of God), the relationship between freedom and necessity presents a major theological and philosophical issue. Until I have the opportunity to develop this at greater length, I place the kind of necessity I attribute to God in quotation marks. There are two kinds of necessity, the necessity of unfreedom, a necessity which is unfree, the necessity of creatures, and secondly, the necessity of freedom, a necessity which is free, the necessity of a Creator. Freedom necessarily chooses the good; unfreedom has the choice between good and evil. Freedom and necessity are not contradictions to be understood in either/or terms alone. In a different way, Thomas Aquinas distinguishes two meanings of necessity in *Summa Theologica,* III, 1, 2.

4. The suffering of God, that God does suffer with us, is another theme which one can find in process thought. In addition to process thinkers, an important work is Jurgen Moltmann's *The Crucified God* (New York: Harper and Row, 1974).

5. This translation of the Holy Spirit as Holy Breath comes from the insight of Donald Gelpi, *Experiencing God* (New York: Paulist Press, 1978), pp. 122-154.

6. This concept of "created gods" is found in mystical literature and theology. E.g. see John Arintero, *The Mystical Evolution in the Development and Vitality of the Church,* vol. 1 (St. Louis: B. Herder Books, 1950), esp. pp. 1-101.

Footnotes to Chapter Eight

1. For further references to this issue, see footnote 7 in Chapter Five.

2. Joachim Jeremias, *New Testament Theology,* pp. 68-75.

3. Ernst Kasemann, *Jesus Means Freedom* (Philadelphia: Fortress Press, 1970).

4. For the development of eschatological and messianic concepts, see Sigmund Mowinckel, *He That Cometh* (Nashville: Abingdon Press, 1954).

5. See Donald Goergen, *Personality-in-Process and Teilhard de Chardin,* unpublished doctoral dissertation, Aquinas Institute, Dubuque, Iowa, 1971, esp. Chapters One and Two. Also see Teilhard de Chardin *Future of Man* (New York: Harper and Row, 1964), pp. 52-57; *Science and Christ* (New York: Harper and Row, 1969), p. 163; *Writings in Time of War* (New York: Harper and Row, 1968), p. 42.

6. An excellent example of a Kenotic Christology is Russell Aldwinckle, *More Than Man* (Grand Rapids: Eerdmans Publishing Co., 1976).

Footnotes to Chapter Nine

1. There are many contemporary expositions of the theology of original sin, e.g., Andre-Marie Dubarle, *The Biblical Doctrine of Original Sin* (New York: Herder and Herder, 1964); Herbert Haag, "The Original Sin Discussion, 1966-

1971)," *Journal of Ecumenical Studies,* vol. 10 (1973), pp. 259-289; Leopold Sabourin, "Original Sin Reappraised," *Biblical Theology Bulletin,* 3 (1973), pp. 51-81; Piet Schoonenberg, *Man and Sin* (South Bend: University of Notre Dame Press, 1964).

2. In this respect, sin is akin to grace. See Thomas O'Meara, *Loose in the World* (New York: Paulist Press, 1974).

3. The important work on psychology and power is Rollo May, *Power and Innocence* (New York: W. W. Norton and Co., Inc., 1972). Also see Rollo May, *The Courage To Create* (New York: W. W. Norton and Co., Inc., 1975); Paul Tillich, *The Courage To Be* (New Haven: Yale University Press, 1952).

4. The philosophy and theology of power has become an important issue in process thought, both Teilhardian and Whiteheadian. Representative discussions would include: John B. Cobb, *God and the World* (Philadelphia: Westminster Press, 1969), Chapter 4; David Ray Griffin, *God, Power and Evil* (Philadelphia: Westminster Press, 1976), Chapters 17 and 18; Bernard Loomer "Two Conceptions of Power," *Process Studies,* vol. 6 (1976), pp. 5-32; Teilhard de Chardin, *The Future of Man* (New York: Harper and Row, 1964), Chapters 11 and 12.

5. Rollo May's understanding of the demonic is important here. See *Love and Will* (New York: W. W. Norton and Co., Inc., 1969), especially Chapters 5 and 6.

6. Thomas Aquinas, *Summa Contra Gentiles,* Book 4, Chapter 21.

7. Thomas Aquinas, *Summa Theologiae,* I, q. 37, a. 1.

8. *Summa Contra Gentiles,* Book 4, Chapter 21.

9. Ibid.

10. Ibid.

11. See Norman Pittenger, *The Holy Spirit* (Philadelphia: United Church Press, 1974); Russell Pregeant, *Christology Beyond Dogma* (Philadelphia: Fortress Press, 1978).

12. See Yves Congar, *The Mystery of the Temple* (Westminster, Md.: Newman Press, 1962).

13. See John A. T. Robinson, *Jesus and His Coming* (New York: Abingdon Press, 1957), esp. pp. 29-30. Also John L. McKenzie, *The Power and the Wisdom* (Milwaukee: Bruce Publishing Co., 1965), p. 67. Also Donald Goergen,

Personality-in-Process and Teilhard de Chardin, unpublished doctoral dissertation, Aquinas Institute, Dubuque, Iowa, Chapter 6.

Footnotes to Appendix I

1. Etienne Gilson and Thomas Longan, *Modern Philosophy: Descartes to Kant* (New York: Random House, 1967), pp. 55-86.
2. Soren Kierkegaard, *Either/Or* (Princeton: Princeton University Press, 1949). Also see Walter Lowrie, *Kierkegaard* (New York: Harper and Row, 1962).
3. Charles Percy Snow, *The Two Cultures and the Scientific Revolution* (New York: Cambridge University Press, 1961). Also C. P. Snow, *The Two Cultures: and a Second Look* (New York: New American Library, 1964).
4. Barbara Tuchman, *A Distant Mirror* (New York: Alfred Knopf, 1978).
5. Frederick Copleston, *A History of Philosophy,* vol. 7, part 1, Fichte to Hegel (Garden City: Doubleday and Co., 1965), p. 203.
6. Jacob Bronowski, *The Origins of Knowledge and Imagination* (New Haven: Yale University Press, 1978), p. 58.
7. Ibid., p. 89.
8. Laurence Thompson, *Chinese Religion: An Introduction* (Belmont: Dickenson Publishing Co., 1969). *The I Ching, or Book of Changes* (New York, 1950). Thompson's book provides excellent further bibliography.
9. E.g., Alfred North Whitehead, *Process and Reality* (New York: Harper and Row, 1960), p. 133. Some introductions to Whitehead's thought include A. H. Johnson, *Whitehead's Theory of Reality* (New York: Dover Publications, 1962); Norman Pittenger, *Alfred North Whitehead* (Richmond: John Knox Press, 1969). More thorough introductions would include William Christian, *An Interpretation of Whitehead's Metaphysics* (New Haven: Yale University Press, 1967); Ivor Leclerc, *Whitehead's Metaphysics* (London: George Allen and Unwin, 1965); Donald Sherburne, *A Key to Whitehead's Process and Reality* (Bloomington: Indiana University Press, 1966).
10. For further discussion of Teilhard see Robert Faricy, *Teil-*

hard de Chardin's Theology of the Christian in the World (New York: Sheed and Ward, 1967); Donald Gray, *The One and the Many* (London: Burns and Oates, 1969); Emile Rideau, *The Thought of Teilhard de Chardin* (New York: Harper and Row, 1967); N. M. Wildiers, *An Introduction to Teilhard de Chardin* (New York: Harper and Row, 1968).

11. Bernard Meland, *Fallible Forms and Symbols* (Philadelphia: Fortress Press, 1976).

12. Jonas Salk, *The Survival of the Wisest* (New York: Harper and Row, 1973), p. 79.

13. Ibid., p. 86-87.

14. Henri Bergson, *Creative Evolution* (New York: Random House, 1944), p. 108.

15. Ibid., p. 150-151.

16. Ibid., p. 150.

17. Ibid., p. 291.

18. Some interesting reading includes: Julian Jaynes, *The Origin of Consciousness in the Breakdown of the Bicameral Mind* (Boston: Houghton Mifflin Co., 1976); Erich Neumann, *The Origins and History of Consciousness* (Princeton: Princeton University Press, 1954).

Footnotes to Appendix II

1. C. S. Lewis, *The Four Loves* (London: Collins, 1965).

2. Rollo May, *Love and Will* (New York: W. W. Norton and Co., 1969), p. 37.

3. Anders Nygren, *Agape and Eros* (Philadelphia: Westminster Press, 1953).

4. See Thor Hall, *Anders Nygren* (Waco: Word Books Publisher, 1978).

5. With this I agree—to a certain extent. It is obvious biblically. There is a kind of priority *diakonia* has. Yet one must call to mind the dangers I raise in Chapter One about any attempt to place the five loves in a hierarchy as being a distortion of them. Of value here is an essay by Karl Rahner, "Reflections on the Unity of the Love of Neighbor and the Love of God," *Theological Investigations*, vol. 6, (Baltimore: Helicon Press, 1969). Note

Nygren's tendency to dichotomize, e.g., p. 210, and then hierarchize, p. 219. This kind of hierarchy is *not* biblical.

6. Nygren's setting aside all forms of self-love is arbitrary as is his interpretation of the text: love your neighbor as yourself. See pp. 100-101.

7. I agree with two of Nygren's four characteristics of *agape: agape* is creative, and God is the initiator. The other two characteristics must be highly qualified: *Agape* is spontaneous and "unmotivated"; *agape* is "indifferent to value" (see pp. 75-81). Nygren writes, "*Agape* does not recognize value, but creates it" (p. 78). True, but then it's not indifferent. As to its being unmotivated in order to be pure, the best biblical treatment of *agape* is still Ceslaus Spicq, *Agape in the New Testament* (St. Louis: B. Herder Co., 1963-1966), 3 volumes. Also see Josef Pieper's excellent *About Love* (Chicago: Franciscan Herald Press, 1974).

8. Plato's *Symposium* would be the important work here.

9. There is a growing body of literature to make us aware that the negativity toward sexuality within Christianity has non-Christian origins. E.g., Vern Bullough's *Sexual Variance in Society and History* (New York: John Wiley and Sons, 1976), esp. chapters 7 and 8.

10. A balanced and helpful perspective here comes from Rollo May's *Love and Will*, especially chapters 2 and 3. Also see my *The Sexual Celibate*.

BIBLIOGRAPHY

This is a bibliography of both classical and contemporary works in the area of spirituality. It is obviously not exhaustive. Of works to which I have referred in this book, I only include those here that pertain to the field of spirituality. I have included some additional works in order to provide a more complete bibliography.

Adler, Alfred. *Superiority and Social Interest*. Edited by Heinz and Rowena Ansbacher. Evanston: Northwestern Univ. Press, 1970.

Aelred of Rievaulx. *Treatise on Pastoral Prayer*. Spencer: Cisterian Publications, 1971.

———. *On Spiritual Friendship*. Washington, D.C.: Cistercian Publications, 1974.

Alexander, Jon. "The American Civil Religion Debate," *Cross and Crown*. 29 (1977):227-236.

Allport, Gordon. *Becoming*. New Haven: Yale University Press, 1955.

Ancelet-Hustache, Jeanne. *Meister Eckhart & The Rhineland Mystics*. New York: Harper Torchbooks, 1957.

Arberry, A. F., trans. *Muslim Saints and Mystics*. London: Routledge & Kegan Paul, 1966.

Arintero, John. *The Mystical Evolution in the Development and Vitality of the Church*, 2 vols. St. Louis: B. Herder Book Co., 1951.

———. *Stages in Prayer*. London: Blackfriars Publications, 1957.

Ashley, Benedict. "Guide to St. Catherine's Dialogue," *Cross and Crown*. 29 (1977):237-249.

———. "A Psychological Model with a Spiritual Dimension," *Pastoral Psychology*. 23 (1972):31-40.

Augustine. *The Confessions*. New York: Doubleday Image, 1960.

———. *The Enchiridion on Faith, Hope and Love*. Chicago: Henry Regnery Co., 1961.

Babuscio, Jack. *We Speak for Ourselves-Experiences in Homosexual Counseling*. Philadelphia: Fortress Press, 1977.

0# DONALD GOERGEN

Bahm, Archie. "Stages in the Development of Religious Experience," *R. M. Bucke Memorial Society Newsletter Review*. Vol. III, No. 1 (1968):26-27.

Bakan, Daniel. *The Duality of Human Existence*. Boston: Beacon Press, 1966.

Balthasar, Hans Urs von. *Prayer*. New York: Sheed & Ward, 1961.

Barry, Wm. A. "Silence and the Directed Retreat," *Review for Religious*. 32 (1973):347-351.

Becker, Ernest. *The Denial of Death*. New York: Free Press, 1973.

Beevers, John, trans. *The Autobiography of St. Therese of Lisieux*. New York: Doubleday Image Books, 1957.

Berrigan, Daniel. *The Dark Night of Resistance*. New York: Doubleday, 1971.

The Bhagavad Gita, trans. by Franklin Edgerton. New York: Harper Torch, 1964.

———. trans. by Juan Mascaro. Baltimore: Penguin Books, 1970.

Blenkinsopp, Joseph. *Sexuality and the Christian Tradition*. Dayton: Pflaum Press, 1969.

Bloesch, Donald. *The Christian Life and Salvation*. Grand Rapids: Eerdmans, 1967.

———. *The Crisis of Piety*. Grand Rapids: Eerdmans, 1968.

———. *Wellsprings of Renewal: Promise in Christian Communal Life*. Grand Rapids: Eerdmans, 1974.

Bloom, Anthony. *God and Man*. New York: Paulist-Newman, 1973.

Bonhoeffer, Dietrich. *The Cost of Discipleship*. New York: Macmillan, 1972.

———. *Life Together*. New York: Harper & Row, 1954.

Bouchard, Charles E. "The Charism of the Community," *Review for Religious*. 37 (1978):350-356.

———. "Journey of Faith," *Review for Religious*. 35 (1977):592-599.

Bouyer, Louis. *The Cistercian Heritage*. Westminster: Newman Press, 1958.

———. *A History of Christian Spirituality,* 3 vols. New York: Seabury, 1977.

———. *Introduction to Spirituality*. Collegeville, Minn.: Liturgical Press, 1961.

——. *Liturgical Piety*. Notre Dame: Notre Dame Press, 1955.

——. *The Spirit and Forms of Protestantism*. Westminster: Newman Press, 1961.

Bowlby, John. *Separation: Anxiety and Anger*. New York: Basic Books, Inc., 1973.

——. *Attachment*. New York: Basic Books, Inc., 1969.

Brain, Robert. *Friends and Lovers*. New York: Simon and Schuster Pocket Books, 1977.

Branden, Nathaniel. *The Disowned Self*. New York: Bantam Books, 1973.

——. *The Psychology of Self-Esteem*. New York: Bantam Books, 1971.

Brennan, James F. "Friendship: The Adlerian Mode of Existence," *Journal of Individual Psychology*. 22 (1966):43-48.

Bro, Bernard. *Christian Asceticism and Modern Man*. New York: Philosophical Library, 1955.

——. *Learning to Pray*. Staten Island: Alba House, 1966.

Browning, Don. *Generative Man*. New York: Dell Publishing Co., 1975.

Bucke, Richard M. *Cosmic Consciousness*. New York: E. P. Dutton & Co., 1969.

Buechner, Frederick. *The Alphabet of Grace*. New York: Seabury Press, 1970.

Bullough, Vern. *Sexual Variance in Society and History*. New York: John Wiley and Sons, 1976.

Burns, Robert. "The Mission of the Christian Church," *Cross and Crown*. 28 (1976):351-361.

Carretto, Carlo. *Letters from the Desert*. Maryknoll: Orbis, 1972.

Carroll, James. *Contemplation*. New York: Paulist Press, 1972.

——. *The Winter Name of God*. New York: Sheed & Ward, 1975.

Chauchard, Paul. *Teilhard de Chardin on Love and Suffering*. Glen Rock: Paulist Press, 1966.

Chenu, M. D. *Faith and Theology*, trans. by Denis Kickey. New York: Macmillan, 1968.

——. "The Need for a Theology of the World", *The Great Ideas of Today*. Chicago: Encyclopedia Britannica, 1967.

Clarke, Thomas E. *New Passion or New Pentecost*. New York: Paulist Press, 1973.

Cloud of Unknowing. Garden City: Doubleday, 1973.

Cobb, John. *God and the World.* Philadelphia: Westminster Press, 1969.

Congar, Marie Joseph. *Mystery of the Temple,* trans. by Reginald Trevett. Westminster: Newman Press, 1962.

Connolly, Wm. "Social Action and the Directed Retreat," *Review for Religious.* 33 (1974):114-118.

———. "Disappointment in Prayer, Prelude to Growth?" *Review for Religious.* 32 (1973):557-560.

Cox, Harvey. *Feast of Fools.* Cambridge: Harvard Univ. Press, 1969.

Cunningham, Francis. *The Christian Life.* Dubuque: The Priory Press, 1959.

Curran, Charles. *Catholic Moral Theology In Dialogue.* Notre Dame: Notre Dame Press, 1976.

Davis, Charles. *Body As Spirit.* New York: Seabury Press, 1976.

———. ed. *English Spiritual Writers.* New York: Sheed & Ward, 1961.

Dechanet, J. M. *Christian Yoga.* New York: Harper & Row, 1960.

DeRougement, Denis. *Love in the Western World.* New York: Harper & Row, 1956.

Dialogues of St. Catherine of Siena. Westminster: Newman Press, 1950.

Discernment of Spirits. Collegeville: Liturgical Press, 1970.

Douglass, James. *The Non-Violent Cross.* New York: Macmillan, 1968.

———. *Resistance and Contemplation.* Garden City: Doubleday, 1972.

Dreikurs, Rudolf. "The Tasks of Life. I. Adler's Three Tasks," *Individual Psychologist.* 4 (1967):18-22.

———. "The Tasks of Life. II. The Fourth Life Task," *Individual Psychologist.* 4 (1967):51-56.

Driver, Tom. "Sexuality and Jesus," *New Theology No. 3.* ed. Marty and Peerman. New York: Macmillan, 1966.

Drummond, Richard. *Gautama the Buddha.* Grand Rapids: Eerdmans, 1974.

———. *Unto the Churches: Jesus Christ, Christianity, and the Edgar Cayce Readings.* Virginia Beach: A.R.E. Press, 1978.

Dufresne, Edward. *Partnership: Marriage and the Committed Life.* New York: Paulist Press, 1975.

Dulles, Avery. *Models of the Church.* Garden City: Doubleday, 1974.

Dunn, James. *Jesus and the Spirit.* London: SCM Press, 1975.

Eliade, Mircea. *Birth and Rebirth.* New York: Harper & Row, 1958.

———. *Cosmos and History.* New York: Harper & Row, 1959.

———. *A History of Religious Ideas.* Chicago: Univ. of Chicago Press, 1978.

———. *Images and Symbols.* New York: Sheed & Ward, 1961.

———. *Mephistopheles and the Androgyne.* New York: Sheed & Ward, 1965.

———. *Myth and Reality.* New York: Harper & Row, 1963.

———. *The Sacred and the Profane.* New York: Harper & Row, 1961.

Ellul, Jacques. *A Critique of the New Commonplaces.* New York: Knopf, 1968.

———. *The Ethics of Freedom.* Grand Rapids: Eerdmans, 1976.

———. *False Presence of the Kingdom.* New York: Seabury, 1972.

———. *Hope in Time of Abandonment.* New York: Seabury, 1973.

———. *The New Demons.* New York: Seabury, 1975.

———. *Prayer and Modern Man.* New York: Seabury, 1973.

———. *The Technological Society.* New York: Knopf, 1965.

———. *Violence.* New York: Seabury, 1969.

English, John. *Choosing Life.* Ramsey: Paulist Press, 1978.

Erikson, Eric. *Childhood and Society.* New York: W. W. Norton & Co., 1963.

Evdokimov, Paul. *The Struggle with God.* Glen Rock: Paulist Press, 1966.

Faricy, R. *Teilhard de Chardin's Theology of the Christian in the World.* New York: Sheed & Ward, 1967.

Farrell, Edward. *Prayer is a Hunger.* Denville: Dimension, 1972.

Finnerty, Adam. *No More Plastic Jesus.* Maryknoll: Orbis Books, 1977.

Fischer, Louis. *Gandhi, His Life and Message for the World.* New York: Mentor Books, 1954.

Fiske, A. "Cassian and Monastic Friendship," *American Benedictine Review.* 12 (1961):190-205.

——. "William of St. Thierry and Friendship," *Citeaux*. 12 (1961):5-27.

——. "Aelred's of Rievaulx Idea of Friendship and Love," *Citeaux*. 13 (1962):5-17; 97-132.

——. "Saint Anselm and Friendship," *Studia Monastica*. 3 (1961):260-290.

Fleming, David. "Beginning Spiritual Direction," *Review for Religious*. 33 (1974):546-550.

Forem, Jack. *Transcendental Meditation*. New York: E. P. Dutton & Co., 1973.

Fox, Matthew. "The Case for Extrovert Meditation," *Spirituality Today*. 30 (1978):164-177.

——. "Catholic Spirituality and the American Spirit: Notes, for a Tricentennial Celebration," *Spiritual Life*. 22 (1976): 44-61.

——. "Elements of a Biblical, Creation-Centered Spirituality," *Spirituality Today*. 30 (1978):360-369.

——. "Hermeneutic and Hagiography," *Spirituality Today*. 30 (1978):263-271.

——. "Learning and Unlearning Spiritualities," *Living Light*. 12 (1975):168-178.

——. *On Becoming a Musical, Mystical Bear*. New York: Harper & Row, 1972.

——. "On Desentimentalizing Spirituality," *Spirituality Today*. 30 (1978):64-76.

——. "The Prayer and Spirituality of Jesus," *Living Light*. 12 (1975): 175-192.

——. *Whee! We, Wee, all the Way Home: A Guide to the New Sensual Spirituality*. Wilmington: Consortium, 1976.

Francis De Sales. *Introduction to the Devout Life*. Westminster: Christian Classics, 1962.

Frankl, Viktor. *Man's Search for Meaning: An Introduction to Logotherapy*. Boston: Beacon Press, 1968.

——. *The Doctor and the Soul: From Psychotherapy to Logotherapy*. New York: Random House, 1973.

Fransen, Peter. *The New Life of Grace*. New York: Seabury, 1973.

Fromm, Erich. *The Art of Loving*. New York: Harper & Row, 1956.

Gallen, Joseph. "Femininity and Spirituality," *Review for Religious.* 20 (1961):237-256.

Gandhi, Mohandas. *Autobiography: The Story of My Experiments With Truth.* Boston: Beacon Press, 1968.

Garrigou-Lagrange, Reginald. *The Love of God and the Cross of Jesus,* 2 vols. St. Louis: B. Herder & Co., 1951.

Gautier, Jean. *Some Schools of Catholic Spirituality.* New York: Desclee, 1959.

Gelpi, Donald. *Charism and Sacrament: A Theology of Christian Conversion.* New York: Paulist Press, 1976.

——. *Discerning the Spirit.* New York: Sheed & Ward, 1970.

——. *Experiencing God: A Theology of Human Experience.* New York: Paulist Press, 1978.

——. *Pentecostalism.* New York: Paulist Press, 1971.

Gilleman, Gerard. *The Primacy of Charity in Moral Theology.* Westminster: Newman Press, 1961.

Gleason, Robert. *Grace.* New York: Sheed & Ward, 1962.

Goble, Frank. *The Third Force.* New York: Grossman Publications, 1970.

Goergen, Donald. "The Eucharistic Presence: A Process Perspective," *The Teilhard Review.* 9 (1974):16-23.

——. *The Sexual Celibate.* New York: Seabury, 1974.

——. "Separation. Anxiety and Celibate Friendship," *Review for Religious.* 35 (1976):256-64.

Graham, Dom Eldred. *Zen Catholicism.* New York: Harcourt, Brace & World, 1963.

Greeley, Andrew. *The Friendship Game.* New York: Doubleday, 1970.

Gutierrez, Gustavo. *A Theology of Liberation.* Maryknoll: Orbis Books, 1973.

Hakenewerth, Quentin. *For the Sake of the Kingdom.* Collegeville: The Liturgical Press, 1971.

Hallier, Amedee. *The Monastic Theology of Aelred of Rievaulx.* Spencer: Cistercian Publications, 1969.

Halpin, Marlene. "Tensions Between Priests and Professional Religious Women," *Spirituality Today.* 30 (1978):24-36.

Happold, F. C. *Mysticism, A Study and an Anthology.* Baltimore: Penguin Books, 1970.

——. *Prayer and Meditation.* Baltimore: Penguin Books, 1971.

Haughey, John. *Should Anyone Say Forever?* Garden City: Doubleday, 1977.

Haring, Bernard. *Blessed are the Pure in Heart: the Beatitudes.* New York: Seabury, 1977.

———. *Celebrating Joy.* New York: Herder & Herder, 1970.

———. *Evangelization Today.* Notre Dame: Fides Publishers, 1974.

———. *Hope is the Remedy.* Garden City: Doubleday, 1972.

———. *Love is the Answer.* Denville: Dimension Books, 1970.

———. *Married Love.* Chicago: Argus Communications, 1970.

———. *Morality is For Persons.* New York: Farrar, Straus & Giroux, 1971.

———. *The Sacraments & Your Everyday Life.* Liguori Publications, 1976.

———. *Sin in the Secular Age.* Garden City: Doubleday, 1974.

———. *A Theology of Protest.* New York: Farrar, Straus & Giroux, 1970.

Harkness, Georgia. *Mysticism, Its Meaning and Message.* Nashville: Abingdon Press, 1973.

Haughton, Rosemary. *The Theology of Experience.* New York: Newman Press, 1972.

Head, J. and Cranston, S. L. *Reincarnation, an East-West Anthology.* Wheaton: Quest Books, 1970.

Henry, Jules. *Culture Against Man.* New York: Vintage Books, 1963.

Heschel, Abraham. *Man's Quest for God.* New York: Charles Scribners, 1954.

Hesse, Hermann. *Narcissus & Goldmund.* New York: Farrar, Straus & Giroux, 1974.

———. *Siddhartha.* New York: New Directions, 1951.

Hick, John. *Death and Eternal Life.* London: Collins, 1976.

———. *Evil and the God of Love.* London: Macmillan, 1977.

Higgins, John. *Merton's Theology of Prayer.* Spencer: Cistercian Publications, 1971.

Hilton, Walter. *The Scale of Perfection.* St. Meinrad: Abbey Press, 1975.

Hinnebusch, Bill. *Dominican Spirituality.* Washington: The Thomist Press, 1965.

Hinnebusch, Paul. *Community in the Lord.* Notre Dame: Ave Maria Press, 1975.

———. "Faith, Prayer and Commitment," *Cross and Crown.* 28 (1976):362-371.

———. *Friendship in the Lord.* Notre Dame: Ave Maria Press, 1974.

———. *Prayer, the Search for Authenticity.* New York: Sheed & Ward, 1969.

———. *Secular Holiness.* Denville: Dimension Books, 1971.

Hocking, William. *The Meaning of God in Human Experience.* New Haven: Yale University Press, 1912.

Holl, Adolf. *Jesus in Bad Company.* New York: Holt, Rinehart & Winston, 1972.

Horner, Tom. *Jonathan Loved David.* Philadelphia: Westminster Press, 1978.

Huizinga, Johan. *Homo Ludens.* Boston: Beacon Press, 1955.

Human Sexuality: New Directions in American Catholic Thought, Catholic Theological Society of America, Anthony Kosnik, et. al. New York: Paulist Press, 1977.

Humphreys, Christian. *Concentration and Meditation.* Baltimore: Penguin Books, 1968.

Illich, Ivan. *Celebration of Awareness: A Call for Institutional Revolution.* Garden City: Doubleday, 1970.

Janssens, Louis. "Norms and Priorities In Love Ethics," *Louvain Studies.* 6 (1977):207-238.

Jaynes, Julian. *The Origins of Consciousness in the Breakdown of the Bicameral Mind.* Boston: Houghton Mifflin Co., 1976.

Jeremias, Joachim. *New Testament Theology.* New York: Charles Scribners, 1971.

———. *The Prayer of Jesus.* Naperville: Allenson, 1967.

Johann, Robert. *The Meaning of Love.* Westminster: Newman, 1959.

Johnston, William. *Christian Zen.* New York: Harper & Row, 1971.

———. *The Mysticism of the Cloud of Unknowing.* St. Meinrad: Abbey Press, 1975.

———. *Silent Music.* New York: Harper & Row, 1974.

———. *The Stillpoint: Reflections on Zen and Christian Mysticism.* New York: Perennial Library, 1970.

Kane, Thomas A. *The Healing Touch of Affirmation.* Whitinsville: Affirmation Books, 1976.

Kanter, Rosabeth. *Commitment and Community.* Cambridge: Harvard Univ. Press, 1974.

Kazantzakis, Nikos. *The Last Temptation of Christ.* New York: Simon and Schuster, 1966.

Keane, Philip. "The Meaning and Functioning of Sexuality in the Lives of Celibates and Virgins," *Review for Religious.* 34 (1975):277-314.

——. *Sexual Morality: A Catholic Perspective.* New York: Paulist Press, 1977.

Keen, Sam. *To A Dancing God.* New York: Harper & Row, 1970.

Kennedy, Eugene. *Sexual Counseling.* New York: Seabury, 1977.

Kierkegaard, Soren. *Purity of Heart is to Will One Thing.* New York: Harper & Row, 1956.

Kiesling, Christopher. "Celibacy, Friendship and Prayer," *Review for Religious.* 30 (1971):595-617.

——. *Celibacy, Prayer and Friendship, a Making-Sense-Out-of-Life Approach.* New York: Alba House, 1978.

Kitagawa, Joseph M. and Charles H. Long, (eds). *Myth and Symbols.* Chicago: University of Chicago Press, 1969.

Kosmicki, Stephen. "Nuclear Weapons: Challenge to Christian Spirituality," *Spirituality Today.* 30 (1978):100-106.

Knox, Ronald. *Enthusiasm.* New York: Oxford University Press, 1961.

Küng, Hans. *On Being a Christian.* Garden City: Doubleday, 1976.

LaPlace, Jean. *Experience the Spirit: An Experience of the Life in the Spirit.* Chicago: Franciscan Herald Press, 1977.

——. *Preparing for Spiritual Direction.* Chicago: Franciscan Herald Press, 1975.

Lepp, Ignace. *The Ways of Friendship.* New York: Macmillan, 1968.

Levinson, Daniel. *The Seasons of a Man's Life.* New York: Alfred Knopf, 1978.

Lewis, Clive Staples. *The Allegory of Love: A Study in Medieval Tradition.* Oxford: The Clarendon Press, 1936.

——. *Beyond Personality.* New York: Macmillan, 1948.

——. *The Four Loves.* London: Collins, 1960.

——. *That Hideous Strength.* New York: Macmillan, 1947.

———. *The Problem of Pain.* New York: Macmillan, 1943.

———. *The Screwtape Letters.* New York: Macmillan, 1944.

Loomer, Bernard. "Two Conceptions of Power," *Process Studies.* 6 (1976):5-32.

Lossky, Vladimir. *The Mystical Theology of the Eastern Church.* London: James Clarke & Co., 1968.

Lotz, Johannes. *Interior Prayer.* New York: Herder & Herder, 1968.

Macquarrie, John. *Christian Hope.* New York: Seabury, 1978.

Madden, James P. (ed.) *Loneliness.* Whitinsville: Affirmation Books, 1977.

Madow, Leo. *Anger.* New York: Charles Scribners, 1972.

Maguire, Daniel C. *The Moral Choice.* Garden City: Doubleday, 1978.

Maloney, George. "Abandonment in Human Love," *Sisters Today.* 49 (1977):231-241.

———. *The Breath of the Mystic.* Denville: Dimension Books, 1974.

———. *Toward Stillness.* Denville: Dimension Books, 1976.

———. *Man, the Divine Icon.* Pecos: Dove Publications, 1973.

Marechal, Joseph. *Psychology of the Mystics.* Albany: Magi Books, 1964.

Marmion, Abbot. *Christ the Life of the Soul.* Westminster: Christian Classics.

Maslow, Abraham. *Motivation and Personality.* New York: Harper & Row, 1970.

———. *Religion, Values, and Peak Experiences.* New York: Viking, 1970.

———. *The Farther Reaches of Human Nature.* New York: Viking, 1972.

May, Rollo. *Courage to Create.* New York: W. W. Norton & Co., 1975.

———. *Love and Will.* New York: W. W. Norton & Co., 1969.

———. *Power and Innocence.* New York: W. W. Norton & Co., 1972.

McGonigle, Thomas. "Second Century Silence," *Spirituality Today.* 30 (1978):45-54.

McInerny, Dennis. *Thomas Merton: The Man and His Work.* Washington, D.C.: Consortium Press, 1974.

McKenzie, John. *The Power and the Wisdom*. Milwaukee: Bruce Publishing Co., 1965.

McNamara, William. *The Art of Being Human*. Milwaukee: Bruce Publishing Co., 1962.

Meister Eckhart. Trans. by B. Blakney. New York: Harper & Row, 1941.

Meltz, Merrill. "Jesus the Model for Ministry," *Spirituality Today*. 30 (1978): 292-303.

Men and Masculinity, edited by Pleck and Sawyer. Englewood Cliffs: Prentice Hall, 1974.

Menninger, Karl. *Man Against Himself*. New York: Harcourt, Brace & World, 1938.

Merton, Thomas. *The Ascent to Truth*. New York: Harcourt, Brace & World, 1951.

———. *Contemplation in a World of Action*. Garden City: Doubleday, 1973.

———. *Contemplative Prayer*. New York: Doubleday, 1971.

———. "Notes for a Philosophy of Solitude," *Disputed Questions*. New York: Farrar, Strauss, Cudahy, 1953.

———. (ed.). *Gandhi On Non-Violence*. New York: New Directions, 1965.

———. *Peace*. New York: McCall's Publishing Co., 1971.

———. *Seeds of Contemplation*. Norfolk: New Directions, 1945.

———. *Thoughts in Solitude*. Garden City: Doubleday, 1968.

———. "The Spiritual Father in the Desert Tradition," *R. M. Bucke Memorial Society Newsletter Review*. Vol. III, No. 1, (1968):7-21.

Metz, Johannes. *Theology of the World*. New York: Seabury, 1969.

Meyer, Charles. *A Contemporary Theology of Grace*. Staten Island: Alba House, 1971.

Mohler, James. *Dimensions of Love: East and West*. Garden City: Doubleday, 1975.

———. *The Heresy of Monasticism*. Staten Island: Alba House, 1971.

Moltmann, Jürgen. *The Crucified God*. New York: Harper & Row, 1974.

———. *Theology of Play*. New York: Harper & Row, 1972.

Montagu, Ashley. *Touching: The Human Significance of the Skin*. New York: Harper & Row, 1972.

Mooney, Christopher, ed. *Prayer: the Problem of Dialogue with God.* New York: Paulist Press, 1969.

Moore, Thomas Verner. *The Life of Man With God.* New York: Harcourt, Brace & Co., 1956.

Moorhouse, Geoffrey. *Against All Reason.* Harmondsworth: Penguin Books, 1972.

Moustakas, Clark. *Loneliness.* Englewood Cliffs: Prentice-Hall, 1961.

———. *Loneliness and Love.* Englewood Cliffs: Prentice-Hall, 1972.

Murphy-O'Connor, Jerome. *Becoming Human Together.* Wilmington: Michael Glazier, 1977.

———. "What is the Religious Life?" *Doctrine and Life.* 11 (1974):3-69.

Murray, Robert. "Spiritual Friendship," *The Way.* 10 (1970): 61-73.

Naranjo, Claudio and Orstein, Robert. *The Psychology of Meditation.* New York: Viking Press, 1971.

Nedoncelle, Maurice. *The Nature and Use of Prayer.* London: Burns & Oates, 1964.

Nelson, James. *Embodiment.* Minneapolis: Augsburg Publishing Co., 1978.

Neumann, Erich. *The Origins and History of Consciousness.* Princeton: Princeton University Press, 1954.

Niebuhr, H. Richard. *Christ and Culture.* New York: Harper & Row, 1956.

Nouwen, Henri. "Compassion: the Core of Spiritual Leadership," *Worship.* 51 (1977):11-23.

———. *Creative Ministry.* Garden City: Doubleday, 1971.

———. *The Genesee Diary.* Garden City: Doubleday, 1976.

———. "Hospitality," *Monastic Studies.* 10 (1974):1-28.

———. *Intimacy.* Notre Dame: Fides Publishers, 1969.

———. *Out of Solitude.* Notre Dame: Ave Maria Press, 1974.

———. *Reaching Out.* Garden City: Doubleday, 1975.

———. "Solitude and Community," *Worship.* 52 (1978):13-23.

———. "Unceasing Prayer," *America.* 139 (1978):46-51.

———. *With Open Hands.* Notre Dame: Ave Maria Press, 1972.

———. *The Wounded Healer.* Garden City: Doubleday, 1962.

———. "The Self-availability of the Homosexual," *Is Gay Good?.* Philadelphia: Westminster Press, 1971.

DONALD GOERGEN

Nygren, Anders. *Agape and Eros.* Philadelphia: Westminster Press, 1953.

O'Brien, Elmer. *Varieties of Mystic Experience.* New York: New American Library, 1964.

O'Connell, Timothy E. *Principles for a Catholic Morality.* New York: Seabury, 1978.

Ochs, Robert. "Imagination, Wit, and Fantasy in Prayer," *Review for Religious.* 29 (1970):521-526.

———. *God is More Present Than You Think.* Paramus: Paulist Press, 1970.

O'Meara, Thomas F. "The Crisis in Ministry Is a Crisis of Spirituality," *Spirituality Today.* 30 (1978):14-23.

———. *Holiness and Radicalism in Religious Life.* New York: Herder & Herder, 1970.

———. *Loose in the World.* New York: Paulist Press, 1974.

———. "Meister Eckhart's Destiny," Pts. 1 and 2, *Spirituality Today.* 30 (1978):250-262; 348-359.

Oraison, Marc. *Being Together: Our Relationship With Other People.* New York: Doubleday, 1971.

———. *The Human Mystery of Sexuality.* New York: Sheed & Ward, 1967.

Osborne, Arthur. "The Two Kinds of Guru," *R. M. Bucke Memorial Society Newsletter Review.* Vol. II, No. 2 (1967): 29-30.

Otto, Rudolf. *Mysticism East and West.* New York: Collier Books, 1962.

Panikkar, Raymond. *The Trinity and the Religious Experience of Man.* New York: Orbis Books, 1973.

———. *The Unknown Christ of Hinduism.* London: Darton, Longman, and Todd, 1964.

———. *Worship and Secular Man.* Maryknoll: Orbis Books, 1973.

The Philosophy of Sarvepalli Radhakrishnan, ed. by Schlipp. New York: Tudor Publishing, 1952.

Phipps, William E. *The Sexuality of Jesus.* New York: Harper & Row, 1973.

Pieper, Josef. *About Love.* Chicago: Franciscan Herald Press, 1974.

———. *Happiness and Contemplation.* New York: Pantheon, 1958.

——. *Leisure, the Basis of Culture.* New York: New American Library, 1963.

Pittenger, Norman. *The Holy Spirit.* Philadelphia: United Church Press, 1974.

——. *Love and Control in Sexuality.* Philadelphia: United Church Press, 1974.

——. *Making Sexuality Human.* Philadelphia: Pilgrim Press, 1972.

——. *Time for Consent: A Christian Approach to Homosexuality.* London: SCM Press, 1970.

Pourrat, Pierre. *Christian Spirituality,* 4 vols. Westminster: Newman Press, 1953.

Powell, John J. *Fully Human.* Niles: Argus Communications, 1976.

——. *A Reason to Live, A Reason to Die.* Niles: Argus Communications, 1972.

——. *The Secret of Staying in Love.* Niles: Argus Communications, 1974.

——. *Why Am I Afraid to Love?* Niles: Argus Communications, 1972.

Radhakrishnan, S. *Eastern Religions and Western Thought.* Oxford: Oxford University Press, 1969.

——. *Religion and Society.* London: George Allen & Unwin, 1966.

Rahner, Hugo. *Man At Play.* New York: Herder & Herder, 1967.

Rahner, Karl, *Belief Today.* New York: Sheed & Ward, 1967.

——. *Christian At the Crossroads.* New York: Seabury, 1975.

——. *Christian In the Market Place.* New York: Sheed & Ward, 1966.

——. *The Christian Commitment.* New York: Sheed & Ward, 1963.

——. *Everyday Faith.* New York: Herder & Herder, 1968.

——. *Foundations of Christian Faith: An Introduction to the Idea of Christianity.* New York: Seabury, 1978.

——. *Marriage.* Denville: Dimension Books, 1970.

——. *Meditations on Hope and Love.* New York: Seabury, 1977.

——. *The Religious Life Today.* New York: Seabury, 1976.

——. *Opportunities for Faith.* New York: Seabury, 1974.

DONALD GOERGEN

——. "Reflections on the Unity of the Love of Neighbor and the Love of God," *Theological Investigations,* Vol. 6. Baltimore: Helican Press, 1969.

——. "The Theology of the Spiritual Life," *Theological Investigations,* Vol. 3. Baltimore: Helicon Press, 1961-1976.

——. "Further Theology of the Spiritual Life," *Theological Investigations,* Vol. 7. Baltimore: Helicon Press, 1961-1976.

——. "Further Theology of the Spiritual Life," *Theological Investigations,* Vol. 8. Baltimore: Helicon Press, 1961-1976.

Richard, Lucien. *The Spirituality of John Calvin.* Atlanta: John Knox Press, 1974.

Robinson, John A. T. *The Body: A Study in Pauline Theology.* London: SCM Press, 1963.

Roustang, Francois. *Growth in the Spirit.* New York: Sheed & Ward, 1966.

Royo, Antonio and Aumann, Jordan. *The Theology of Christian Perfection.* Dubuque: The Priory Press, 1962.

Russell, Letty. *Human Liberation in a Feminist Perspective.* Philadelphia: Westminster Press, 1974.

Scannell, Mark. "Help At Life's Turning Points," *Spirituality Today.* 30 (1978):323-333.

Scanzoni, Letha and Mollenkott, Virginia. *Is the Homosexual My Neighbor.* New York: Harper & Row, 1978.

Schachter, Rabbi Zalman. "The Spiritual Director in Judaism," *R. M. Bucke Memorial Society Newsletter Review.* Vol. II, No. 2, (1967):4-8.

Schillebeeckx, E. *Celibacy.* New York: Sheed & Ward, 1968.

Scholem, Gershom G. *Major Trends in Jewish Mysticism.* New York: Schocken Books, 1969.

Schoonenberg, Piet. *Man and Sin.* South Bend: University of Notre Dame Press, 1964.

Schumacher, E. F. *Small Is Beautiful: Economics As If People Mattered.* New York: Harper & Row, 1973.

Segundo, Juan Luis. *The Community Called Church.* Maryknoll: Orbis Books, 1973.

——. *Evolution and Guilt.* Maryknoll: Orbis Books, 1974.

——. *Grace and the Human Condition.* Maryknoll: Orbis Books, 1973.

——. *The Liberation of Theology.* Maryknoll: Orbis Books, 1976.

Sen, K. M. *Hinduism.* Baltimore: Penguin Books, 1970.

Smith, Huston. *The Religions of Man.* New York: Harper & Row, 1965.

Smith, Bradford. *Meditation: The Inward Art.* Philadelphia: J. P. Lippincott Co., 1963.

Soelle, Dorothee. *Death by Bread Alone.* Philadelphia: Fortress Press, 1978.

——. *Political Theology.* Philadelphia: Fortress Press, 1974.

——. *Suffering.* Philadelphia: Fortress Press, 1975.

Spicq, Ceslaus. *Agape in the New Testament,* 3 vols. St. Louis: B. Herder Co., 1963-1966.

The Spiritual Exercises of St. Ignatius. Trans. Louis Puhl. Chicago: Loyola University Press, 1951.

Squire, Aelred. *Asking the Fathers.* New York: Morehouse-Barlow, 1973.

Sugrue, Thomas. *There is a River.* New York: Dell Publishing Co., 1967.

Suzuki, D. T. *An Introduction to Zen Buddhism.* New York: Grove Press, 1964.

——. *Mysticism, Christian and Buddhist.* New York: Harper & Row, 1971.

Switzer, David. *The Dynamics of Grief.* New York: Abingdon Press, 1970.

Tart, Charles T. (ed.) *Altered States of Consciousness.* New York: Wiley, 1969.

Teilhard de Chardin, Pierre. *Christianity and Evolution.* New York: Harcourt, Brace and Jovanovich, 1971.

——. *The Divine Mileu.* New York: Harper & Row, 1960.

——. *How I Believe.* New York: Harper & Row, 1969.

——. *Human Energy.* New York: Harcourt, Brace and Jovanovich, 1970.

——. *Hymn of the Universe.* New York: Harper & Row, 1965.

——. *Science and Christ.* New York: Harper & Row, 1969.

——. *Writings in Time of War.* New York: Harper & Row, 1968.

Thurian, Max. *Marriage and Celibacy.* London: SCM Press, 1969.

Tillard, Jean Marie Roger. *A Gospel Path: The Religious Life.* Bruxelles: Lumen Vitae, 1977.

——. *The Mystery of Religious Life.* St. Louis: Herder Book Co., 1967.

——. *There Are Charism and Charisms: The Religious Life.* Bruxelles: Lumen Vitae, 1977.

Tolstoy, Leo. *The Kingdom of God and Peace Essays.* New York: Oxford U., 1936.

Tugwell, Simon. *Did You Receive the Spirit?* New York: Paulist Press, 1972.

——. *New Heaven? New Earth? An Encounter With Pentecostalism.* London: Darton, Longman and Todd, 1976.

——. *Prayer.* Springfield: Templegate Publishers, 1975.

——. *Prayer In Practice.* Springfield: Templegate Publishers, 1974.

Underhill, Evelyn. *Mysticism.* New York: E. P. Dutton, 1961.

Van Breeman, Peter. *Called By Name.* Denville: Dimension Books, 1976.

Van Kaam, Adrian Leo. *The Dynamics of Spiritual Self Direction.* Denville: Dimension Books, 1976.

——. *Envy & Originality.* Garden City: Doubleday, 1972.

——. *Personality Fulfillment in the Spiritual Life.* New York: Dimension Books, 1966.

——. *Personality Fulfillment in the Religious Life.* Denville: Dimension Books, 1967.

——. *The Vowed Life.* Denville: Dimension Books, 1968.

Vann, Gerald. *To Heaven with Diana.* Chicago: Henry Regnery Co., 1965.

——. *The Heart of Man.* New York: Longmans, Green, 1945.

Viviano, Benedict T. "Origins of Christian Study," *Cross and Crown.* 29 (1977):216-226.

——. "St. Paul and the Ministry of Women," *Spirituality Today.* 30 (1978):37-44.

Vatican II: Conciliar and Post Conciliar Documents. Ed. by Austin Flannery. Northport: Costello Publishing Co., 1975.

Waddell, Helen. *The Desert Fathers.* Ann Arbor: University of Michigan Press, 1966.

Ware, Tallistos. *The Power of the Name.* Oxford: SLG Press, 1974.

Watts, Allan. *The Joyous Cosmology*. New York: Vintage, 1962.

Weber, Richard K. "Defective Male or Defective Theology: Women and Ministry in the Medieval Experience," *Spirituality Today*. 30 (1978):55-63.

Weil, Simone. *Waiting on God*. London: Collins Fontana Books, 1968.

Wildiers, N. M. *An Introduction to Teilhard de Chardin*. New York: Harper & Row, 1968.

Williams, Daniel Day. *The Spirit and the Forms of Love*. New York: Harper & Row, 1968.

Woods, Richard "Foundations of a Gay Spirituality," *Spirituality Today*. 30 (1978):107-125.

Zaehner, Robert. *Christianity and Other Religions*. New York: Hawthorn Books, 1964.

——. *Evolution in Religion*. Oxford: Clarendon Press, 1971.

——. *Hindu and Muslim Mysticism*. London: Athlone Press, 1960.

——. *Hinduism*. New York: Oxford University Press, 1962.

——. *Matter and Spirit*. New York: Harper & Row, 1963.

——. *Mysticism, Sacred and Profane*. Oxford: Oxford University Press, 1961.

——. *The Bhagavad Gita With a Commentary Based on the Original Sources*. Oxford: Clarendon Press, 1969.